Real-Resumes for Manufacturing Jobs...
including real resumes used to change careers and transfer skills to other industries

Anne McKinney, Editor

PREP PUBLISHING

FAYETTEVILLE, NC

PREP Publishing
1110½ Hay Street
Fayetteville, NC 28305
(910) 483-6611

Library of Congress Cataloging-in-Publication Data

Real-resumes for manufacturing jobs : including real resumes used to change careers and transfer skills to other industries / Anne McKinney, editor.
     p. cm. -- (Real-resumes series)
  ISBN 1-885288-23-9 (trade pbk.)
    1. Résumés (Employment) 2. Manufacturing industries. I. McKinney, Anne, 1948- II. Series.

  HF5383 .R39587 2002
  650.14′2--dc21   2002020596
                                          CIP

Printed in the United States of America

By PREP Publishing

Business and Career Series:

RESUMES AND COVER LETTERS THAT HAVE WORKED

RESUMES AND COVER LETTERS THAT HAVE WORKED FOR MILITARY PROF

GOVERNMENT JOB APPLICATIONS AND FEDERAL RESUMES

COVER LETTERS THAT BLOW DOORS OPEN

LETTERS FOR SPECIAL SITUATIONS

RESUMES AND COVER LETTERS FOR MANAGERS

REAL-RESUMES FOR COMPUTER JOBS

REAL-RESUMES FOR MEDICAL JOBS

REAL-RESUMES FOR FINANCIAL JOBS

REAL-RESUMES FOR TEACHERS

REAL-RESUMES FOR STUDENTS

REAL-RESUMES FOR CAREER CHANGERS

REAL-RESUMES FOR SALES

REAL ESSAYS FOR COLLEGE & GRADUATE SCHOOL

REAL-RESUMES FOR AVIATION & TRAVEL JOBS

REAL-RESUMES FOR POLICE, LAW ENFORCEMENT & SECURITY JOBS

REAL-RESUMES FOR SOCIAL WORK & COUNSELING JOBS

REAL-RESUMES FOR CONSTRUCTION JOBS

REAL-RESUMES FOR MANUFACTURING JOBS

Judeo-Christian Ethics Series:

SECOND TIME AROUND

BACK IN TIME

WHAT THE BIBLE SAYS ABOUT...Words that can lead to success and happiness

A GENTLE BREEZE FROM GOSSAMER WINGS

BIBLE STORIES FROM THE OLD TESTAMENT

Fiction:

KIJABE...An African Historical Saga

Table of Contents

A WORD FROM THE EDITOR:
ABOUT THE REAL-RESUMES SERIES

Welcome to the Real-Resumes Series. The Real-Resumes Series is a series of books which have been developed based on the experiences of real job hunters and which target specialized fields or types of resumes. As the editor of the series, I have carefully selected resumes and cover letters (with names and other key data disguised, of course) which have been used successfully in real job hunts. That's what we mean by "Real-Resumes." What you see in this book are *real* resumes and cover letters which helped real people get ahead in their careers.

The Real-Resumes Series is based on the work of the country's oldest resume-preparation company known as PREP Resumes. If you would like a free information packet describing the company's resume preparation services, call 910-483-6611 or write to PREP at 1110½ Hay Street, Fayetteville, NC 28305. If you have a job hunting experience you would like to share with our staff at the Real-Resumes Series, please contact us at preppub@aol.com or visit our website at http://www.prep-pub.com.

The resumes and cover letters in this book are designed to be of most value to people already in a job hunt or contemplating a career change. If we could give you one word of advice about your career, here's what we would say: Manage your career and don't stumble from job to job in an incoherent pattern. Try to find work that interests you, and then identify prosperous industries which need work performed of the type you want to do. Learn early in your working life that a great resume and cover letter can blow doors open for you and help you maximize your salary.

This book is dedicated to those seeking jobs in the manufacturing field. We hope the superior samples will help you manage your current job campaign and your career so that you will find work aligned to your career interests.

Real-Resumes for Manufacturing Jobs...
including real resumes used to change careers
and transfer skills to other industries

Anne McKinney, Editor

As the editor of this book, I would like to give you some tips on how to make the best use of the information you will find here. Because you are considering a career change, you already understand the concept of managing your career for maximum enjoyment and self-fulfillment. The purpose of this book is to provide expert tools and advice so that you *can* manage your career. Inside these pages you will find resumes and cover letters that will help you find not just a job but the type of work you want to do.

**Introduction:
The Art of
Changing
Jobs...
and Finding
New Careers**

Overview of the Book

Every resume and cover letter in this book actually worked. And most of the resumes and cover letters have common features: most are one-page, most are in the chronological format, and most resumes are accompanied by a companion cover letter. In this section you will find helpful advice about job hunting. Step One begins with a discussion of why employers prefer the one-page, chronological resume. In Step Two you are introduced to the direct approach and to the proper format for a cover letter. In Step Three you learn the 14 main reasons why job hunters are not offered the jobs they want, and you learn the six key areas employers focus on when they interview you. Step Four gives nuts-and-bolts advice on how to handle the interview, send a follow-up letter after an interview, and negotiate your salary.

The cover letter plays such a critical role in a career change. You will learn from the experts how to format your cover letters and you will see suggested language to use in particular career-change situations. It has been said that "A picture is worth a thousand words" and, for that reason, you will see numerous examples of effective cover letters used by real individuals to change fields, functions, and industries.

The most important part of the book is the Real-Resumes section. Some of the individuals whose resumes and cover letters you see spent a lengthy career in an industry they loved. Then there are resumes and cover letters of people who wanted a change but who probably wanted to remain in their industry. Many of you will be especially interested by the resumes and cover letters of individuals who knew they definitely wanted a career change but had no idea what they wanted to do next. Other resumes and cover letters show individuals who knew they wanted to change fields and had a pretty good idea of what they wanted to do next.

Whatever your field, and whatever your circumstances, you'll find resumes and cover letters that will "show you the ropes" in terms of successfully changing jobs and switching careers.

Before you proceed further, think about why you picked up this book.
- Are you dissatisfied with the type of work you are now doing?
- Would you like to change careers, change companies, or change industries?
- Are you satisfied with your industry but not with your niche or function within it?
- Do you want to transfer your skills to a new product or service?
- Even if you have excelled in your field, have you "had enough"? Would you like the stimulation of a new challenge?
- Are you aware of the importance of a great cover letter but unsure of how to write one?
- Are you preparing to launch a second career after retirement?
- Have you been downsized, or do you anticipate becoming a victim of downsizing?
- Do you need expert advice on how to plan and implement a job campaign that will open the maximum number of doors?
- Do you want to make sure you handle an interview to your maximum advantage?

- Would you like to master the techniques of negotiating salary and benefits?
- Do you want to learn the secrets and shortcuts of professional resume writers?

Using the Direct Approach

As you consider the possibility of a job hunt or career change, you need to be aware that most people end up having at least three distinctly different careers in their working lifetimes, and often those careers are different from each other. Yet people usually stumble through each job campaign, unsure of what they should be doing. Whether you find yourself voluntarily or unexpectedly in a job hunt, the direct approach is the job hunting strategy most likely to yield a full-time permanent job. The direct approach is an active, take-the-initiative style of job hunting in which you choose your next employer rather than relying on responding to ads, using employment agencies, or depending on other methods of finding jobs. You will learn how to use the direct approach in this book, and you will see that an effective cover letter is a critical ingredient in using the direct approach.

The "direct approach" is the style of job hunting most likely to yield the maximum number of job interviews.

Lack of Industry Experience Not a Major Barrier to Entering New Field

"Lack of experience" is often the last reason people are not offered jobs, according to the companies who do the hiring. If you are changing careers, you will be glad to learn that experienced professionals often are selling "potential" rather than experience in a job hunt. Companies look for personal qualities that they know tend to be present in their most effective professionals, such as communication skills, initiative, persistence, organizational and time management skills, and creativity. Frequently companies are trying to discover "personality type," "talent," "ability," "aptitude," and "potential" rather than seeking actual hands-on experience, so your resume should be designed to aggressively present your accomplishments. Attitude, enthusiasm, personality, and a track record of achievements in any type of work are the primary "indicators of success" which employers are seeking, and you will see numerous examples in this book of resumes written in an all-purpose fashion so that the professional can approach various industries and companies.

Using references in a skillful fashion in your job hunt will inspire confidence in prospective employers and help you "close the sale" after interviews.

The Art of Using References in a Job Hunt

You probably already know that you need to provide references during a job hunt, but you may not be sure of how and when to use references for maximum advantage. You can use references very creatively during a job hunt to call attention to your strengths and make yourself "stand out." Your references will rarely get you a job, no matter how impressive the names, but the way you use references can boost the employer's confidence in you and lead to a job offer in the least time.

You should ask from three to five people, including people who have supervised you, if you can use them as a reference during your job hunt. You may not be able to ask your current boss since your job hunt is probably confidential.

A common question in resume preparation is: "Do I need to put my references on my resume?" No, you don't. Even if you create a references page at the same time you prepare your resume, you don't need to mail, e-mail, or fax your references page with the resume and cover letter. Usually the potential employer is not interested in references until he meets you, so the earliest you need to have references ready is at the first interview. Obviously there are exceptions to this standard rule of thumb; sometimes an ad will ask you to send references with your first response. Wait until the employer requests references before providing them.

An excellent attention-getting technique is to take to the first interview not just a page of references (giving names, addresses, and telephone numbers) but an actual letter of reference written by someone who knows you well and who preferably has supervised or employed you. A professional way to close the first interview is to thank the interviewer, shake his or her hand, and then say you'd like to give him or her a copy of a letter of reference from a previous employer. Hopefully you already made a good impression during the interview, but you'll "close the sale" in a dynamic fashion if you leave a letter praising you and your accomplishments. For that reason, it's a good idea to ask supervisors during your final weeks in a job if they will provide you with a written letter of recommendation which you can use in future job hunts. Most employers will oblige, and you will have a letter that has a useful "shelf life" of many years. Such a letter often gives the prospective employer enough confidence in his opinion of you that he may forego checking out other references and decide to offer you the job on the spot or in the next few days.

With regard to references, it's best to provide the names and addresses of people who have supervised you or observed you in a work situation.

Whom should you ask to serve as references? References should be people who have known or supervised you in a professional, academic, or work situation. References with big titles, like school superintendent or congressman, are fine, but remind busy people when you get to the interview stage that they may be contacted soon. Make sure the busy official recognizes your name and has instant positive recall of you! If you're asked to provide references on a formal company application, you can simply transcribe names from your references list. In summary, follow this rule in using references: If you've got them, flaunt them! If you've obtained well-written letters of reference, make sure you find a polite way to push those references under the nose of the interviewer so he or she can hear someone other than you describing your strengths. Your references probably won't ever get you a job, but glowing letters of reference can give you credibility and visibility that can make you stand out among candidates with similar credentials and potential!

The approach taken by this book is to (1) help you master the proven best techniques of conducting a job hunt and (2) show you how to stand out in a job hunt through your resume, cover letter, interviewing skills, as well as the way in which you present your references and follow up on interviews. Now, the best way to "get in the mood" for writing your own resume and cover letter is to select samples from the Table of Contents that interest you and then read them. A great resume is a "photograph," usually on one page, of an individual. If you wish to seek professional advice in preparing your resume, you may contact one of the professional writers at Professional Resume & Employment Publishing (PREP) for a brief free consultation by calling 1-910-483-6611.

Part One: Some Advice About Your Job Hunt

What if you don't know what you want to do?

Your job hunt will be more comfortable if you can figure out what type of work you want to do. But you are not alone if you have no idea what you want to do next! You may have knowledge and skills in certain areas but want to get into another type of work. What *The Wall Street Journal* has discovered in its research on careers is that most of us end up having at least three distinctly different careers in our working lives; it seems that, even if we really like a particular kind of activity, twenty years of doing it is enough for most of us and we want to move on to something else!

That's why we strongly believe that you need to spend some time figuring out *what interests you* rather than taking an inventory of the skills you have. You may have skills that you simply don't want to use, but if you can build your career on the things that interest you, you will be more likely to be happy and satisfied in your job. Realize, too, that interests can change over time; the activities that interest you now may not be the ones that interested you years ago. For example, some professionals may decide that they've had enough of retail sales and want a job selling another product or service, even though they have earned a reputation for being an excellent retail manager. We strongly believe that interests rather than skills should be the determining factor in deciding what types of jobs you want to apply for and what directions you explore in your job hunt. Obviously one cannot be a lawyer without a law degree or a secretary without secretarial skills; but a professional can embark on a next career as a financial consultant, property manager, plant manager, production supervisor, retail manager, or other occupation if he/she has a strong interest in that type of work and can provide a resume that clearly demonstrates past excellent performance in *any* field and *potential* to excel in another field. As you will see later in this book, "lack of exact experience" is the last reason why people are turned down for the jobs they apply for.

> Figure out what interests you and you will hold the key to a successful job hunt and working career. (And be prepared for your interests to change over time!)

> "Lack of exact experience" is the last reason people are turned down for the jobs for which they apply.

How can you have a resume prepared if you don't know what you want to do?

You may be wondering how you can have a resume prepared if you don't know what you want to do next. The approach to resume writing which PREP, the country's oldest resume-preparation company, has used successfully for many years is to develop an "all-purpose" resume that translates your skills, experience, and accomplishments into language employers can understand. What most people need in a job hunt is a versatile resume that will allow them to apply for numerous types of jobs. For example, you may want to apply for a job in pharmaceutical sales but you may also want to have a resume that will be versatile enough for you to apply for jobs in the construction, financial services, or automotive industries.

Based on more than 20 years of serving job hunters, we at PREP have found that your best approach to job hunting is **an all-purpose resume** and **specific cover letters tailored to specific fields** rather than using the approach of trying to create different resumes for every job. If you are remaining in your field, you may not even need more than one "all-purpose" cover letter, although the cover letter rather than the resume is the place to communicate your interest in a narrow or specific field. An all-purpose resume and cover letter that translate your experience and accomplishments into plain English are the tools that will maximize the number of doors which open for you while permitting you to "fish" in the widest range of job areas.

Your resume will provide the script for your job interview.

When you get down to it, your resume has a simple job to do: Its purpose is to blow as many doors open as possible and to make as many people as possible want to meet you. So a well-written resume that really "sells" you is a key that will create opportunities for you in a job hunt.

This statistic explains why: The typical newspaper advertisement for a job opening receives more than 245 replies. And normally only 10 or 12 will be invited to an interview.

But here's another purpose of the resume: it provides the "script" the employer uses when he interviews you. If your resume has been written in such a way that your strengths and achievements are revealed, that's what you'll end up talking about at the job interview. Since the resume will govern what you get asked about at your interviews, you can't overestimate the importance of making sure your resume makes you look and sound as good as you are.

So what is a "good" resume?

Very literally, your resume should motivate the person reading it to dial the phone number or e-mail the screen name you have put on the resume. When you are relocating, you should put a local phone number on your resume if your physical address is several states away; employers are more likely to dial a local telephone number than a long-distance number when they're looking for potential employees.

If you have a resume already, look at it objectively. Is it a limp, colorless "laundry list" of your job titles and duties? Or does it "paint a picture" of your skills, abilities, and accomplishments in a way that would make someone want to meet you? Can people understand what you're saying? If you are attempting to change fields or industries, can potential employers see that your skills and knowledge are transferable to other environments? For example, have you described accomplishments which reveal your problem-solving abilities or communication skills?

How long should your resume be?

One page, maybe two. Usually only people in the academic community have a resume (which they usually call a *curriculum vitae*) longer than one or two pages. Remember that your resume is almost always accompanied by a cover letter, and a potential employer does not want to read more than two or three pages about a total stranger in order to decide if he wants to meet that person! Besides, don't forget that the more you tell someone about yourself, the more opportunity you are providing for the employer to screen you out at the "first-cut" stage. A resume should be concise and exciting and designed to make the reader want to meet you in person!

Should resumes be functional or chronological?

Employers almost always prefer a chronological resume; in other words, an employer will find a resume easier to read if it is immediately apparent what your current or most recent job is, what you did before that, and so forth, in reverse chronological order. A resume that goes back in detail for the last ten years of employment will generally satisfy the employer's curiosity about your background. Employment more than ten years old can be shown even more briefly in an "Other Experience" section at the end of your "Experience" section. Remember that your intention is not to tell everything you've done but to "hit the high points" and especially impress the employer with what you learned, contributed, or accomplished in each job you describe.

Your resume is the "script" for your job interviews. Make sure you put on your resume what you want to talk about or be asked about at the job interview.

The one-page resume in chronological format is the format preferred by most employers.

Once you get your resume, what do you do with it?
You will be using your resume to answer ads, as a tool to use in talking with friends and relatives about your job search, and, most importantly, in using the "direct approach" described in this book.

When you mail your resume, always send a "cover letter."
A "cover letter," sometimes called a "resume letter" or "letter of interest," is a letter that accompanies and introduces your resume. Your cover letter is a way of personalizing the resume by sending it to the specific person you think you might want to work for at each company. Your cover letter should contain a few highlights from your resume—just enough to make someone want to meet you. Cover letters should always be typed or word processed on a computer—never handwritten.

Never mail or fax your resume without a cover letter.

1. Learn the art of answering ads.
There is an "art," part of which can be learned, in using your "bestselling" resume to reply to advertisements.

Sometimes an exciting job lurks behind a boring ad that someone dictated in a hurry, so reply to any ad that interests you. Don't worry that you aren't "25 years old with an MBA" like the ad asks for. Employers will always make compromises in their requirements if they think you're the "best fit" overall.

What about ads that ask for "salary requirements?"
What if the ad you're answering asks for "salary requirements?" The first rule is to avoid committing yourself in writing at that point to a specific salary. You don't want to "lock yourself in."

What if the ad asks for your "salary requirements?"

There are two ways to handle the ad that asks for "salary requirements."
First, you can ignore that part of the ad and accompany your resume with a cover letter that focuses on "selling" you, your abilities, and even some of your philosophy about work or your field. You may include a sentence in your cover letter like this: "I can provide excellent personal and professional references at your request, and I would be delighted to share the private details of my salary history with you in person."

Second, if you feel you must give some kind of number, just state a range in your cover letter that includes your medical, dental, other benefits, and expected bonuses. You might state, for example, "My current compensation, including benefits and bonuses, is in the range of $30,000-$40,000."

Analyze the ad and "tailor" yourself to it.
When you're replying to ads, a finely tailored cover letter is an important tool in getting your resume noticed and read. On the next page is a cover letter which has been "tailored to fit" a specific ad. Notice the "art" used by PREP writers of analyzing the ad's main requirements and then writing the letter so that the person's background, work habits, and interests seem "tailor-made" to the company's needs. Use this cover letter as a model when you prepare your own reply to ads.

Date

Exact Name of Person
Exact Title
Exact Name of Company
Address
City, State, Zip

Dear Exact Name of Person (or Dear Sir or Madam if answering a blind ad):

With the enclosed resume, I would like to make you aware of my interest in the position as Chief Operating Officer.

A resourceful management style with creative problem-solving ability

As you will see from my resume, I offer a management style which is committed to achieving lowest total production costs in the process of producing superior quality products. After earning my B.S. in Biology and prior to earning my master's degree, I developed new waste water technologies for a Fortune 500 company that saved the company $2 million annually. I then became Plant Manager for a plant which serviced the Rohm & Haas corporation, and in that capacity I developed processes to recover precious metals from hazardous waste which saved $25 million yearly. Because of my outstanding bottom-line results, I was recruited by a Florida company to manage its technical services. I have contributed numerous common-sense solutions to manufacturing problems and spearheaded the development of more than 20 new products. I have also developed numerous cost-saving manufacturing solutions such as a system I developed for a customer company which saved the company nearly a quarter of a million dollars annually. I am a resourceful individual who thrives on developing plans for new areas of technology.

Common-sense manager with outstanding team building skills

Currently as the #2 manager in a company generating revenues of $120 million annually, I am excelling in a position which was created especially for me—Director of Operations. When I joined the company, its revenues were only $300,000 a month. Although I am held in the highest regard in my current company, I am selectively exploring opportunities in companies that can use a strong problem-solver committed to aggressive improvements in quality, profitability, and customer satisfaction.

If my background and skills interest you, I hope you will contact me to suggest a time when we could meet in person to discuss your needs. I can provide outstanding references.

Yours sincerely,

Edmond J. Warren

Employers are trying to identify the individual who wants the job they are filling. Don't be afraid to express your enthusiasm in the cover letter!

2. Talk to friends and relatives.

Don't be shy about telling your friends and relatives the kind of job you're looking for. Looking for the job you want involves using your network of contacts, so tell people what you're looking for. They may be able to make introductions and help set up interviews.

About 25% of all interviews are set up through "who you know," so don't ignore this approach.

3. Finally, and most importantly, use the "direct approach."

The "direct approach" is a strategy in which you choose your next employer.

More than 50% of all job interviews are set up by the "direct approach." That means you actually mail, e-mail, or fax a resume and a cover letter to a company you think might be interesting to work for.

To whom do you write?

In general, you should write directly to the *exact name* of the person who would be hiring you: say, the vice-president of marketing or data processing. If you're in doubt about to whom to address the letter, address it to the president by name and he or she will make sure it gets forwarded to the right person within the company who has hiring authority in your area.

How do you find the names of potential employers?

You're not alone if you feel that the biggest problem in your job search is finding the right names at the companies you want to contact. But you can usually figure out the names of companies you want to approach by deciding first if your job hunt is primarily geography-driven or industry-driven.

In a **geography-driven job hunt,** you could select a list of, say, 50 companies you want to contact **by location** from the lists that the U.S. Chambers of Commerce publish yearly of their "major area employers." There are hundreds of local Chambers of Commerce across America, and most of them will have an 800 number which you can find through 1-800-555-1212. If you and your family think Atlanta, Dallas, Ft. Lauderdale, and Virginia Beach might be nice places to live, for example, you could contact the Chamber of Commerce in those cities and ask how you can obtain a copy of their list of major employers. Your nearest library will have the book which lists the addresses of all chambers.

In an **industry-driven job hunt,** and if you are willing to relocate, you will be identifying the companies which you find most attractive in the industry in which you want to work. When you select a list of companies to contact **by industry,** you can find the right person to write and the address of firms by industrial category in *Standard and Poor's, Moody's,* and other excellent books in public libraries. Many Web sites also provide contact information.

Many people feel it's a good investment to actually call the company to either find out or double-check the name of the person to whom they want to send a resume and cover letter. It's important to do as much as you feasibly can to assure that the letter gets to the right person in the company.

On-line research will be the best way for many people to locate organizations to which they wish to send their resume. It is outside the scope of this book to teach Internet research skills, but librarians are often useful in this area.

What's the correct way to follow up on a resume you send?

There is a polite way to be aggressively interested in a company during your job hunt. It is ideal to end the cover letter accompanying your resume by saying, "I hope you'll welcome my call next week when I try to arrange a brief meeting at your convenience to discuss your current and future needs and how I might serve them." Keep it low key, and just ask for a "brief meeting," not an interview. Employers want people who show a determined interest in working with them, so don't be shy about following up on the resume and cover letter you've mailed.

STEP THREE: Preparing for Interviews

It pays to be aware of the 14 most common pitfalls for job hunters.

But a resume and cover letter by themselves can't get you the job you want. You need to "prep" yourself before the interview. Step Three in your job campaign is "Preparing for Interviews." First, let's look at interviewing from the hiring organization's point of view.

What are the biggest "turnoffs" for potential employers?

One of the ways to help yourself perform well at an interview is to look at the main reasons why organizations *don't* hire the people they interview, according to those who do the interviewing.

Notice that "lack of appropriate background" (or lack of experience) is the *last* reason for not being offered the job.

The 14 Most Common Reasons Job Hunters Are Not Offered Jobs *(according to the companies who do the interviewing and hiring):*

1. Low level of accomplishment
2. Poor attitude, lack of self-confidence
3. Lack of goals/objectives
4. Lack of enthusiasm
5. Lack of interest in the company's business
6. Inability to sell or express yourself
7. Unrealistic salary demands
8. Poor appearance
9. Lack of maturity, no leadership potential
10. Lack of extracurricular activities
11. Lack of preparation for the interview, no knowledge about company
12. Objecting to travel
13. Excessive interest in security and benefits
14. Inappropriate background

Department of Labor studies have proven that smart, "prepared" job hunters can increase their beginning salary while getting a job in *half* the time it normally takes. (4½ months is the average national length of a job search.) Here, from PREP, are some questions that can prepare you to find a job faster.

Are you in the "right" frame of mind?

It seems unfair that we have to look for a job just when we're lowest in morale. Don't worry *too* much if you're nervous before interviews. You're supposed to be a little nervous, especially if the job means a lot to you. But the best way to kill unnecessary fears about job hunting is through 1) making sure you have a great resume and 2) preparing yourself for the interview. Here are three main areas you need to think about before each interview.

Do you know what the company does?

Don't walk into an interview giving the impression that, "If this is Tuesday, this must be General Motors."

Find out before the interview what the company's main product or service is. Where is the company heading? Is it in a "growth" or declining industry? (Answers to these questions may influence whether or not you want to work there!)

Research the company before you go to interviews.

Information about what the company does is in annual reports, in newspaper and magazine articles, and on the Internet. If you're not yet skilled at Internet research, just visit your nearest library and ask the reference librarian to guide you to printed materials on the company.

Do you know what you want to do for the company?

Before the interview, try to decide how you see yourself fitting into the company. Remember, "lack of exact background" the company wants is usually the last reason people are not offered jobs.

Understand before you go to each interview that the burden will be on you to "sell" the interviewer on why you're the best person for the job and the company.

How will you answer the critical interview questions?

Put yourself in the interviewer's position and think about the questions you're most likely to be asked. Here are some of the most commonly asked interview questions:

Anticipate the questions you will be asked at the interview, and prepare your responses in advance.

Q: "What are your greatest strengths?"
A: Don't say you've never thought about it! Go into an interview knowing the three main impressions you want to leave about yourself, such as "I'm hard-working, loyal, and an imaginative cost-cutter."

Q: "What are your greatest weaknesses?"
A: Don't confess that you're lazy or have trouble meeting deadlines! Confessing that you tend to be a "workaholic" or "tend to be a perfectionist and sometimes get frustrated when others don't share my high standards" will make your prospective employer see a "weakness" that he likes. Name a weakness that your interviewer will perceive as a strength.

Q: "What are your long-range goals?"
A: If you're interviewing with Microsoft, don't say you want to work for IBM in five years! Say your long-range goal is to be *with* the company, contributing to its goals and success.

Q: "What motivates you to do your best work?"
A: Don't get dollar signs in your eyes here! "A challenge" is not a bad answer, but it's a little cliched. Saying something like "troubleshooting" or "solving a tough problem" is more interesting and specific. Give an example if you can.

Q: "What do you know about this organization?"

A: Don't say you never heard of it until they asked you to the interview! Name an interesting, positive thing you learned about the company recently from your research. Remember, company executives can sometimes feel rather "maternal" about the company they serve. Don't get onto a negative area of the company if you can think of positive facts you can bring up. Of course, if you learned in your research that the company's sales seem to be taking a nose-dive, or that the company president is being prosecuted for taking bribes, you might politely ask your interviewer to tell you something that could help you better understand what you've been reading. Those are the kinds of company facts that can help you determine whether or not you want to work there.

Go to an interview prepared to tell the company why it should hire you.

Q: "Why should I hire you?"

A: "I'm unemployed and available" is the wrong answer here! Get back to your strengths and say that you believe the organization could benefit by a loyal, hard-working cost-cutter like yourself.

In conclusion, you should decide in advance, before you go to the interview, how you will answer each of these commonly asked questions. Have some practice interviews with a friend to role-play and build your confidence.

STEP FOUR: Handling the Interview and Negotiating Salary

Now you're ready for Step Four: actually handling the interview successfully and effectively. Remember, the purpose of an interview is to get a job offer.

A smile at an interview makes the employer perceive of you as intelligent!

Eight "do's" for the interview

According to leading U.S. companies, there are eight key areas in interviewing success. You can fail at an interview if you mishandle just one area.

1. **Do wear appropriate clothes.**
   You can never go wrong by wearing a suit to an interview.

2. **Do be well groomed.**
   Don't overlook the obvious things like having clean hair, clothes, and fingernails for the interview.

3. **Do give a firm handshake.**
   You'll have to shake hands twice in most interviews: first, before you sit down, and second, when you leave the interview. Limp handshakes turn most people off.

4. **Do smile and show a sense of humor.**
   Interviewers are looking for people who would be nice to work with, so don't be so somber that you don't smile. In fact, research shows that people who smile at interviews are perceived as more intelligent. So, smile!

5. **Do be enthusiastic.**
   Employers say they are "turned off" by lifeless, unenthusiastic job hunters who show no special interest in that company. The best way to show some enthusiasm for the employer's operation is to find out about the business beforehand.

6. Do show you are flexible and adaptable.

An employer is looking for someone who can contribute to his organization in a flexible, adaptable way. No matter what skills and training you have, employers know every new employee must go through initiation and training on the company's turf. Certainly show pride in your past accomplishments in a specific, factual way ("I saved my last employer $50.00 a week by a new cost-cutting measure I developed"). But don't come across as though there's nothing about the job you couldn't easily handle.

7. Do ask intelligent questions about the employer's business.

An employer is hiring someone because of certain business needs. Show interest in those needs. Asking questions to get a better idea of the employer's needs will help you "stand out" from other candidates interviewing for the job.

8. Do "take charge" when the interviewer "falls down" on the job.

Go into every interview knowing the three or four points about yourself you want the interviewer to remember. And be prepared to take an active part in leading the discussion if the interviewer's "canned approach" does not permit you to display your "strong suit." You can't always depend on the interviewer's asking you the "right" questions so you can stress your strengths and accomplishments.

Employers are seeking people with good attitudes whom they can train and coach to do things their way.

An important "don't": Don't ask questions about salary or benefits at the first interview.
Employers don't take warmly to people who look at their organization as just a place to satisfy salary and benefit needs. Don't risk making a negative impression by appearing greedy or self-serving. The place to discuss salary and benefits is normally at the second interview, and the employer will bring it up. Then you can ask questions without appearing excessively interested in what the organization can do for you.

Now...negotiating your salary
Even if an ad requests that you communicate your "salary requirement" or "salary history," you should avoid providing those numbers in your initial cover letter. You can usually say something like this: "I would be delighted to discuss the private details of my salary history with you in person."

Once you're at the interview, you must avoid even appearing *interested* in salary before you are offered the job. Make sure you've "sold" yourself before talking salary. First show you're the "best fit" for the employer and then you'll be in a stronger position from which to negotiate salary. **Never** bring up the subject of salary yourself. Employers say there's no way you can avoid looking greedy if you bring up the issue of salary and benefits before the company has identified you as its "best fit."

Don't appear excessively interested in salary and benefits at the interview.

Interviewers sometimes throw out a salary figure at the first interview to see if you'll accept it. You may not want to commit yourself if you think you will be able to negotiate a better deal later on. Get back to finding out more about the job. This lets the interviewer know you're interested primarily in the job and not the salary.

When the organization brings up salary, it may say something like this: "Well, Mary, we think you'd make a good candidate for this job. What kind of salary are we talking about?" You may not want to name a number here, either. Give the ball back to the interviewer. Act as though you hadn't given the subject of salary much thought and respond something like this: "Ah, Mr. Jones, I wonder if you'd be kind enough to tell me what salary you had in mind when you advertised the job?" Or ... "What is the range you have in mind?"

Don't worry, if the interviewer names a figure that you think is too low, you can say so without turning down the job or locking yourself into a rigid position. The point here is to negotiate for yourself as well as you can. You might reply to a number named by the interviewer that you think is low by saying something like this: "Well, Mr. Lee, the job interests me very much, and I think I'd certainly enjoy working with you. But, frankly, I was thinking of something a little higher than that." That leaves the ball in your interviewer's court again, and you haven't turned down the job either, in case it turns out that the interviewer can't increase the offer and you still want the job.

Salary negotiation can be tricky.

Last, send a follow-up letter.

Mail, e-mail, or fax a letter right after the interview telling your interviewer you enjoyed the meeting and are certain (if you are) that you are the "best fit" for the job. The people interviewing you will probably have an attitude described as either "professionally loyal" to their companies, or "maternal and proprietary" if the interviewer also owns the company. In either case, they are looking for people who want to work for *that* company in particular. The follow-up letter you send might be just the deciding factor in your favor if the employer is trying to choose between you and someone else. You will see an example of a follow-up letter on page 16.

A follow-up letter can help the employer choose between you and another qualified candidate.

A cover letter is an essential part of a job hunt or career change.

Many people are aware of the importance of having a great resume, but most people in a job hunt don't realize just how important a cover letter can be. The purpose of the cover letter, sometimes called a **"letter of interest,"** is to introduce your resume to prospective employers. The cover letter is often the critical ingredient in a job hunt because the cover letter allows you to say a lot of things that just don't "fit" on the resume. For example, you can emphasize your commitment to a new field and stress your related talents. The cover letter also gives you a chance to stress outstanding character and personal values. On the next two pages you will see examples of very effective cover letters.

A cover letter is an essential part of a career change.

Please do not attempt to implement a career change without a cover letter such as the ones you see in Part Two of this book. A cover letter is the first impression of you, and you can influence the way an employer views you by the language and style of your letter.

Special help for those in career change

We want to emphasize again that, especially in a career change, the cover letter is very important and can help you "build a bridge" to a new career. A creative and appealing cover letter can begin the process of encouraging the potential employer to imagine you in an industry other than the one in which you have worked.

As a special help to those in career change, there are resumes and cover letters included in this book which show valuable techniques and tips you should use when changing fields or industries. The resumes and cover letters of career changers are identified in the table of contents as "Career Change" and you will see the "Career Change" label on cover letters in Part Two where the individuals are changing careers.

Date

Exact Name of Person
Exact Title
Exact Name of Company
Address
City, State, Zip

Dear Exact Name of Person (or Dear Sir or Madam if answering a blind ad):

I would appreciate an opportunity to talk with you soon about how I could contribute to your organization through my education, experience, and knowledge.

As you will see from my enclosed resume, I received my B.S. in Electrical Engineering, Manufacturing concentration, from Arizona State University. In order to complete this rigorous degree program, I was required to pass graduate-level courses in Digital Signal Processing, Project Management for Engineers, and Switching Theory. Since earning my degree, I have supplemented my education with additional courses in AUTOCAD V.15, C Programming, and Java.

I earned rapid advancement with Concord, Inc., a division of Varsity Corporation located in Santa Fe, NM, and was working at the Varsity Corporation's Automotive Division in Santa Fe. Originally hired as a Production Technician, I rapidly advanced to a shift supervisor's job before my selection as a Quality Technician. I had completed the screening and interviewing process and was offered a position as an Engineering Intern when I was laid off due to serious business declines. I was, however, offered a job as an Assembly Technician at a company site in another state. Because of personal reasons, however, I do not wish to relocate at this time.

Among my strongest skills are my ability to anticipate problems, analyze situations, and develop the solutions which will result in increasing productivity and profitability. In earlier jobs in shipping and receiving operations, as well as in technical jobs with Varsity, I have initiated changes which have resulted in reduced man-hours and lowered costs.

If you can use a positive, results-oriented professional with diversified technical skills related to manufacturing operations, I hope you will contact me soon to arrange a time when we might meet to discuss your needs. I can assure you in advance that I have an excellent reputation and can provide outstanding references.

Sincerely,

Gary Andrew Laredo

Addressing the Cover Letter: Get the exact name of the person to whom you are writing. This makes your approach personal.

First Paragraph: This explains why you are writing.

Second Paragraph: You have a chance to talk about whatever you feel is your most distinguishing feature.

Third Paragraph: You bring up your next most distinguishing qualities and try to sell yourself.

Fourth Paragraph: Here you have another opportunity to reveal qualities or achievements which will impress your future employer.

Final Paragraph: He asks the employer to contact him. Make sure your reader knows what the "next step" is.

Alternate Final Paragraph: It's more aggressive (but not too aggressive) to let the employer know that you will be calling him or her. Don't be afraid to be persistent. Employers are looking for people who know what they want to do.

Date

Exact Name of Person
Exact Title
Exact Name of Company
Address
City, State, Zip

Dear Exact Name of Person (or Dear Sir or Madam if answering a blind ad):

I would appreciate an opportunity to talk with you soon about how I could contribute to your organization through my strong communication and organizational skills as well as my highly motivated nature and "can-do" attitude.

Most recently I excelled in manufacturing jobs, first at Jones Manufacturing and then at Crosby Manufacturing. At Crosby, I was credited with making contributions which allowed the company to achieve its goal of "zero defects" in on-time shipping, and I was a member of a department which qualified for ISO 9000 certification on the company's first attempt.

While I was highly regarded by my employer and can provide excellent references at the appropriate time, recent downturns in business forced the company to reduce its workforce, displacing myself and many of my co-workers. I have taken the opportunity to strengthen my administrative and financial skills with a Bank Teller training course from Carson City Community College. I am confident that my outgoing personality and excellent work habits would be well suited to any environment that requires strict attention to detail.

In a previous position, I worked in a clerical/secretarial capacity for Classic Hair Coifs in Carson City. I essentially performed the functions of an office manager or administrative assistant, scheduling appointments, ordering supplies, operating a multi-line phone system, and handling all correspondence.

If your organization could benefit from a motivated, detail-oriented young professional with exceptional organizational, customer service, and communication skills, I hope you will contact me to suggest a time when we could meet to discuss your needs. I assure you in advance that I have an excellent reputation and could quickly become a strong asset to your company.

Sincerely,

Karen Marie Steardon

CC: Mr. Michael Reardon

Date
Three blank spaces

Address

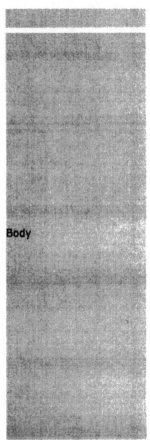

Salutation
One blank space

Body

One blank space

Signature

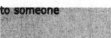
cc: Indicates you are sending a copy of the letter to someone

Date

Exact Name of Person
Title or Position
Name of Company
Address (number and street)
Address (city, state, and zip)

Dear Exact Name:

I am writing to express my appreciation for the time you spent with me on 9 December, and I want to let you know that I am sincerely interested in the position of Controller which you described.

I feel confident that I could skillfully interact with your 60-person work force in order to obtain the information we need to assure expert controllership of your manufacturing company, and I would cheerfully travel as your needs require. I want you to know, too, that I would not consider relocating to Salt Lake City to be a hardship! It is certainly one of the most beautiful areas I have ever seen.

As you described to me what you are looking for in a controller, I had a sense of "déjà vu" because my current boss was in a similar position when I went to work for him. He needed someone to come in and be his "right arm" and take on an increasing amount of his management responsibilities so that he could be freed up to do other things. I have played a key role in the growth and profitability of his multi-unit business, and he has come to depend on my sound financial and business advice as much as my day-to-day management skills.

It would be a pleasure to work for a successful individual such as yourself, and I feel I could contribute significantly to your business not only through my accounting and business background but also through my strong qualities of loyalty, reliability, and trustworthiness. I am confident that I could learn Quick Books rapidly, and I would welcome being trained to do things your way. I send best wishes for the holidays, and I look forward to hearing from you again soon.

Yours sincerely,

Jacob Evangelisto

In this section, you will find resumes and cover letters of manufacturing professionals—and of people who want to work in the manufacturing field. How do manufacturing professionals differ from other job hunters? Why should there be a book dedicated to people seeking jobs in the manufacturing field? Based on more than 20 years of experience in working with job hunters, this editor is convinced that resumes and cover letters which "speak the lingo" of the field you wish to enter will communicate more effectively than language which is not industry-specific. This book is designed to help people (1) who are seeking to prepare their own resumes and (2) who wish to use as models "real" resumes of individuals who have successfully launched careers in the manufacturing industry or advanced in the field. You will see a wide range of experience levels reflected in the resumes in this book. Some of the resumes and cover letters were used by individuals seeking to enter the field; others were used successfully by senior professionals to advance in the field.

Newcomers to an industry sometimes have advantages over more experienced professionals. In a job hunt, junior professionals can have an advantage over their more experienced counterparts. Prospective employers often view the less experienced workers as "more trainable" and "more coachable" than their seniors. This means that the mature professional who has already excelled in a first career can, with credibility, "change careers" and transfer skills to other industries.

Newcomers to the field may have disadvantages compared to their seniors. Almost by definition, the inexperienced manufacturing professional—the young person who has recently entered the job market, or the individual who has recently received certifications respected by the industry—is less tested and less experienced than senior managers, so the resume and cover letter of the inexperienced professional may often have to "sell" his or her potential to do something he or she has never done before. Lack of experience in the field she wants to enter can be a stumbling block to the junior manager, but remember that many employers believe that someone who has excelled in anything—academics, for example—can excel in many other fields.

Some advice to inexperienced professionals...
If senior professionals could give junior professionals a piece of advice about careers, here's what they would say: Manage your career and don't stumble from job to job in an incoherent pattern. Try to find work that interests you, and then identify prosperous industries which need work performed of the type you want to do. Learn early in your working life that a great resume and cover letter can blow doors open for you and help you maximize your salary.

Special help for career changers...
For those changing careers—either out of manufacturing or into manufacturing—you will find useful the resumes and cover letters marked "Career Change" on the following pages. Consult the Table of Contents for page numbers showing career changers.

Exact Name of Person
Exact Title
Exact Name of Company
Address
City, State, Zip

ADMINISTRATIVE ASSISTANT

Dear Exact Name of Person (or Dear Sir or Madam if answering a blind ad):

With the enclosed resume, I would like to introduce you to my background as a natural leader with a talent for training and supervising others along with strong administrative skills which I could put to work for your organization.

As you will see from my resume, I have been with GMC Engineering Inc. for more than twelve years, and I have earned a reputation as a detail-oriented quick learner known for high levels of creativity and initiative. I have become recognized as a young professional who can be counted on to give my time freely to advise and guide others. With excellent skills in many areas, I have been effective in training others to achieve superior results in office operations, professional skills, and technical areas.

Skilled in many areas, I offer special knowledge of engineering and other computer systems. With a reputation as a team player, I am known for my willingness to help others and pass my knowledge on to co-workers. Through my professionalism and ability to learn quickly, I earned advancement to Administrative Assistant.

If you can use a talented young professional who meets challenges head-on and thrives on them, please contact me to suggest a time when we might meet to discuss your goals and how my background might serve your needs. I can provide outstanding references at the appropriate time.

Sincerely,

Vanessa C. Mither

Alternate Last Paragraph:
I hope you will welcome my call soon to arrange a brief meeting when we might meet to discuss your needs and goals and how my background might serve them. I can provide outstanding references at the appropriate time.

VANESSA C. MITHER

1110½ Hay Street, Fayetteville, NC 28305 • preppub@aol.com • (910) 483-6611

OBJECTIVE   To benefit an organization that can use a self-motivated and experienced office manager, administrative assistant, or data entry professional with exceptional computer skills and a background in purchasing and inventory control, manufacturing, and supervision.

EDUCATION   Division System Specialist Program, GMC training program, 2001.
Continuous Flow Workshop, GMC training program, 1999.
Completed courses in Customer Service (1987) and Basic First Aid (1997), Springfield Community College, Springfield, IL.

COMPUTERS   *Office:* Microsoft Word, Excel, PowerPoint, and Outlook
Manufacturing and Mainframe: Skilled in the operation of the IBM AS-400, IBM S/36, and IBM S/38 computer systems; FoxBase engineering software and EDI ordering system.

EXPERIENCE   *With GMC Engineering, Inc., have been promoted to positions of increasing responsibility in this busy manufacturing facility, Springfield, IL:*
2000-present: **ADMINISTRATIVE ASSISTANT.** Performed a variety of clerical and administrative duties for this electronics manufacturing operation.
- Assist and instruct employees on the operation of the various components of the Microsoft Office suite, including Word, Excel, PowerPoint, and Outlook.
- Read engineering drawings and entered data into an IBM AS-400 computer.
- Release customer orders for manufacture and shipment.
- Oversee the maintenance and distribution of the travel reimbursement fund; book all travel and entertainment arrangements for employees and their guests.
- Purchase office supplies and reduced office supply expenditures by 50%.
- Responsible for troubleshooting and correction of order processing problems.

1993-1999: **COORDINATOR OF ADMINISTRATIVE SERVICES.** Was promoted to this position; utilized my organizational and problem-solving skills to ensure that administrative support was provided to the facility in an efficient and effective manner.
- Processed engineered customer orders and released them for manufacture.
- Assisted the scheduler with the purchase of production materials.
- Read engineering drawings and entered pertinent data into an IBM AS-400 or IBM System 38 computer system.
- Learned the FoxBase engineering program, as well as Excel and PowerPoint.
- Filled in for customer service representatives and engineers as needed.

1990-1993: **COMPUTER TERMINAL OPERATOR.** In addition to administrative and clerical tasks, I was responsible for purchasing and served as customer service representative for seven service centers.
- Entered purchase orders and receipts into IBM System/36 and System/38 computers.
- Expedited and purchased production materials as needed and purchased hardware under the direction of the senior buyer.

Other experience:
SALES ASSOCIATE/SWITCHBOARD OPERATOR. Readicut Lumber Company, Springfield, IL (1987-1989). Operated the telephone switchboard and worked the sales floor, providing customer service, processing government contracts, and compiling billing statements.

PERSONAL   Outstanding personal and professional references are available upon request.

Date

Exact Name of Person
Exact Title
Exact Name of Company
Address
City, State, Zip

Dear Exact Name of Person (or Dear Sir or Madam if answering a blind ad):

I would appreciate an opportunity to talk with you soon about how I could contribute to your organization through my versatile experience and skills in office operations, computer applications, and quality control.

As you will see from my enclosed resume, I am a self-motivated professional who believes in the importance of customer satisfaction and quality products and services. I enjoy the challenge of developing methods of improving productivity and effectiveness while reducing costs. Through my excellent verbal and written communication skills, I have become known as one who can be counted on to prepare accurate and timely reports and correspondence and to work well with others in leadership roles while contributing to team efforts.

In my most recent job as an Administrative Assistant at Cruller Inc., I handled a wide range of office and production activities. I prioritized work, provided quality assurance support, controlled inventory, and typed/word processed a variety of reports, documents, and spreadsheets. I also filed and answered multiline phones and then directed calls to appropriate personnel.

I am confident that my willingness to meet challenges head on and dedicate my efforts to increasing efficiency and reducing costs would make me a valuable asset to any organization seeking a dedicated hard worker. I hope you will contact me to suggest a time when we might meet to discuss your needs. I can assure you in advance that I could rapidly become an asset to your organization.

Sincerely,

Elizabeth M. Wordsworth

ELIZABETH M. WORDSWORTH

1110½ Hay Street, Fayetteville, NC 28305   •   preppub@aol.com   •   (910) 483-6611

OBJECTIVE
To benefit an organization that can use my knowledge and experience in office operations, computer applications, and quality control along with my reputation as a self-motivated leader who excels in finding ways to increase productivity while reducing costs.

EDUCATION & TRAINING
Completed a year of general studies at the University of Hawaii, Honolulu, HI, and 1-1/2 years in the Dental Hygiene program at Dayton Technical Community College, OH.
Have completed numerous training programs and seminars on subjects such as:

Team leading concepts	Continuous flow technology	Workplace Safety
Small business operations	Advertising	Small business taxes
Testing/wiring motor control units		Chemical hazard safety

SPECIAL SKILLS
Offer specialized knowledge and experience which includes:
Computers: MS Office, Microsoft Windows, WordPerfect 8.0, and MS Word
Office operations and procedures: preparing special reports, providing quality control, processing work orders, prioritizing jobs, ordering equipment, and preparing spreadsheets

EXPERIENCE
ADMINISTRATIVE ASSISTANT. Cruller Inc., Dayton, OH (2000-02). Handled a wide range of operational activities related to production planning and quality control as well as leading a 20-person team of specialists.
- Made decisions about which procedures and jobs were of greatest priority and organized work flow so that high-dollar jobs were properly completed in a timely manner.
- Reviewed spreadsheets and determined whether needed parts were in stock or were to be ordered from outside vendors.
- Applied my computer skills while processing memos, letters, and reports.
- Provided quality assurance and ensured schematics were followed.
- Answered incoming calls on a multiline system and routed them to the correct person.
- Achieved a perfect first-time no-defects records on units going through testing.
- Established standardized locations for schematic drawings and labels.

TREASURER. Student Government Association, Dayton Technical Community College, Dayton, OH (1997-00). Gained leadership experience and was able to play a role in finding economical ways to improve student quality of life while maintaining budget records and obtaining approval for spending for school activities.
- Compiled and presented reports to the school dean and the association.
- Served as chairperson of the five-member budget committee.

FULL-TIME STUDENT. DTCC, Dayton, OH, and the University of Hawaii, Honolulu, HI (1994-97). Refined my time management and organizational skills while also working to finance my education.

ADMINISTRATIVE ASSISTANT. Hawaii Blueprint Company, Honolulu, HI (1993-94). Held multiple responsibilities related to approving bids and processing the contracts for architectural drawings and building blueprints for state and county planning divisions.
- Filed billing and sales records.
- Learned how to sell and how to prepare bids which resulted in profits for the company.
- Became known for my service orientation and ability to ensure high quality and customer satisfaction.

PERSONAL
Work well with others in team settings or while filling leadership roles.

Exact Name of Person
Exact Title
Exact Name of Company
Address
City, State, Zip

ASSEMBLY PRODUCTION MANAGER

Dear Exact Name of Person (or Dear Sir or Madam if answering a blind ad):

With the enclosed resume, I would like to make you aware of my interest in discussing employment opportunities with your company. I am interested in contributing to an organization that could benefit from my broad background in the food industry where the emphasis has been on providing technical support for sanitation and public health concerns.

As you will see from my resume, I am an effective communicator and manager who excels in working with people ranging from unskilled workers, to skilled workers, to professionals in manufacturing, industrial, and support services environments. Presently the Production Manager for a contract manufacturing firm for several internationally known manufacturers of power tools, I manage a 120-person work force. I have been instrumental in managing the growth of this company from 12 employees to its present level of 120 in just 15 months. In addition to acting as the safety and quality control expert, I ensure compliance with all safety and health standards while advising the General Manager on personnel issues.

An experienced technical instructor and developer of educational programs, I became a subject matter expert on food inspection and sanitation, hygiene, quality control, and workplace safety while working for the United States Department of Agriculture (USDA). In one job I was handpicked as Operations Manager for Food Inspection and Sanitation Support Services for a three-state region. Prior to that assignment, I served as Chief of Food Hygiene, Safety, and Quality Assurance in a region which included all poultry processing plants in northern South Carolina.

If you can use a mature and experienced professional with expert knowledge of sanitation and cleaning along with superior instructional, communication, and planning skills, I hope you will call me soon to arrange a brief meeting at your convenience to discuss your current and future needs and how I might serve them. Thank you in advance for your time and consideration.

Sincerely,

Eric W. Hayman

ERIC W. HAYMAN

1110½ Hay Street, Fayetteville, NC 28305   •   preppub@aol.com   •   (910) 483-6611

OBJECTIVE

To contribute to an organization that can use my knowledge of the food processing industry, experience in providing technical support for sanitation and public health concerns, as well as my excellent communication, customer service, and managerial skills.

EDUCATION & TRAINING

Completed 30 hours in the **Industrial Management and Food Service** program, Fountain Technical Community College, FL, 1996-98.
Studied Liberal Arts at St. Leo College, FL.
Extensive training in food hygiene, safety, sanitation, quality assurance, and food inspection while serving in the U.S. Department of Agriculture.

SPECIAL KNOWLEDGE

Offer special knowledge and skills in numerous areas:
- Familiar with Hazard Analysis Critical Control Points (HACCP) and Good Manufacturing Practices (GMP) programs for food plants
- Routinely work with all regulatory agencies (state and federal)
- Evaluating and certifying food processors worldwide to ensure product safety
- Making decisions in the proper selection of proper cleaning and sanitizing chemicals and methods of application (CIP)
- Developing, writing, implementing, and monitoring food safety programs
- Interpreting microbiological results for plant management to take appropriate action
- Teaching and providing educational support to industry

EXPERIENCE

PRODUCTION MANAGER. Big E Enterprises, Charles City, IA (1998-present). Supervise and coordinate workers in all areas of the assembly process for a subcontracting firm supporting several internationally known manufacturers of power tools.
- Manage 120 employees in a company which has grown from an original work force of 12 people in only a 15-month period.
- Monitor quality control support and have been credited with developing quality checklists as well as methods for improving production procedures.
- Have become familiar with industrial safety procedures and safe handling of chemicals; conduct safety committee meetings, develop guidelines, and regulate safety concerns.
- Oversee production, estimate man-hour requirements, and adjust assembly operations in order to meet consumer demand and scheduling goals.
- Apply technical knowledge while interpreting specifications, blueprints, and job orders.
- Develop production guidelines and instruct personnel.
- Maintain production records; review and chart daily production figures.

Became recognized as a subject matter expert in food sanitation and as a knowledgeable and skilled professional while serving in the United States Department of Agriculture (USDA):
OPERATIONS MANAGER FOR FOOD INSPECTION AND SANITATION SUPPORT SERVICES. Richmond, VA (1993-97). Oversaw sanitary and food inspection operations for red meat processing plants in three states.

CHIEF OF FOOD HYGIENE, SAFETY, AND QUALITY ASSURANCE. Columbia, SC (1989-93). Excelled at the highest levels of my field as the **Food Safety Officer** and subject matter expert for a region which included all poultry processing plants in the northern areas of South Carolina.

PERSONAL

Articulate, self-motivated individual with top-notch communication skills.

Exact Name of Person
Exact Title
Exact Name of Company
Address
City, State, Zip

ASSEMBLY TEAM LEADER   Dear Exact Name of Person (or Dear Sir or Madam if answering a blind ad):

I would appreciate an opportunity to talk with you soon about how I could contribute to your organization through my education, experience, and knowledge.

As you will see from my enclosed resume, I received my B.S. in Electrical Engineering from Arizona State University. In order to complete this rigorous degree program, I was required to pass graduate-level courses in Digital Signal Processing, Project Management for Engineers, Introduction to Neural Processing, and Switching Theory. Since earning my degree, I have supplemented my education with additional courses in AUTOCAD V.15 (Parts 1 and 2) and C Programming.

I earned rapid advancement with Concord, Inc., a division of Varsity Corporation located in Santa Fe, NM, and am currently working at the Varsity Corporation's Automotive Division in Santa Fe. Originally hired by Concord as a Production Technician, I rapidly advanced to a shift supervisor's job before my selection as a Quality Technician. I had completed the screening and interviewing process and been offered a position as an Engineering Intern when I was laid off due to serious business declines and offered a job as an Assembly Technician at another company site.

I am confident that among my strongest skills are my ability to anticipate problems, analyze situations, and develop the solutions which will result in increasing productivity and profitability. In earlier jobs in shipping and receiving operations as well as in technical jobs with Varsity, I have initiated changes which have resulted in reduced man-hours and lowered costs.

If you can use a positive, results-oriented professional with strong technical skills related to automation and production operations, I look forward to hearing from you soon. I can assure you in advance that I have an excellent reputation and would quickly become a valuable asset to your company.

Sincerely,

Gary Andrew Laredo

GARY ANDREW LAREDO

1110½ Hay Street, Fayetteville, NC 28305　　•　　preppub@aol.com　　•　　(910) 483-6611

OBJECTIVE　　To offer my technical abilities to an organization that can benefit from my outstanding problem-solving, decision-making, and leadership skills.

EDUCATION
& TRAINING　　Received a **B.S. in Electrical Engineering,** Arizona State University, Scottsdale, AZ, 1991. To complete this rigorous degree program, was required to pass the following graduate-level courses: Digital Signal Processing, Project Management for Engineers, Introduction to Neural Processing, and Switching Theory.
Have completed additional course work which includes: C Programming, Galen Technical Community College, Galen, NM, 1996; AUTOCAD V.15, Parts I and 2, Logan Technical Community College, Loch, NM, 2001

TECHNICAL
EXPERTISE　　*Operating systems:* UNIX, TOPS10, VAX/VMS, and Windows 2000
Software/languages: Java, C-Programming, FORTRAN, Pascal, Excel, and Lotus 1-2-3

EXPERIENCE　　*Advanced with the Varsity Corporation in the following "track record":*
ASSEMBLY TECHNICIAN and **ACTING TEAM LEADER.** Loch, NM (2001-present). Cross-trained extensively while contributing through my versatility and knowledge to a team which ensures quality, productivity, safety, and customer service for this operation manufacturing climate control modules for automotive air conditioning systems. After only four months, was promoted to acting Team Leader.
- Participate in operations including hand assembly, calibration, testing, and packaging.
- Use hand and power tools, machines, and charging equipment as well as precision gauges and measurement devices to complete assembly operations.
- Member of the team that achieved QS-9000 certification for this facility.

PRODUCTION TECHNICIAN, QUALITY TECHNICIAN, AND SHIFT LEADER. Santa Fe, NM (1999-2000). Originally hired as a Production Technician, after two months was promoted to Team Leader, manufacturing motor control units for air compressors and elevators. Earned rapid promotion with this custom OEM manufacturer.
- Promoted to Quality Technician in May 1999, and was interviewed for and hired as an Engineering Intern just prior to widespread company layoffs due to business declines.
- Made suggestions on improvements or changes to wiring diagrams and specifications.
- Managed as many as eight employees in the production of motor control units.
- As a Quality Technician, ensured units were correctly assembled and wired according to customer and engineering specifications and all electrical components were functioning properly; installed UL (Underwriters Laboratory) labels after units passed inspection.
- Made important contributions that allowed the facility to achieve ISO-9000 certification.

SHIPPING AND RECEIVING CLERK. Phoenix Sales Company, Inc., Phoenix, AZ (1996-98). Suggested procedural changes which resulted in cost reductions for the packaging and shipping department while assisting in picking items, packing, shipping, and receiving.

ASSISTANT SUPERVISOR. Royal Kingdom Corporation, Phoenix, AZ (1989-95). Supervised five employees in a textile printing company with two warehouses; oversaw shipping and receiving for chemicals, as well as printed and unprinted textiles.

Highlights of earlier experience: Completed the set up and complete check of electrical connections and operability of production machinery, Camelback Incorporated, Phoenix, AZ.

Date

Exact Name of Person
Exact Title
Exact Name of Company
Address
City, State, Zip

Dear Exact Name of Person (or Dear Sir or Madam if answering a blind ad):

With the enclosed resume, I would like to make you aware of my experience in logistics and inventory management as well as my desire to put that experience to work for the benefit of your organization.

As you will see from my resume, I was promoted ahead of my peers while serving my country in the U.S. Army and earning a reputation as a creative problem solver. In one job, on my own initiative I saved my employer more than $1 million through identifying and correcting problems related to manufacturer overpricing as well as the receipt of shortaged and damaged goods. I received a respected medal for my contributions.

I am skilled in operating equipment related to warehousing, including forklifts of 10K and below. Highly safety conscious, I have maintained an error-free, accident- free perfect safety record, and I have trained others in safe methods of equipment operation.

Automated logistics operation is an area in which I have had more than five years of experience, and I am experienced with bar code technology. On numerous occasions I have prepared reports and visual aids which have identified problems, recommended solutions, and resulted in the saving of time and money. I have utilized specialized software programs used for inventory control and logistics management, and I am skilled at conducting research through technical manuals and publications.

You will notice that I am an experienced supervisor. In one job I managed 10 employees in an electronics department. In another job, I supervised a staff of 10 people. In my most recent job, I supervised five individuals. I offer a proven ability to train and motivate others, and I am well aware of the need to instill in others an attitude of attention to detail as well as a respect for utilizing available resources in the most time-efficient and cost-effective manner.

If you can use a hard-working and enthusiastic young professional known for an exemplary attitude and work ethic, I would enjoy the opportunity to meet with you in person. I am single and can relocate worldwide according to your needs, and I can provide outstanding personal and professional references at the appropriate time.

Sincerely,

Beth Ann Charo

BETH ANN CHARO

1110½ Hay Street, Fayetteville, NC 28305   •   preppub@aol.com   •   (910) 483-6611

OBJECTIVE

To contribute to an organization that can benefit from my seven years of experience in warehousing, inventory control, shipping and receiving, and automated logistics management.

EDUCATION

Completed extensive training in logistics, materials handling, and computer automated logistics management, U.S. Army Quartermaster School, Ft. Lee, VA. 1995.

LICENSE

Licensed to operate forklifts of 10K and below; certified in CPR.
Have a seven-year accident-free track record in operating all kinds of heavy equipment.

EXPERIENCE

AUTOMATED LOGISTICS SPECIALIST & SUPERVISOR. U.S. Army, Ft. Dix, NJ (2000-present). Was promoted ahead of my peers to this job which involved supervising a staff of five people in the receiving section for aviation equipment.

- Earned a respected medal for my initiative and resourcefulness in saving the company more than $1 million; identified manufacturer overpricing problems and corrected problems related to the receipt of damaged and shortaged equipment.
- Prepared reports of discrepancy; tracked status of costs and equipment on hand and on order; packaged incoming and outgoing supplies by various methods.
- With extensive responsibility for quality control and quality assurance, inspected incoming repair parts for correct letters of documentation and met with department supervisors to explain problems with requests.
- Prepared reports for upper management which were praised for their clarity in identifying problems and recommending solutions.
- Became skilled in all aspects of bar code technology.

COMPUTER-AUTOMATED LOGISTICS SPECIALIST. U.S. Army, Camp Hovey, Korea (1998-99). Supervised a staff of 10 people while managing the distribution of multimillion-dollar weapons components; tracked and assigned man-hour reports, and was responsible for utilizing labor costs in the most efficient manner.

- Provided extensive customer service while communicating by phone with customers and vendors from all over the world.
- Became known for my resourcefulness in resolving complex problems related to parts availability; creatively solved problems in constantly changing circumstances.
- Maintained and operated equipment including 4K generators and 5-ton tractor trailer while also operating forklifts of 10K and below.
- Produced production reports for 12 departments; communicated verbally and in writing.
- Became skilled in utilizing technical manuals and publications for research.

MATERIAL HANDLING & STORAGE SPECIALIST. U.S. Army, Ft. Hood, TX (1994-98). Was promoted ahead of my peers in this job, and received a prestigious medal for my initiative in designing a new method of inventory management which eliminated five jobs and reduced equipment costs.

- Supervised 10 individuals while maintaining an extensive electronics inventory.
- Conducted daily, weekly, monthly, and semiannual inventory inspections.
- Composed productivity and efficiency graphs that I compiled from raw data.
- Supervised shipping and receiving related to the supply of HAWK missile system components to their correct destinations.

PERSONAL

Single; will relocate worldwide. Proven ability to manage multimillion-dollar inventory and related logistics responsibilities. Exemplary work ethic.

Date

Dear Exact Name
Exact Title
Exact Name of Company
Address
City, State Zip

CHEMICAL TECHNICIAN   Dear Exact Name of Person (or Dear Sir or Madam if answering a blind ad):

I would appreciate an opportunity to talk with you soon about the contributions I could make to your operation through my strong customer service focus and proven ability to supervise, train, and motivate personnel.

As you will see, I have extensive experience in high-volume, dynamic retail environments where the primary emphasis was customer service. I have excelled in staff development and am known as an articulate communicator and natural leader.

In my current position as a Chemical Technician at Smith's Lone Creek facility in Dayton, I oversee distribution operations, receiving raw materials to feed the production line and shipping finished product. Recognized as a flexible and reliable professional, I serve as a "floater," serving in any area of the distribution department and managing distribution activities in the absence of the supervisor.

I began my management career with Modern Auto Parts, Inc. After only seven months as a sales representative, I was promoted to manage the store and, in my first year as a manager, took sales from $800,000 to $1,100,000 without any increase in payroll. I was selected Manager of the Year.

At The Auto Shop, I managed a "superstore" with four assistant managers and more than 30 employees, while producing dramatic increases in sales, increased profit as a percentage of sales, and cut payroll as a percentage of the operating budget. I became known for "setting the standard" for customer service and was even featured in written articles because of my commitment to outstanding customer service.

Although I am highly regarded by my present employer, and can provide excellent personal and professional references at the appropriate time, I am interested in exploring other options, where I can better utilize my highly-developed customer service and communication skills. I am skilled at simultaneously coordinating numerous functional areas ranging from sales, to personnel training, to inventory control, and I feel that my experience would make me a valuable addition to your company.

I hope you will call or write me soon to suggest a time when we might meet and discuss your current and future needs and how I might serve them. Thank you in advance for your time.

Sincerely yours,

Kenneth Winston

KENNETH WINSTON

1110½ Hay Street, Fayetteville, NC 28305   •   preppub@aol.com   •   (910) 483-6611

OBJECTIVE

To contribute to an organization that can use an articulate management professional with a strong focus on customer service and the proven ability to train and motivate personnel who offers natural leadership ability as well as supervisory experience in distribution.

EXPERIENCE

CHEMICAL TECHNICIAN. Smith Chemical Co., Dayton, OH (2000-present). Recognized as a reliable professional, have been cross-trained in all distribution department positions, including management of the operation in the absence of the Distribution Manager; served as Customer Service Representative, Material Handler, and Stores Clerk.
- Manage inventory levels of raw material, keeping adequate stock on hand to maintain production levels; oversee scheduling and delivery of all rail cars and trailers.
- Inspect and perform preventive maintenance on all plant equipment; troubleshoot and repair equipment that is not functioning properly to prevent loss of production.
- Assist in the planning and organization of shipping/receiving activities.
- Cross-reference analyses of raw materials received with production specifications.
- Oversee and perform handling, storage, and disposal of all hazardous materials according to company and OSHA safety regulations and guidelines.
- Have supervised as many as 16 employees while overseeing all aspects of the operation of the department in the absence of the Distribution Supervisor.
- As Customer Service Representative, answer a large number of telephone calls, taking orders, answering customer inquiries, and dealing with complaints.

STORE MANAGER. The Auto Shop, Dayton, OH (1994-00). Became known for "setting the standard" for customer service in this company, and was featured in publications because of my commitment to outstanding service; have come to believe that superior customer service is the key to competing in today's marketplace.
- Supervised four assistant managers and more than 30 employees, overseeing both the retail parts and automotive service departments.
- Have excelled in customer service as well as in key management areas which include profit, inventory control, personnel development, sales, and store appearance.
- With a customer base of 150,000 customers per year, 1994 retail sales were $3.2 million.
- From 1994 to 1997, steadily increased profit from 9% to 16% as a percentage of sales.
- Cut payroll from 10.5% to 8.5% of the store's total budget.
- Produced a 26% increase in sales in 1996 compared to 1995.

STORE MANAGER. Modern Auto Parts, Inc., Dayton, NC (1987-94). Began as a Sales Representative and, after only seven months, was promoted to manage the store; in my first year as a manager, took sales from $800,000 to $1,100,000 without any increase in payroll!
- Supervised a unit with more than 10 employees producing $1.2 million in annual sales on a customer base of 100,000 people a year.
- Was selected as *Manager of the Year, 1990*, a selection made from among 15 other managers based on personnel development, shrinkage, sales, and profits.
- Led the store to consistently rank first out of 100 stores in the volume of special orders.

EDUCATION

Hold an Automotive Service Certificate, Dayton Technical Community College; have become knowledgeable in numerous aspects of automotive service including engine repair, brakes, manual drive trains/axles, suspension and steering, and heating and air conditioning.

PERSONAL

Offer the ability to get along with others. Am self-motivated and flexible. Outstanding personal and professional references are available upon request.

Date

Exact Name of Person
Exact Title
Exact Name of Company
Address
City, State, Zip

DATA COORDINATOR   Dear Exact Name of Person (or Dear Sir or Madam if answering a blind ad):

With the enclosed resume, I would like to acquaint you with my exceptional organizational and communication skills as well as my background in data management, purchasing and inventory control, quality assurance, and manufacturing.

As you will see, I have excelled in a variety of positions with Anderson-Smith. I was rewarded for my leadership, organizational skills, and hard work during the opening of a new facility with a promotion to Materials Coordinator, where I oversaw materials purchasing and inventory control, quickly mastering the EDI ordering system. This position was vital to the operation of the plant, as I was responsible for ensuring an adequate supply of materials to maintain production levels.

In my current position as Data Coordinator for the facility, I act as liaison among supervisors, shop employees, OEM customers, and the business manager. I have sharpened my computer skills and refined my knowledge of the AS-400 computer system and the Microsoft Office suite. In addition to my duties as Data Coordinator, I also relieve the receptionist when necessary, answering multi-line phones, typing, and filing.

In the evenings, I am pursuing an Associate's degree in Business Marketing, and have completed numerous training courses for Anderson-Smith, including the Zinger-Miller course on problem-solving and team concepts. I feel that my strong motivational skills, leadership ability, and experience would be valuable additions to your company.

I hope you can use a motivated, articulate professional with strong organizational, communication, and clerical/secretarial skills along with a background in purchasing and inventory control, quality assurance, manufacturing, and data management. I can assure you that I have an excellent reputation and could quickly become a valuable asset to your organization. Please contact me if my skills and talents are of interest to you, and thank you in advance for your consideration.

Sincerely,

Marie Joan White

MARIE JOAN WHITE

1110½ Hay Street, Fayetteville, NC 28305 • preppub@aol.com • (910) 483-6611

OBJECTIVE   To benefit an organization that can use a self-motivated and experienced office manager, administrative assistant or data entry professional with exceptional computer skills and a background in purchasing and inventory control, quality assurance, manufacturing, and data management.

EDUCATION   Enrolled in business marketing courses in the evenings at Stratford Technical College.
Zinger-Miller course, Stratford Technical College, 2002.
AutoCad I course, Stratford Technical College, 2001.
Statistical Process Control course, Stratford Technical College, 2000.

COMPUTERS   *Am proficient with the following computer software and hardware*:
- *Office*: Microsoft Works, Excel, PowerPoint, and Access
- *Manufacturing Mainframe*: Skilled in the operation of the IBM AS-400 computer and the EDI ordering system

EXPERIENCE   *With Anderson-Smith Company (formerly a division of General Electric), have been promoted to positions of increasing responsibility in a busy OEM manufacturing facility.*
2000-present: DATA COORDINATOR. Stratford, CT. Was promoted to this position from Materials Coordinator; act as liaison among supervisors, customer service, shop employees, and the business manager.
- Modify assemblies from engineered bills of materials in preparation for manufacturing production; verify accuracy of all assemblies, ensuring that they are correct according to customer and engineering specifications.
- Assemble packets and distribute jobs to the shop.
- Gained extensive knowledge of the IBM AS-400 computer system.
- Helped mainstream the front end production flow.

1999: **MATERIALS COORDINATOR.** Stratford, CT. Promoted to Materials Coordinator due to my strong organizational skills; responsible for ensuring adequate supply of materials to maintain production levels.
- Expedited material orders and worked closely with the engineering department to determine appropriate substitutes when materials were not available.
- Quickly mastered the EDI computer ordering system.
- Willingly put in the extra effort required to keep production afloat and meet customer demands during a critical transition phase for the company.

1998: **MANUFACTURING TECHNICIAN.** Stamford, CT. Was selected as a member of the start-up team for this expansion of our existing manufacturing operations; was instrumental in the successful start-up of production.
- Identified materials and set up material storage locations.
- Trained new hires in assembly and electrical wiring and performed final inspections.

1991-1998: **MANUFACTURING TECHNICIAN.** Stratford, CT. Worked at this facility performing duties in various departments.
- Fabricated motor control structures, installing the wiring harnesses and wiring cells.
- Modified components according to customer and engineering specifications.
- Was trained in Statistical Process Control as well as mastering the reading of wiring diagrams and schematics.

Date

Mr. Larry Smith
Director of Human Resources
Swift Manufacturing
500 North Broad Street
Lakeland, NJ 28339

DEPARTMENT MANAGER Dear Mr. Smith:

With the enclosed resume, I would like to make you aware of my background as an experienced management professional with a strong manufacturing background. I offer proven leadership ability and strong communication skills along with the ability to develop and implement new programs and procedures that increase efficiency and lower production costs.

As you will see, I am currently excelling as a Department Manager at SpinCare Industries at the facility in Peachtree, Georgia. In this position, I manage seven supervisors and a production team of 140 employees producing 250,000 pounds of finished product per week. I manage and develop supply and project budgets totaling more than $800,000 and am responsible for the maintenance and accountability of over $7 million worth of manufacturing equipment. I started with SpinCare as a Product Manager, where I quickly distinguished myself by producing two-thirds of the written documentation for implementing I.S.O. procedures. Due in large part to my efforts, the Denniston facility was the first SpinCare plant to achieve I.S.O. 9002 certification.

Prior to joining SpinCare, I proudly served as a Captain in the United States Marine Corps, where I served as a HAWK missile Firing Platoon Commander during the Persian Gulf War. I managed 70 personnel and was responsible for the maintenance, security, and accountability of more than $45 million worth of advanced equipment. I received a number of prestigious awards and medals for my exemplary performance.

I have earned a Bachelor of Arts degree from Georgia State University, which I have supplemented with my military training as well as with professional development courses related to manufacturing, leadership, and management.

If you can use an experienced management professional whose strong supervisory and communication skills have been tested in a variety of challenging environments, I hope you will contact me to suggest a time when we might meet to discuss your needs. I can assure you in advance that I could rapidly become an asset to your organization.

Sincerely,

Jason T. Argo

JASON T. ARGO

1110½ Hay Street, Fayetteville, NC 28305   •   preppub@aol.com   •   (910) 483-6611

OBJECTIVE   To benefit an organization that can use a management professional with a strong manufacturing background and excellent communication and leadership skills.

EXPERIENCE   *At SpinCare Industries, have advanced in the following "track record" of increasing responsibility with this large textiles manufacturer:*
2000-present: **DEPARTMENT MANAGER II.** Peachtree, GA. Due to my success in managing the Spinning and Winding department, was entrusted with the supervision of an additional department (Carding).
- Directly manage seven supervisors and 140 employees producing 250,000 pounds of finished product per week.
- Develop and manage a quarterly supply budget of $120,000 as well as an $80,000 quarterly projects budget; total budgetary responsibility is $800,000 per year.
- Am directing a pilot project which has increased spinning frame production by 6%.
- Responsible for the maintenance and accountability of more than $7 million worth of textile manufacturing equipment
- Coordinated an interdepartmental technical trial which resulted in detection of a critical processing defect, correction of which would greatly improve quality and runnability.
- Respond to all Customer Action Requests (CAR) and I.S.O. documentation involving manufacturing process.

1998-99: **DEPARTMENT MANAGER II.** Peachtree, GA. Promoted to this position; managed the Spinning/Winding department.
- Developed a program which resulted in a minimum annual energy savings of $60,000.
- Implemented procedures resulting in a 3% capacity increase on one production line.

1996-98: **DEPARTMENT MANAGER I.** Crawford, GA. Promoted to this position from a Product Manager/Supervisor position; managed the Spinning/Winding department consisting of four supervisors and 80 employees.
- Developed new programs for producing tencel and high-twist yarn.
- Achieved and maintained 16% improvement in S+E labor cost.

1993-95: **PRODUCT MANAGER, SUPERVISOR.** Denniston, GA. Performed texturing process during shift assignment. Produced two-thirds of the written documentation for implementing I.S.O. procedures including all of the Manufacturing and Quality Control sections; our facility was the first SpinCare plant to achieve I.S.O. 9002 certification.

With the United States Marine Corps, achieved the rank of Captain and proudly served in the Persian Gulf War:
OFFICER, U.S.M.C. Cherry Point, NC (1989-1993). As a HAWK missile Platoon Commander, managed 70 personnel and $45 million worth of advanced equipment and effectively presented a new training program involving senior agencies that was adopted in preparation for Operation Desert Storm.
- Received numerous prestigious awards and medals for exemplary service.

EDUCATION   Bachelor of Arts degree in Political Science, Georgia State University, 1989.
Supplemented my education with numerous professional development courses.

PERSONAL   Have excellent communication skills and have published nine hunting stories in a national magazine. Excellent personal and professional references are available upon request.

Exact Name of Person
Exact Title
Exact Name of Company
Address
City, State, Zip

DIRECTOR OF
OPERATIONS
SEEKING
CHIEF
EXECUTIVE OFFICER
POSITION

Dear Exact Name of Person (or Dear Sir or Madam if answering a blind ad):

With the enclosed resume, I would like to make you aware of my interest in the position as Chief Operating Officer.

A resourceful management style with creative problem-solving ability

As you will see from my resume, I offer a management style which is committed to achieving lowest total production costs in the process of producing superior quality products. After earning my B.S. in Biology and prior to earning my master's degree, I developed new waste water technologies for a Fortune 500 company that saved the company $2 million annually. I then became Plant Manager for a plant which serviced the Rohm & Haas corporation, and in that capacity I developed processes to recover precious metals from hazardous waste which saved $25 million yearly. Because of my outstanding bottom-line results, I was recruited by a Florida company to manage its technical services. I have contributed numerous common-sense solutions to manufacturing problems and spearheaded the development of more than 20 new products. I have also developed numerous cost-saving manufacturing solutions such as a system I developed for a customer company which saved the company nearly a quarter of a million dollars annually. I am a resourceful individual who thrives on developing plans for new areas of technology.

Common-sense manager with outstanding teambuilding skills

Currently as the #2 manager in a company generating revenues of $120 million annually, I am excelling in a position which was created especially for me—Director of Operations. Although I am held in the highest regard in my current company, I am selectively exploring opportunities in companies that can use a strong problem-solver committed to aggressive improvements in quality, profitability, and customer satisfaction.

If my background and skills interest you, I hope you will contact me to suggest a time when we could meet in person to discuss your needs. I can provide outstanding references.

Yours sincerely,

Edmond J. Warren

EDMOND J. WARREN

1110½ Hay Street, Fayetteville, NC 28305   •   preppub@aol.com   •   (910) 483-6611

OBJECTIVE   To contribute to an organization that can use an experienced executive and resourceful problem solver who has achieved strong bottom-line results while managing functions including manufacturing, accounting, purchasing, logistics, and management information systems.

EDUCATION   **Masters in Public Administration,** Florida State University, Gainesville, FL, 1992.
B.S. in Biology, University of Maryland, Baltimore, MD, 1983.
Certification in Production and Inventory Management (CPIM), 2002.

EXPERIENCE   1995-present. <u>Animal Husbandry.</u> Colersville, FL. Have progressed to the number two management position in this international company while playing a key role in growing revenues from $300,000 a month in 1995 to its current level of $10 million a month:
DIRECTOR OF OPERATIONS (2000-present). This position was specially created for me. Oversee transportation of manufactured products from three warehouses and three manufacturing sites to 140 "ship-to" locations. As a biologist by education, provide expertise on matters including HACCP and bio-security to poultry packing plants and farms.
- Increased inventory turnover from 5.7 to 12.8 turns within 18 months.
- Reduced shipping errors from 60 per 10,000 to one per 10,000.
- Reduced work-in-process inventory by 35% and increased output by 38%.
- Decreased staff by 11% while improving quality assurance and customer satisfaction.
- Have invented numerous cost-saving manufacturing solutions; reduced costs 15% through a dry packaging system I developed, and saved a customer company nearly a quarter million dollars annually through a common-sense system I devised for packaging materials.
- Supervised the design of hardware/software systems to provide an efficient flow of information.

TECHNICAL SERVICES DIRECTOR (1995-99). Because of my innovative problem-solving within Rohm & Haas, was recruited by Animal Husbandry to develop environmentally friendly materials for a vast network of hog and poultry producers and packers.
- Set up and managed chemical operations; spearheaded the development of 21 new products and improved 17 replacements at an annual cost savings of $2.3 million.
- Developed protocols for and coordinated use of products to maintain bio-security; created a more environmentally friendly workplace and reduced potential corporate liability by reducing chemical usage 22%.
- Coordinated HACCP plans for multiple poultry packing plant sanitation projects.

1984-95. <u>Diversified Industries, Baltimore, MD.</u> Excelled as **PLANT MANAGER & TECHNICAL SERVICES DIRECTOR** for a company which provided contracted services to Rohm & Haas. Managed a plant with 130 people.
- Developed proprietary processes to recover precious materials from catalysts, filter media, film emulsion, and solutions designated as "hazardous waste;" cut costs by $15 million yearly.
- Directed the startup of operations processing up to 900,000 pounds monthly of raw material valued at $285 million annually.
- Developed technology and processes that complied with air quality and solid waste regulations.

PERSONAL   Excellent references. Extensive ISO 9000 experience. Reputation as visionary thinker.

Date

Exact Name of Person
Exact Title
Exact Name of Company
Address
City, State, Zip

ELECTRICAL TECHNICIAN

Dear Exact Name of Person (or Dear Sir or Madam if answering a blind ad):

With the enclosed resume, I would like to make you aware of my considerable technical electronics and electrical skills as well as my experience in managing the repair of armament and electrical systems.

As you will see from my resume, I have served my country with distinction since 1997. While being promoted ahead of my peers and receiving several medals for distinguished technical knowledge and management skills, I have earned a reputation as a skilled troubleshooter and problem solver.

In my most recent assignments I excelled in managing up to seven individuals involved in maintaining aircraft/missile systems including electrical systems. I have become accustomed to working in environments in which there was "no room for error" because a mistake by me or one of my associates could cost the loss of human lives and assets. On the formal written citation for one medal which I received, I was praised for my "superb work ethic and troubleshooting ability" and I was also described in writing as "the key to the maintenance effort" during a major project involving 24 helicopters.

With a belief that strong training programs produce highly skilled technicians, I have on my own initiative developed training programs which improved the skill levels of electricians and armament fire control specialists. I have been praised in formal performance evaluations for "unwavering commitment to improving the skills of subordinates," and I have been described in writing as "one of the most trusted and respected electrical troubleshooters."

Although I have been promoted ahead of my peers and was strongly encouraged to remain in the military, I have decided to leave the U.S. Army and seek civilian employment. I am available for relocation and travel according to your needs.

If you can use a creative young professional who responds to challenges and pressure with hard work and dedication, I hope you will contact me to suggest a time when we might meet to discuss your needs. I can assure you that I could quickly become an asset to your organization and can provide outstanding references at the appropriate time.

Sincerely,

Daniel Shirley

DANIEL SHIRLEY

1110½ Hay Street, Fayetteville, NC 28305 • preppub@aol.com • (910) 483-6611

OBJECTIVE

To offer excellent technical electronics skills, with an emphasis on armament and electrical systems repair, to an organization that can use an adaptable quick learner with extensive diagnostic, troubleshooting, and problem-solving experience.

EDUCATION & TRAINING

Completed nearly a year of college coursework, Delta College, MA.
Extensive U.S. Army training in electricity and armaments repair.

TECHNICAL EXPERTISE

Use and interpret: layout drawings, schematics, and diagrams to solve problems; skilled at troubleshooting to the circuit level using tools and equipment including:

amp meters	multimeters	tensiometers	electrical carts
auxiliary power units	heaters	hydraulic test carts	light carts

Aircraft expertise: AH-64.

Awards & Medals: Won **nine prestigious medals** recognizing my expertise as an electrician, management skills, hard work, positive attitude, and resourcefulness.

- On one citation, was praised for "superb work ethic and troubleshooting ability which enabled all unit aircraft to complete six table gunnery and harmonize gun systems."
- On the formal write-up for one medal, was described as "the key to the maintenance effort" during special operations in assuring that 24 Apache helicopters were operational.

EXPERIENCE

Built a reputation as a knowledgeable technical expert, U.S. Army:

SUPERVISOR & ELECTRICAL TECHNICIAN. U.S. Army, Korea (2002-present). Supervise seven employees and shop equipment valued at $100,000.

- Led six team projects which completed more than 50 work orders which were interrupting mission capability.
- Was selected as Assistant Maintenance Supervisor over four other mid-managers based on my vast technical abilities.
- Emphasized training and retraining and was noted for my "unwavering commitment to improving the skills of subordinates;" cross-trained ten armament technicians in electrical component repair, and implemented a new advanced skill level training program which greatly improved customer support.
- Supervise and perform aviation unit, intermediate, and depot maintenance on the AH-64 electrical and instrument systems and the electrical, electronic, mechanical, and pneudraulics systems associated with the AH-64 armament and fire control systems.
- Have become noted for my skill in diagnosing and repairing malfunctions in electrical, instrument, and fire control systems and components including solid state and transistorized subsystems according to technical devices and instruments.

AH-64A ARMAMENT FIRE CONTROL REPAIRER. U.S. Army, Ft. Benning, GA (1997-01). Performed the same duties as those described above while managing a squad of seven employees in an attack helicopter battalion capable of worldwide relocation at any time.

- Maintained aircraft/missile systems to include electrical systems; performed maintenance on aircraft weapons components, fire control, sighting elements, electronic and mechanical devices for a fleet of 24 AH-64A Apache helicopters.
- Was accountable for $4.5 million in tools and ground support equipment.
- Was described in writing as **"one of the unit's most trusted and respected electrical troubleshooters"** and praised for "excellent squad supervision and problem-solving techniques which helped the unit achieved an exceptional readiness rating."

PERSONAL

Outstanding personal and professional references. Held Secret security clearance.

LENNY SOUTHEBY

1110½ Hay Street, Fayetteville, NC 28305

preppub@aol.com

(910) 483-6611

OBJECTIVE

To benefit an organization that can use a skilled troubleshooter, and versatile problem solver with expertise related to the electrical, mechanical, field engineering, as well as the instrumentation and control disciplines.

EDUCATION & TRAINING

Completed EMT training, Midwestern Community College, MI, as well as numerous technical, quality assurance, and management courses sponsored by companies including Michigan Power & Light, Lansing Nuclear Power Training Center, and others.

At Lansing Nuclear Plant of MP&L, gained hands-on experience related to:

terminating	meggering of power and instrument control cables
clearance training	coaxial cable splicing
breaker testing	I&C training

Graduated from Cerro Gordo High School, Cerro Gordo, CA.

CERTIFICATIONS Certified **Electrician.**

EXPERIENCE

Summary of experience: In the following track record of professional advancement, have acquired more than 20 years of industrial experience.
- Extensive experience in nuclear generating plants.
- Experienced in the installation and corrective/preventive maintenance of AC/DC electrical instrumentation control and distribution systems.
- Experienced in document review and work package final review for closeout.
- Known as a highly adept troubleshooter while working with I&C/electrical trouble tickets, routes, and calibration of electrical and instrumentation devices such as thermocouples, RTDs, transducers, level and flow switches, temperature indicators, pressure and level transmitters, 480 and 4160 Volt Breaker Testing.

GENERAL FOREMAN. Doleman Plant of Michigan Electric, Wabash, MI (2000-present). Supervised the Foreman in the layout and planning of pre-shutdown and shutdown activities.
- Oversaw activities which included installation of new motor drives, replacement of motors and instrumentation loops, and relocation and rewiring of switchgear.

ELECTRICIAN SPECIALIST. Sunshine, Inc. (PGI), Hollywood, MI (1999-2000). Installed barcode scanners and computers throughout the plant; installed and maintained lighting, receptacles and motors according to prescribed schedule.

ELECTRICIAN SPECIALIST AND FOREMAN. Andrews Industrial Constructors, Johnson Steel, Richmond, IA (1999). Supervised pulling and termination of wire and cable in switchgear, MCCs, starters, and motors.

ELECTRICIAN SPECIALIST. Southern Constructors, Polymer Group, Inc., Benson, NC (1998-1999). Pulled/terminated wire and cable in switchgear, MCCs, starters, motors, and PLC controls on the Miratec addition.

ELECTRICIAN SPECIALIST. Power Services, Holtrachem Manufacturing, Riegelwood, NC (1998). Researched and rerouted existing underground electrical power and controls for the construction of new facilities.

ELECTRICIAN SPECIALIST. Rust Construction Company, International Paper, Riegelwood, NC (1997). Installed conduit and cable tray; pulled and terminated wire and cable in switchgear, MCCs, starters and motors; completed PLC and DCS controls on the #4 bleach plant addition and modification.

ELECTRICAL QA/QC SPECIALIST. McIntosh Inc., Florence, SC (1996). Inspected switchgear, MCCs, starters, motors, lighting, and receptacles for correct installation. Tested and started up the listed systems with punch list items resolved and tested upon completion.
*   Performed static testing on Teflon process piping throughout the launch building under the direction of the Roche electrical engineer.

ELECTRICIAN SPECIALIST AND FOREMAN. B.E.&K. Construction Company, three consecutive projects (1995-96):
*   *International Paper,* Richmond, VA: Supervised Phase I, II, and III at the lime kiln and pressure washer/dregs areas to include installing DCS controls for 480V/4160V motors and for new and existing instrumentation.
*   *Champion Paper,* Duluth, MN: Supervised work for a paper machine shutdown to include installing PLC and DCS systems, terminating field instruments, MCC controls, and motors.
*   *Roche Nevada,* Las Vegas, NV: Installed conduit and supports; pulled cable and terminated cable and wiring to instruments in the "Pilot" building.

ELECTRICIAN SPECIALIST AND ELECTRICAL FIELD FOLLOW. Dallas Construction Company, Dallas, TX (1990-95). Reviewed modification work package for workability and paperwork while keeping all work steps signed off and assisting craftsmen with questions about job installation or plant procedures.
*   Installed seismic conduit supports and conduit, pulled cable, and carried out control work.
*   Assisted in the installation of HVAC upgrade for unit 1 and 2 control rooms and the addition of smoke detectors in unit 1 heater drain pump rooms.
*   Was Lead Electrician on installation of chlorine detection systems for unit 1 and 2 reactor and turbine buildings; assisted on the acceptance testing and startup of new systems.
*   Ran conduit, pulled wire/cable, control work; worked on installation of fire seals upgrade modifications; assisted on acceptance test on system upgrade of motor-operated valves.
*   Assisted on a project to upgrade all essential plant equipment working with CP&L plant electricians on modifications.

ELECTRICIAN SPECIALIST. Duckworth Electric Co., BMW Plant, Spartanburg, SC (1988-90). Installed wireway and conduit, cable pulling, termination of wiring in PLC panels and HI/LO/Brake Termination in 480V motors. Worked closely with Durr Engineering to resolve field installation and punchlist items on conveyors and paint booth systems.

PERSONAL   Married with children. Outstanding personal and professional reputation and can provide exceptionally strong references from all previous employers. Nonsmoker and nondrinker.

Exact Name of Person
Exact Title
Exact Name of Company
Address
City, State, Zip Code

ELECTRICIAN Dear Exact Name of Person (or Dear Sir or Madam if answering a blind ad):

With the enclosed resume, I would like to acquaint you with my skills as an experienced commercial and industrial electrician with a solid background in the wiring, maintenance, troubleshooting, and repair of electrical systems.

As you will see from my enclosed resume, I have extensive training in various types of wiring and electrical systems. In my most recent position at Gorham Industries, I assembled, wired, and performed troubleshooting on motor control units for industrial and commercial grade air compressors and chillers. Through our efforts, the department was awarded ISO 9002 certification while achieving the company's goal of "zero defects" in on-time shipping.

At Berenger Electric I acquired valuable experience in new construction wiring and installation as well as applying my knowledge in reading blueprints and schematics while working on the new Morehouse Medical Center building.

During my years of experience, I have learned to troubleshoot and repair high-tension systems and electrical substations, as well as working with the wiring and electrical systems of a wide variety of ships and power equipment. In addition to the Electrical Wireman Journeyman's Course, I have completed supplementary training courses at Washington University and Payne Technical College. I feel that my extensive industry experience and education will be a strong asset to your organization.

If you can benefit from the services of a highly experienced electrician whose skills have been tested in a wide variety of industrial and commercial environments, please contact me to suggest a time when we might meet to discuss your needs and how I might meet them. Thank you in advance for your time and consideration.

Sincerely,

Roy L. Munster

ROY L. MUNSTER

1110½ Hay Street, Fayetteville, NC 28305 • preppub@aol.com • (910) 483-6611

OBJECTIVE   To benefit an organization that can use an experienced electrician with a solid background in wiring, maintenance, troubleshooting, and repair of industrial and commercial electrical systems.

EDUCATION   General Manufacturing (GMC) Course, Payne Technical College, 1998.
Zinger-Miller Course, Payne Technical College, 1998.
Electrical Equipment Testing & Maintenance, Washington University, 1989.
How to Charge Substation Batteries course, Canal Zone Vocational School, 1988.
Graduated from Canal Zone Vocational School's Electrical Wireman Journeyman's course, Panama.

SPECIAL SKILLS   Offer expertise in the following areas and with the following equipment:

troubleshooting all electrical devices	Lincoln & Hobart welders
wire machines	machine shop
heat treating equipment	electrical circuit design
plumbing	AC/DC motors & generators
fabrication	3-phase 480 volt wiring
3-phase 208 volt wye delta controls	electrical controls

EXPERIENCE   **QUALITY TECHNICIAN.** Gorham Industries, Payne, OR (2000-present). Perform various electrical assembly and wiring tasks in this fast-paced factory environment.
- Read wiring diagrams, schematics, and engineering order specifications to ensure units were completed according to requirements and proper standards.
- Assemble, wire, and perform troubleshooting on motor control units for industrial and commercial grade air compressors and chillers.
- Learned testing and troubleshooting of a wide variety of motor control units from different manufacturers.
- Was credited with making contributions which allowed the company to reach its goal of "zero defects" in on-time shipping.
- Member of a department which successfully qualified for ISO 9002 certification.

ELECTRICIAN. Berenger Electric Company, Payne, OR (1998-00). Primary responsibility was wiring and electrical installation of new construction at the Morehouse Medical Center job site.
- Installed junction boxes; mounted and wired electrical panels.
- Cut, bent, and installed electrical conduit of various sizes.
- Ran wires and cables through conduit to junction boxes, panels, and breaker boxes.

Other experience: WIREMAN/ELECTRICIAN. Panama Canal Zone, Balboa, Panama. Started with Panama Canal Zone as Electrician Apprentice at Canal Zone Vocational School; advanced to Wireman/Electrician after completing the program.
- Performed routine maintenance, troubleshooting, and repair on air and oil circuit breakers of electrical substations.
- Maintained various power equipment, including forklifts, high-capacity battery chargers, welding machines, magnetic drills, etc.
- Learned to troubleshoot and repair high-tension electrical systems.
- Worked on wiring, electrical systems, and batteries for ships, barges, beacons, and buoys.

PERSONAL   Excellent personal and professional references are available upon request.

Date

Dear Sir or Madam:

With the enclosed resume, I would like to make you aware of my background as an experienced industrial equipment specialist who offers a track record of success in operations management and training related to maintenance, repair, and operations of heavy equipment.

In my most recent position as an Instructor and Quality Control Inspector for Vimax International, I was responsible for conducting in-service inspections to ensure that equipment delivered to the Army was safe and fully operational. I trained civilian and military personnel in the performance of troubleshooting to the component level, repair and replacement of defective parts and systems, and maintenance of new Family of Medium Tactical Vehicles (FMTV) equipment. As a Manufacturing Equipment Specialist, I instructed employees in the proper operation and maintenance of the full range of ground support equipment.

With a Bachelor of Science in Business Management from Central Wyoming Community College as well as a two-year diploma in Manufacturing Maintenance Technology, I have a strong educational background to support my years of practical experience.

If you can use an accomplished management professional whose knowledge of industrial equipment maintenance and repair and exceptional training abilities have been tested in challenging environments, then I look forward to hearing from you soon. I assure you in advance that I have an excellent reputation and would quickly become an asset to your organization.

Sincerely,

Samuel D. Dylan

SAMUEL D. DYLAN

1110½ Hay Street, Fayetteville, NC 28305   •   preppub@aol.com   •   (910) 483-6611

OBJECTIVE

To benefit an organization that can use an experienced manufacturing equipment specialist and instructor with strong communication and motivational skills who offers experience in managing all phases of heavy equipment maintenance, repair, and operations.

EDUCATION

Bachelor of Science in **Business Management**, Central Wyoming Community College, Elkhart, WY.
Completed a two-year diploma program in **Manufacturing Maintenance Technology**, Central Wyoming Community College, Elkhart, WY.
Completed a tractor-trailer operator course, Fort Bragg, NC.

LICENSES

Hold a Class "A" Commercial Driver's License (CDL).

EXPERIENCE

INSTRUCTOR and **QUALITY CONTROL INSPECTOR.** Vimax, Fort Bragg, NC (2000-present). Because of my vast knowledge of automotive manufacturing, was specially selected for this position which involved inspecting the new Family of Medium Tactical Vehicles (FMTV) equipment and road-testing all FMTVs to ensure that the vehicles being delivered to the Army were safe and fully operational before they were put into service.
- Conducted a complete inspection of all vehicles, checking for vehicle damage, missing parts, and proper fluid levels as well as safety and correct operation of all moving parts.
- Performed troubleshooting to the component level to determine the cause of any system malfunctions and repaired or replaced defective parts before issuing the vehicle.
- Served as Assistant Instructor for the FMTV Unit Maintenance and Direct Support level Maintenance Courses.
- Trained military personnel in troubleshooting, maintenance, and repair of electrical, hydraulic, and pneumatic systems, as well as the engine and drive train of FMTVs.
- Provided operator training to military personnel for all truck models, with additional training on the dump truck, cargo crane, and wrecker.

MANUFACTURING EQUIPMENT SPECIALIST. ATCOM, St. Louis, MO (1987-1999). While working for a government contractor, traveled worldwide to provide new equipment training to mechanics and equipment operators in supported units as well as technical, logistical, and supply assistance.
- Attended numerous New Equipment Instructor Training courses in order to effectively coach maintenance and operations personnel on appropriate procedures.
- Conducted Component Testing and Repair classes for Direct Support Level Maintenance Mechanics.
- Trained personnel on the operation and maintenance of various types of equipment to support the ground operation of troops, which included:

Generators	Air Conditioners	Water Purification Units
Tank & Pump Units	Mobile Field Kitchens	Refrig/Cold Storage Units
Bridge Boats	Laundry & Bath Units	Herman Nelson Heaters

Highlights of other Experience:
Provided my industrial maintenance technology expertise while excelling in positions as a **POWER GENERATOR MECHANIC, HEAVY EQUIPMENT MECHANIC,** and **POWER PLANT MAINTENANCE MECHANIC** at locations throughout the Fort Bragg military installation.

PERSONAL

Excellent personal and professional references are available upon request.

Date

Exact Name of Person
Exact Title
Exact Name of Company
Address
City, State, Zip

FOOD PRODUCTION MANAGER

Dear Exact Name of Person (or Dear Sir or Madam if answering a blind ad):

With the enclosed resume, I would like to make you aware of my recent background in management as well as my previous experience in sales.

As you will see from my resume, I am currently excelling as a Production Manager with McAdam Foods, a company which has rewarded my strong problem-solving and communication skills by promoting me in a rapid track record of advancement. In my current position managing three supervisors and three departments, I indirectly supervise 125 people and am regarded as an articulate communicator with a flair for getting my point across.

Prior to earning my Bachelor of Business Administration degree, I worked briefly in the jewelry business, and that job allowed me to discover my natural marketing ability and talent for sales.

With a reputation as an aggressive and goal-oriented individual, I thrive on the challenge of tackling ambitious goals. On my own initiative, I have developed and designed process improvements in two of the departments I manage, and under my direction, equipment troubleshooting guides were created which significantly aided my junior supervisors in achieving high production goals.

If you can use a dynamic individual and resourceful problem solver who thrives on the challenge of a fast-paced environment, I hope you will contact me to suggest a time when we might meet to discuss your goals and how I might help you achieve them. Thank you in advance for your time.

Sincerely,

Kelly J. Richards

KELLY JUNE RICHARDS

1110½ Hay Street, Fayetteville, NC 28305   •   preppub@aol.com   •   (910) 483-6611

OBJECTIVE

To benefit an organization that can use an enthusiastic, highly motivated professional with strong communication skills and proven sales ability who offers a reputation as a disciplined hard worker and creative problem solver known for persistence and perseverance.

EDUCATION & TRAINING

Earned **Bachelor of Business Administration**, Houghton University, Houghton, AL, 1993.

Excelled in extensive management and technical training through McAdams Foods.

EXPERIENCE

With McAdams Foods – Mexican Original, a large national food service manufacturer in Houghton, AL, have advanced in the following "track record" of promotion while earning a reputation as a dynamic individual and resourceful problem-solver who thrives on the challenge of a fast-paced environment:

PRODUCTION MANAGER. (2000-present). Report to the plant manager; was promoted to this position from Shift Superintendent; manage all aspects of first-shift production operations and direct the work of three supervisors and two processing departments.

- Interview, hire, and train new personnel; motivate, discipline, and counsel up to 125 employees.
- Consistently achieve or exceed objectives in all areas of production management; meet ambitious production quotas and keep turnover, absenteeism, and safety issues within prescribed goals.
- On my own initiative, designed and implemented process improvements in the corn and flour departments; under my direction, troubleshooting guides were created for packaging, corn, and die-cut equipment to aid in solving machine/product problems.
- Have become known for my ability to maintain effective working relationships at all levels of the organization; lead by example through my strong work ethic.

SHIFT SUPERINTENDENT. (1996-00). Oversaw first-shift production in the flour and corn departments, providing supervisory oversight to five supervisors and 150 team members and coordinating with other shifts to maintain work flow and ensure that production objectives were met or exceeded.

- On my own initiative, created a new troubleshooting guide for supervisors and operators.
- Established evaluation procedures and reviewed all team members' performance appraisals written by supervisors whom I managed.
- Provided oversight for a training program for production personnel to prevent repetitive motion injuries and reduce inefficiency.
- Increased production yields on small press lines from 125 to 136 in a three-month period.
- Approved all work orders and requisitioned equipment for production.

DEPARTMENT SUPERVISOR. (1994-96). Managed all phases of first shift production on the taco lines, tostado line, and chip line, supervising more than 50 team members.

- Trained operators and team leaders; prepared performance evaluations on all employees and became known for my excellent writing and counseling skills.
- Conducted research and development testing to monitor customer reaction to new products.

Previous sales experience:

Excelled in all aspects of sales and demonstrated my excellent communication and customer service skills while selling jewelry for Saslow's Jewelers, Houghton, AL.

PERSONAL

Am an aggressive, goal-oriented individual who thrives on tackling ambitious goals.

Career Change

Tom Smith
Director of Production
Woodlake, AZ 25555

FORCE VARIATION MACHINE OPERATOR

Here you see an example of an individual in career transition. With the manufacturing industry in temporary distress, this manufacturing machine operator anticipates being downsized and he has decided to put out "feelers" to assess his chances of returning to his former field of employment -- golfing.

Dear Mr. Smith:

With the enclosed resume, I would like to make you aware of my interest in a position as an Assistant Golf Pro.

You will notice from my resume that I excelled as a golfing professional prior to transitioning into the manufacturing industry. I have continued teaching and mentoring golfing enthusiasts while employed in the manufacturing industry, so my skills are current.

If you can use a talented golf professional with exceptional teaching skills along with a proven ability to motivate and inspire improvement in students of all levels, I hope you will contact me soon to suggest a time when we might meet to discuss your needs. I can assure you in advance that I have an outstanding reputation and could quickly become an asset to your organization.

Sincerely,

Ward H. Yeats

WARD H. YEATS

1110½ Hay Street, Fayetteville, NC 28305 • preppub@aol.com • (910) 483-6611

OBJECTIVE

To benefit an organization that can use a dedicated machining professional with a proven ability to meet ambitious goals for productivity, safety, and quality assurance.

EXPERIENCE

With Manville Tire Company, have advanced in the following "track record" of increasing responsibility with this busy tire manufacturing plant:

1998-present: **FORCE VARIATION MACHINE OPERATOR.** Nashua, IA. Operate a machine in the Final Finish department that inflates the tire to test for holes, spins the tire to check the balance, and grinds off any imperfections in the tread, then applies a load to ensure that the tire can bear the appropriate amount of weight.

- Responsible for the safety and maintenance of more than $9 million worth of equipment.
- Order tires to be routed to the machines, scheduling them on the computer according to their assigned bar codes; sort finished tires onto pallets for shipping.
- Ensure that all machines are functioning properly and report any malfunctions or problems immediately to minimize any adverse effects on production.

1990-98: **FLOOR COORDINATOR.** Nashua, IA. Coordinated tire assignments in accordance with production schedules for the week, based on customer orders, available materials, and other factors.

1980-89: **TIRE BUILDER.** Nashua, IA. Started with Manville operating a tire machine in the production area of this busy manufacturing facility; strove to reach production quotas while safely performing the functions of the job.

ASSISTANT GOLF PROFESSIONAL. Fountain Country Club, Charles City, IA (1979-1980). Provided managerial oversight and supervision to pro shop personnel, while performing additional duties in events coordination, golf instruction, and public relations.

- Supervised six pro shop employees; interviewed, hired, and trained all new personnel.
- Managed all operational aspects of the pro shop at this prestigious country club; scheduled tee times and rented golf carts.
- Assisted customers in the selection of new equipment; increased equipment sales by making expert recommendations based on knowledge of the customer's specific needs.
- Scheduled golf tournaments and other events, coordinating with local businesses and private individuals to obtain their sponsorship and support.
- Oversaw the setup and preparation for golf tournaments; worked closely with the greens superintendent to ensure the course was ready for the event.
- Filled in for the head professional, giving golf lessons when he was not available; analyzed the specific problems of the student's game and provided solutions.
- Taught school clinics for local youth groups and assisted the coach of the Erwin High School golf team, providing supplemental instruction to the members of his team.
- Conducted periodic inventories of equipment and supplies, reordering as needed.

EDUCATION

Have studied with five different golf pros, including Howard Smith, in order to improve my teaching skills and learn new strategies for improving student performance.

Completed a 24-hour course on Grounds Maintenance, Iowa State University, Ames, IA.

PERSONAL

Excellent personal and professional references are available upon request.

Personnel/Human Resources Manager
Johnson Tire and Rubber Company
St. Mary's, OH

**FORCE VARIATION
MACHINE OPERATOR**

Dear Sir or Madam:

With the enclosed resume, I would like to make you aware of an experienced manufacturing professional with excellent communication and organizational skills as well as a background in tire production, quality control, and the mixing and testing of rubber butylene products.

In my current position with Hopkins Tire Company, I supervise five sorters in the operation of nine manufacturing machines. I assure the security and proper functioning of more than $9 million worth of manufacturing equipment, reporting any maintenance problems or malfunctions to minimize the effect on production. On numerous occasions, I have had the highest production in my department, and was a member of the team that implemented procedural changes for correction factors, enabling the plant to achieve QS-9002 certification.

In earlier positions at Concrete Material, Inc. and United Technologies, I further honed my skills in manufacturing and quality control. At Concrete Materials, I mixed rubber, fed materials to extruders, and conducted viscosity testing of rubber butylene products. While working for United Technologies, I ensured that wire manufactured for use in automotive wiring harnesses met engineering specifications, pull-testing for rated strength and inspecting the number of copper strands in each wire. In addition, I improved the pull-testing process by recommending a shield on the pull tester to prevent buildup of debris.

As you will see, I have completed five years of a degree program in Mechanical Engineering at Pensacola Christian College. My course work included numerous classes in which I first learned, then utilized AutoCAD as well as other courses with direct application to a manufacturing environment. I feel that my strong combination of education and experience will make me a valuable addition to your operation.

If you can use a motivated, experienced manufacturing professional with a background in tire and rubber production and quality control, I hope you will contact me to suggest a time when we might meet to discuss your needs and how I might meet them. I can assure you in advance that I have an excellent reputation and could quickly become an asset to your organization.

Sincerely,

Randolph N. Browning

RANDOLPH N. BROWNING

1110½ Hay Street, Fayetteville, NC 28305   •   preppub@aol.com   •   (910) 483-6611

OBJECTIVE

To benefit an organization that can use an experienced manufacturing professional with excellent communication and organizational skills who offers a background in tire production.

EDUCATION

Completed five years of a degree program in Mechanical Engineering, including numerous courses in AutoCAD 12 & 13, at Pensacola Christian College, Pensacola, FL.

EXPERIENCE

MACHINE OPERATOR. Hopkins Tire Company, Savannah, NE (2000-present). Work in the Final Finish department, operating a machine that inflates the finished tire to test for holes, spins it to check the balance, and grinds off any imperfections or uneven spots in the tread, then applies a load to ensure that the tire can bear the appropriate amount of weight.
- Supervise five sorters in the operation of nine force variation machines.
- Responsible for the safety and security of more than $9 million worth of equipment.
- Order tires to be routed to the machines, scheduling them on the computer by assigned bar codes.
- Ensure that all machines are functioning properly and report any malfunctions or problems immediately so that any effect on production is minimized.
- Oversee the sorting of scheduled tires onto pallets for shipping and remove unscheduled tires from laterals, returning them to stock until they are scheduled for testing.
- Was a member of the team that implemented procedural changes for correction factors, which allowed the plant to achieve QS-9002 certification.
- On numerous occasions, have had the highest daily production in my department.

MANUFACTURING ASSISTANT. Evans Properties, Pensacola, FL (1996-99). Performed various maintenance, manufacturing, and construction duties for this rental management company while working another part-time job and attending college full-time.
- Prepped, sanded, and painted interior walls, trim, and ceilings as well as exterior walls.
- Installed ceramic tile and linoleum in kitchens and bathrooms.
- Cleaned and installed gutters and installed exterior siding.

PRODUCTION WORKER. Concrete Materials, Inc., New Carlisle, OH (1995-96). In a summer job while attending college, performed a number of manufacturing, testing, and warehousing duties for this manufacturer of rubber butylene sealants.
- Mixed rubber, fed materials to extruders, and carried out pentrometer testing for viscosity of rubber butylene products.
- Packaged finished product and operated a forklift, slotting finished product in the appropriate area of the warehouse.

QUALITY CONTROL INSPECTOR. United Technologies, Zanesville, OH (1994). Worked in Process Inspection and analyzed circuits, terminals, and retainers in electrical wiring harnesses manufactured for automotive applications.
- Read wiring diagrams, schematics, and blueprints.
- Ensured that wire manufactured for use in wiring harnesses met engineering specifications, pull-testing for rated strength and inspecting the number of copper strands in each wire.
- Improved pull-testing process by recommending a shield on the pull tester to prevent buildup of debris.

PERSONAL

Excellent personal and professional references are available upon request.

FORKLIFT MECHANIC

Dear Sir or Madam:

With the enclosed resume, I would like to make you aware of my interest in applying for the position as Forklift Mechanic on the 1B shift.

As you will see from my resume, I am qualified by Smart-Mart to operate the RC, Slip, and Clamp forklifts, and I previously repaired, tested, and maintained 4K, 6K, and 20,000-lb. forklifts while serving my country as an Aviation Support Equipment Mechanic and Inspector in the U.S. Navy. As an Equipment Repair Specialist, Mechanic, and Inspector, I won numerous awards in recognition of my accomplishments in decreasing downtime, boosting organizational efficiency, and developing new systems that streamlined efficiency. I trained and developed personnel who became knowledgeable of operational inspection techniques, and I was singled out by the Navy for jobs as Work Center Safety Officer and Inspector because of my excellent technical knowledge and unquestioned reliability.

A skilled maintenance professional, I am proficient at maintaining hydraulic systems, reading schematics, and troubleshooting electrical systems. While in the Navy, I excelled in numerous schools and courses which refined my technical knowledge and trouble-shooting abilities, and I became skilled in repairing, maintaining, and testing not only forklifts but also all types of ground support equipment.

After leaving the Navy and prior to joining Smart-Mart, I worked as a Maintenance Mechanic for a private company where I was involved in building, installing, and repairing industrial equipment used in institutions such as jails and hospitals.

I am a responsible and hard-working individual who prides myself on my ability to make any activity function more efficient and I would enjoy the opportunity to apply my strong technical knowledge for the benefit of Smart-Mart as a Forklift Mechanic.

Sincerely,

Terrance James Washington

TERRANCE JAMES WASHINGTON

1110½ Hay Street, Fayetteville, NC 28305   •   preppub@aol.com   •   (910) 483-6611

OBJECTIVE   I want to further contribute to the Smart-Mart organization as a 1B Shift Forklift Mechanic so that I can benefit the organization through my extensive preventive maintenance, safety, and quality assurance background as well as my knowledge of and dedication to Smart-Mart.

LICENSES   Qualified and licensed by Smart-Mart to operate the RC, Slip, and Clamp forklifts

SKILLS   Skilled maintenance professional; maintain hydraulic systems; skilled in reading schematics; troubleshoot electrical systems

EDUCATION   Through training/experience while serving in the U.S. Navy, became skilled in repairing, maintaining, and testing **forklifts (4K, 6K, & 20,000-lbs.)** and aircraft ground support equipment including:

tow tractors	liquid oxygen carts	hydraulic units
gas turbine compressors	firefighting unit	mobile electric power plants

Completed ASE Class "A1" School; ASE GTC-85 Turbine Engine Course; ASE GTCP-100 Gas Turbine Engine Course.
Completed a six-week arc and gas welding course at a community college.

EXPERIENCE   **UNLOADER.** Smart-Mart, Spiral, FL (2000-present). Began as a Staple Stock Unloader on 2A shift in June 2000 and then moved to DA Unloader on 1B in Dec 2000.
* Safely and skillfully operate all three forklifts used by Smart-Mart.

MAINTENANCE MECHANIC. X & Y Equipment, Orlando, Tampa, and Clearwater, FL (1996-99). For a private company, serviced and maintained coin-operated laundry equipment; built laundromats and installed large, commercial laundry equipment in institutions such as jails and hospitals.
* Functioned as the company's mechanic, and troubleshot maintenance problems in multiple cities where the company installed and serviced equipment.
* Since the owner of the company also owned a 49-unit trailer home park, also maintained the park's plumbing system and well.
* As the owner's "right arm," made regular visits to laundromats owned by the company to collect and count receipts, make bank deposits, complete maintenance and repair, and handle any customer service or operational problems; supervised other employees.

Served my country in the U.S. Navy and was promoted ahead of my peers because of my exceptional skills related to preventive maintenance, quality assurance, and safety:
EQUIPMENT MECHANIC & INSPECTOR. NAS Whidbey Island, WA (1995). Won several medals in recognition of my achievements in reducing downtime and boosting organizational efficiency, and cited as a major contributor to the air station's selection for the 1995 Installation of Excellence Award.
* Was selected to oversee a support activity in which 2300 items of equipment for 22 customer units were properly issued, received, and accounted for.
* Developed well-trained personnel who were thoroughly knowledgeable of pre- and post-operational inspection techniques.
* Implemented a system which made scanning repair/maintenance boards easier to read.
* Was singled out for the critical position of Work Center Safety Officer.

PERSONAL   Responsible and hard-working individual who excels in technical problem solving.

Date

Exact Name of Person
Title or Position
Name of Company
Address (number and street)
Address (city, state, and zip)

HEAVY EQUIPMENT OPERATOR & MANUFACTURING CONSULTANT

Dear Exact Name of Person (or Sir or Madam if answering a blind ad):

With the enclosed resume, I would like to acquaint you with my strong leadership skills and manufacturing industry knowledge including my extensive background in manufacturing management and crew supervision.

While serving as Operations Manager and General Manager of teams consisting of up to 20 people, I have supervised machine operators in a variety of manufacturing environments. As a consultant, I have led consulting teams involved in traveling worldwide to resolve welding problems in manufacturing plants all over the globe.

I offer a reputation as a skilled heavy equipment operator and welder with years of supervisory and heavy construction experience. I am proficient in mig and arc welding and familiar with tig; I own my own welding truck with a complete inventory of welding equipment.

If your organization can benefit from the services of a hardworking and versatile individual with extensive supervisory experience, heavy equipment operation skills, and welding expertise, please contact me to suggest a time when we could meet to discuss your needs and how I might serve them. I can provide outstanding personal and professional references.

Sincerely,

Howard E. Radley

HOWARD E. RADLEY

1110½ Hay Street, Fayetteville, NC 28305   •   preppub@aol.com   •   (910) 483-6611

OBJECTIVE   To contribute to an organization that can benefit from the services of an experienced heavy equipment operator and welder with an extensive background in crew supervision, commercial and industrial construction, as well as welding and parts fabrication.

EDUCATION   Am completing two Associate's degree programs, one in Welding Applications and one in General Studies; have completed more than 42 college credit hours in welding.
Am seven classes short of finishing these two degrees; will finish in my spare time.
Graduated from Wilson High School, Wilson, OK, 1989.
- Was one of the school's most outstanding students in Agricultural Mechanics classes which included welding; was selected to represent my high school in a statewide welding competition.

Excelled in numerous military management and technical construction training programs.

SKILLS   **Welding:** Proficient in mig and arc welding; familiar with tig welding; own my own welding truck with a complete inventory of welding equipment.
Blueprints and surveys: Skilled in reading blueprints, surveys, and land transits.

EXPERIENCE   **OPERATIONS MANAGER.** General Manufacturing Corporation, Tempe, AZ (2000-present). Supervise and am responsible for training and developing a staff of 12 manufacturing machining operators.
- Trained and supervised operators of front-end loaders and graders and dump trucks.
- Maintained an excellent safety record while completing heavy construction projects, always coming in under deadline and within budget.
- Managed the security, maintenance, and accountability of $600,000 worth of equipment.
- Estimated materials required and completed engineering work estimate forms.
- Managed crews engaged in vertical, road, bridge and airfield construction as well as rigging, bridging, and demolition activities.

MANUFACTURING LIAISON. Myaflex Inc., Houston, TX (1996-2000). Managed a seven-person team in providing manufacturing expertise and consulting to organizations through-out the world; earned respect for my expertise related to all aspects of welding.
- Managed security, maintenance, and accountability of over $455,000 worth of equipment.
- Was commended for my "brilliant recommendations" during a major project.

MACHINE SHOP FOREMAN. Dynamic Engineering Company, Houston, TX (1994-1996). Started as a Team Leader and was promoted to Squad Leader while supervising and taking responsibility for the training, health, and welfare of up to 10 machinists.
- Accounted for $300,000 in equipment. Assisted engineers and bridge and powered-bridge specialists; read, interpreted, and plotted maps, overlays, and photos; assisted with technical operations.
- Was manager of a mobile metal machine shop; performed arc welding on vehicles and fabricated parts for tanks.

Prior military experience: COMBAT ENGINEER. 37TH Engineering Battalion, Ft. Bragg, NC and Central America (1990-1994). Entered the U.S. Army as a Combat Engineer; was promoted to Sergeant (E-4) and Squad Leader in just one year and three months; supervised a 9-person squad of Combat Engineers.

PERSONAL   Excellent references on request. Nonsmoker and nondrinker.

Exact Name of Person
Title or Position
Name of Company
Address (no., street)
Address (city, state, zip)

INDUSTRIAL ENGINEER

Dear Exact Name of Person: (or Dear Sir or Madam if answering a blind ad.)

I would appreciate an opportunity to talk with you soon about how I could contribute to your organization through my industrial engineering background including my experience in managing cost reduction programs, planning capital expenditures, and supporting new product design.

In my current job as an Industrial Engineer and Cost Reduction Manager, I have implemented the new manufacturing concept known as continuous process flow cells and have functioned as the "in-house expert" in training my associates in this area. While managing a $700,000 cost reduction program, I investigate and implement cost reductions through alternative materials and manufacturing processes as well as design modifications. I am involved on a daily basis in on-the-floor problem solving, costing of component processing, tooling and gauging, and capital equipment acquisitions. I have had extensive experience in project management.

Prior to graduating with my B.S. degree in Industrial Engineering, I worked my way through college in jobs in which I was involved in producing computer-aided drawings and participating in new product design. Although I worked my way through college, financing 80% of my education, I excelled academically and received the Outstanding Senior Award.

I am knowledgeable of numerous popular software and drafting packages. I offer a proven ability to rapidly master new software and adapt it for specific purposes and environments.

Single and willing to relocate, I can provide outstanding personal and professional references. I am highly regarded by my current employer and have been credited with making numerous contributions to the company through solving problems, cutting costs, determining needed capital equipment, and implementing new processes. I am making this inquiry to your company in confidence because I feel there might be a fit between your needs and my versatile areas of expertise.

I hope you will call or write me soon to suggest a time convenient for us to meet and discuss your current and future needs and how I might serve them. Thank you in advance for your time.

Sincerely yours,

Douglas Atkinson

DOUGLAS ATKINSON

1110½ Hay Street, Fayetteville, NC 28305 • preppub@aol.com • (910) 483-6611

OBJECTIVE

To add value to an organization that can use an accomplished young industrial engineer who offers specialized know-how in coordinating cost reductions, experience in both manufacturing and process engineering, proven skills in project management, and extensive interaction with product design, quality control, vendor relations, and capital expenditures.

EDUCATION

Bachelor of Science (B.S.) degree, Industrial Engineering Major; concentration in manufacturing, Western Carolina University, Asheville, NC, 1990.
- Achieved a 3.5 GPA (3.8 in my major); inducted into National Honor Fraternity.
- Received Outstanding Senior Award in manufacturing concentration.
- Worked throughout college and financed 80% of my education.

Associate of Applied Science (A.A.S.) degree, Mechanical Engineering and Design Technology Major, Richmond Community College, Richmond, VA, 1986; 3.7 GPA.

From 1990-present, completed business courses at Virginia Beach Community College, Virginia Beach, VA.

Participated in continuing education sponsored by Ingersoll-Rand, Ford Motor Company, and the George Group in these and other areas:

ISO 9002 Internal Auditing	Root Cause Analysis
Total Quality Management	Value Engineering/Value Analysis
Continuous Flow Manufacturing	Synchronous Manufacturing

TECHNICAL KNOWLEDGE

Software: Quattro Pro, Freelance, PowerPoint, Word, Fox Pro, UNIX
Drafting: VERSACAD, CADCAM, Cascade, Intergraph, Unigraphics Machining:
Knowledge of machining processes and tooling and gaging equipment; experience in programming CNC equipment.
Certification: Certified Manufacturing Technologist; Certified ISO 9002 Internal Auditor

EXPERIENCE

INDUSTRIAL ENGINEER & COST REDUCTION MANAGER. Delbert Smith Co., Virginia Beach, VA (1992-present). Manage the processing of machined components from raw material to finished product while also coordinating a $700,000 annual cost reduction program; investigate and implement cost reductions by exploring the possibility of alternative materials, other manufacturing processes, and design modifications.
- Involved on a daily basis in on-the-floor problem solving, costing of component processing, tooling and gauging, and capital equipment acquisitions.
- Implemented and coordinated continuous process flow cells, a new concept in the manufacturing area; completed extensive training and trained my associates.
- Performed cost justifications and complete equipment installs for capital equipment acquisitions totaling half million dollars.
- Continuously interact with new product teams, problem-solving groups, purchasing specialists, vendors, as well as manufacturing and quality control personnel.
- Evaluated ergonomic equipment in assembly environment to reduce operator fatigue.

Other experience:
- **DESIGNER.** For the Precision Controls Division of Dana Corporation, produced computer-aided drawings and actively participated in new product design while interacting with engineering and manufacturing. Was part of the team that introduced the first microprocessor-controlled cruise control.
- **DEPARTMENT ASSISTANT.** On a part-time work scholarship, produced drawings on VERSACAD computer-aided drafting system for Richmond Community College.

PERSONAL

Society of Manufacturing Engineers, Roanoke Division; National Association of Industrial Technology; Epsilon Pi Tau International Honorary Fraternity for Education in Technology.

MATTHEW HOWARD

1110½ Hay Street, Fayetteville, NC 28305

preppub@aol.com   •   (910) 483-6611

INDUSTRIAL
MAINTENANCE
MECHANIC

OBJECTIVE

To offer excellent technical skills related to industrial maintenance and electronics as well as expert knowledge of hydraulics, pneudraulics, flight control, landing gear, and jet engine maintenance to an organization that can use a professional dedicated to maintaining high standards of quality and safety.

EXPERIENCE

INDUSTRIAL MAINTENANCE MECHANIC. Folger Brothers, Holston, MA (2001-present). For a company which makes preformed plywood for furniture, was the sole maintenance mechanic.

- Worked on L&L hydraulic pumps and presses and on dependable hydraulic pumps and presses; worked on radio wave generators; applied my knowledge of L&L radio wave generators.
- Handled repair and servicing of Black Brother glue spreaders; also repaired and serviced all wood-cutting band saws, table saws, rip saws, and boring machines.
- Applied my knowledge of thermwood computer-controlled boring/router machine; also applied my knowledge related to the servicing of wood chipping grinder.
- Handled maintenance of wood boring incinerator; performed general maintenance of servicing of wood dust collecting system and auger system.
- Became knowledgeable of 480V motor control system.
- Handled general maintenance and servicing of forklifts including Whites, TCM, and Komatsu (3000, 4000, and 6000 IBS class); worked on Sullair air compressor system.

INDUSTRIAL MAINTENANCE MECHANIC. Oriole Industries, Holston, MA (1999-01). Was one of two maintenance mechanics for a company which prints sports apparel including shorts and t-shirts for distribution and sale worldwide.

- Serviced and maintained M&R pneumatic printing press, M&R manual printing press, M&R gas fired dryer oven, Harrco electric dryer oven, and electric forklifts.
- Applied my knowledge while servicing hyrol conveyor systems, Ingersol-Rand compressor, strapper machine, and hydro blaster system.

AIRCRAFT MANUFACTURING TECHNICIAN. Raytheon, Seattle, WA (1993-99). Became widely recognized as a skilled and talented professional familiar with every aspect of aircraft maintenance activities including major and minor troubleshooting of all systems including hydraulic, pneudraulic, environmental, primary and secondary flight controls, landing gear, and spoiler systems.

- Was an important contributor within an organization which became the company's first quality support service maintenance unit.

AIRCRAFT MANUFACTURING TECHNICIAN. U.S. Air Force, Laughlin AFB, TX (1989-92). Earned a reputation as a highly skilled technician and knowledgeable professional while performing preflight, thruflight, and postflight inspections as well as 125- and 250-hour inspections while ensuring that unscheduled maintenance was performed in a timely manner.

- Became skilled in performing operational checks as well as servicing and inspecting hydraulic, pneudraulic, and environmental aircraft systems.
- Was consistently praised for my willingness to work long, hard hours and set the example for my co-workers.
- Provided technical knowledge and skills which had a positive impact on the unit achieving "zero defects" and "excellent" ratings in numerous postflight inspections.
- Learned to install and remove T-37B environmental systems.
- Gained experience in administrative activities including ordering parts, monitoring the status of orders for assigned aircraft, and maintaining forms and records.
- Was entrusted with a Secret security clearance.

Highlights of earlier experience: Gained valuable experience in jobs calling for skills in operating heavy equipment such as metal-forming presses, jig welders, and injection molders as well as drill presses, grinders, and sanders. Also gained sales and customer service experience and warehouse operations knowledge.

EDUCATION	Completed 42 hours toward a degree in Aircraft Maintenance and Manufacturing, Community College of the Air Force.

Excelled in 555 hours of USAF training programs which led to qualification in areas such as aircraft maintenance, field detachment training for tactical aircraft maintenance, dedicated crew chief classes, engine removal and installation for the J-69-T-25A, T-37B, environmental and hydraulics cut training, refueling supervision, hazardous waste supervision and handling, safety procedures for exiting aircraft, security police training, ATC maintenance information system, aircraft maintenance, corrosion control, and others. T-37B engine-run qualified and Red "X" qualified

SPECIAL SKILLS

Through training and experience, am familiar with jet engine troubleshooting and assembly, metal fabrication, and major/minor mechanical troubleshooting.

Use standard and specialized test equipment including multimeters and am experienced in using various equipment such as the following:

pipe benders	H1 heaters	protractors
clinometers	tensiometers	torque tools
NF2 Lite-alls	dial calipers	drill presses
pipe threaders	aircraft jacks	MD-3 power units
alignment jigs	I.D. micrometers	hydraulic presses
cutting torches	depth micrometers	nitrogen service carts
tap and die sets	MC2A air compressors	oxygen test equipment
engine hoists	engine dollies	MC1A air compressors
oxygen service carts	engine roll-over stands	nitrogen service carts

TTU-228E hydraulic test stands
MA-1-A pneumatic power units
B-1, B-2, B-4, B-5, and C-1 aircraft maintenance stands

Qualified to perform maintenance on aircraft including OA/T-37B Cessna, F-5, T-38, AT-38, Northrop, and McDonnell Douglas RF4/F4

PERSONAL

Work well with others. Extensive automated process ordering experience using various computer systems including CAMMS.

Date

Exact Name of Person
Exact Title
Exact Name of Company
Address
City, State, Zip

**LOADING AND
SHIPPING MANAGER**

Dear Exact Name of Person (or Dear Sir or Madam if answering a blind ad):

With the enclosed resume, I would like to make you aware of a motivated, experienced professional with strong communication, organizational, and supervisory skills and a background in office administration, manufacturing, and warehouse supervision.

As Area Manager in the shipping department of Glory Tire Company, I oversee all aspects of the shipping operation for a facility with an inventory of more than $1 million dollars, supervising up to 26 associates. I prioritize daily tasks and assign personnel to ensure that all tasks are completed while controlling hours to minimize overtime. In previous positions as a Tire Classifier and Tire Inspector, I was responsible for identifying defects in tires coming off the production line and for determining whether the product was salvageable or would have to be scrapped. Earlier, I performed a variety of office administration and clerical tasks as a Receptionist in my first job with the company.

In addition to a year of college coursework at New Jersey State University, I have completed a Real Estate licensing course and numerous courses related to leadership, personnel development, manufacturing, and communications through Glory Tire.

Although I am highly regarded by my present employer and can provide excellent personal and professional references at the appropriate time, I am interested in exploring other career opportunities where I can utilize my strong communication skills in a service environment.

If you can use an experienced professional with excellent communication skills and a desire to work with the public, then I look forward to hearing from you soon, to arrange a time when we might meet to discuss your needs. I can assure you in advance that I have an excellent reputation, and would quickly become a valuable asset to your company.

Sincerely,

Rosemary A. Deere

ROSEMARY A. DEERE

1110½ Hay Street, Fayetteville, NC 28305 • preppub@aol.com • (910) 483-6611

OBJECTIVE

To benefit an organization that can use a motivated, experienced professional with strong supervisory, communication, and organizational skills as well as a background in office administration, manufacturing, and warehouse management.

EXPERIENCE

With Glory Tire Company, have advanced in the following "track record" of increasing responsibilities:

2000-present: **AREA MANAGER.** Camden, NJ. Promoted from a Tire Classifier position after completing the Assessment Center program for management training; manage all aspects of the shipping operations for a tire warehouse with more than $1 million in inventory.
- Supervise 26 associates in the loading and shipping of finished tires.
- Responsible for the maintenance and security of over $300,000 worth of equipment.
- Prepare weekly employee schedules and control labor hours to curtail overtime.
- Counsel marginal employees to improve job performance and encourage excellence.
- Interact with union representatives in response to the grievances of specific employees.
- Oversee the loading of outbound freight to ensure maximum safe loads.

1996-2000: **TIRE CLASSIFIER.** Camden, NJ. Advanced to a position of greater responsibility within the quality control department after working as a Tire Inspector.
- Received defective product from the Tire Inspectors and determined proper disposition of the defective tire.
- Examined defective tires to determine if they were salvageable or had to be scrapped.
- Communicated various patterns of defects and problems to defect analysts.

1988-1996: **TIRE INSPECTOR.** Camden, NJ. Moved to the production area as a Tire Inspector after a position as a Receptionist.
- Visually inspected product for any obvious defects.
- Marked the defective area of a finished tire and placed it on the conveyor belt for transport to the Tire Classifier.

1987-1988: **RECEPTIONIST.** Camden, NJ. Performed a variety of office administration and clerical tasks as a Receptionist for this large tire manufacturing facility.
- Answered multi-line phones and handled the switchboard, receiving all incoming calls and directing them to the appropriate personnel or taking messages.
- Sorted and distributed all incoming mail to the correct person or department.
- Processed shipping orders via the teletype machine.

Other Experience: OFFICE MANAGER. Radio Station WKMC, Camden, NJ (1986). Served in a number of administrative and clerical capacities with WKMC.
- Planned and scheduled placement of advertising to ensure that client's radio spots ran in the time brackets they had purchased and peak hours were not overbooked.

EDUCATION

Completed one year of college course work at New Jersey State University.
Completed a Real Estate Licensing course; awarded New Jersey Real Estate License, 1988.
Have completed numerous training courses through Glory Tire Company, including courses on leadership development, management, personnel development, quality assurance, and a recent course on policies and procedures for ISO 9000 certification.

PERSONAL

Excellent personal and professional references are available upon request.

Exact Name of Person
Exact Title
Exact Name of Company
Address
City, State, Zip

LOCKSMITH   Dear Exact Name of Person (or Dear Sir or Madam if answering a blind ad):

With the enclosed resume, I would like to make you aware of my interest in exploring employment opportunities with your organization.

As you will see from my resume, I am an experienced and certified locksmith and have completed Advanced Locksmithing and Professional Locksmithing Courses. I am especially experienced at working in manufacturing environments.

While in military service, I served as an Ammunition Specialist and then as a Mechanic. I earned rapid promotion ahead of my peers to supervisory roles, and I became known as a strong troubleshooter and problem solver. In one job as a Team Chief, I played a key role in testing a new, enhanced howitzer and refined my mechanical skills while participating in numerous simulated combat missions. After being handpicked for one job as a Maintenance Manager, I developed a new quality control program on my own initiative and implemented new safety procedures which resulted in no incidents or accidents. In a subsequent job as a Artillery Repairman, I performed quality control checks and trained artillery repairmen in technical skills, and I was praised as "a teacher and innovator who consistently displays technical expertise."

You will notice from my resume that I graduated from Bellwood Antis High School. My wife is also from Pennsylvania, and we are eager to return to Pennsylvania.

If you feel my background and skills could benefit your organization, I hope you will contact me to suggest a time when we could meet in person to discuss your needs. Thank you.

Yours sincerely,

Lee Drake Summer

LEE DRAKE SUMMER

1110½ Hay Street, Fayetteville, NC 28305   •   preppub@aol.com   •   (910) 483-6611

OBJECTIVE   To contribute to an organization that can use an experienced locksmith who has served earned respect for strong problem-solving skills.

EDUCATION   Completed Management and Manufacturing course work, Central Texas College.
Completed Advanced Locksmithing Course and Professional Locksmithing Course, Foley-Belsaw Institute, 2000.
Graduated from Wheel Recovery School; extensive training by the U.S. Army related to handling hazardous cargo; also graduated from the Army's Primary Leadership Development Course.
Graduated from Bellwood Antis High School, Bellwood, PA, 1990; curriculum emphasized advanced courses including Calculus, Geometry, and Advanced Math.

CERTIFICATION   Certified Locksmith credentials earned at Foley-Belshaw Institute.
Licensed to operate 4- and 6-ton forklifts; 10-ton trucks and below; and tow trucks.

EXPERIENCE   **LOCKSMITH.** Surety Locksmith, Wayne, NC (2000-present). Began part-time as a locksmith working nights and weekends, and then moved to full-time after receiving an honorable discharge from the U.S. Army. Specialize in autos, foreign and domestic.

- Re-key and install locks in new and existing residential and commercial buildings; design key and lock systems including computerized systems; install, repair, and maintain electromagnetic latching systems; wire and install card reading/scanning devices.
- Establish key lock and related systems which permit controlled access to buildings.
- Clean, lubricate, and adjust locks; machine new pieces to fit hardware.
- Order and maintain inventory of key and lock materials and supplies and maintain related computerized systems; inventory old locks from remodeled jobs.
- Maintain computerized record system for keys and locks.
- Rebuild and reinforce door frames to accommodate new and specialized hardware.
- Lubricate, adjust, and rebuild panic devices, door closures, coordinators, hinges, automatic hardware, fire doors, and alarm systems.
- Design and build custom security devices; estimate time and material for job costs.

ARTILLERY REPAIRMAN. U.S. Army, Ft. Bragg, NC (1999-2000). Performed quality assurance and quality control checks for maintenance, and trained artillery repairmen in technical skills which enabled them to keep howitzers operational.

MAINTENANCE MANAGER. U.S. Army, Ft. Bragg, NC (1997-98). Was selected over my peers for this position; supervised five people while managing the troubleshooting and testing related to 24 howitzers valued at $1.5 million.

- On my own initiative, developed a quality control program where none had existed before and implemented new safety procedures; as a result, we consistently exceeded the 97% standard expected by the Army.

TEAM CHIEF. U.S. Army, Ft. Bragg, NC (1995-97). Advanced ahead of my peers to manage up to 10 people while playing a key role in testing the new, enhanced version of the M198 howitzer.

- Received a respected medal praising my "superior service and exceptional leadership."

Other U.S. Army experience (1991-95): locations worldwide.
Received several medals in recognition of my superior contributions and achievements.

CAREER CHANGE

Date

TO: Rich Smith
FROM: Nathan Bowles

**MACHINE OPERATOR &
MANUFACTURING
SUPERVISOR**

Here you see the resume of
an experienced
manufacturing industry
professional who is
relocating and seeking a
change. He communicates
in his cover letter that his
skills and competencies are
transferable to other
industries. Notice that he
has recently returned to an
academic environment in
order to refresh his
computer skills. This
resume is a blend of a
chronological and
functional resume, which
works well for an individual
who has worked for only
one employer.

Dear Mr. Smith:

With the enclosed resume, I would like to follow up on our recent telephone conversation and make you aware of my interest in exploring employment opportunities with your organization.

As you will see from my resume, I have served the same company for the past 30 years and once won an award for a five-year period of perfect attendance. Within a Fortune 500 company environment, I have served in both supervisory and production operation capacities. As a supervisor, I managed up to 52 people involved in the daily production of automotive parts, and I became known for my strong communication skills and ability to maintain excellent communications between maintenance and production personnel. As a machine operator, I operated machinery in a state-of-the-art computerized environment and maintained constant vigilance of quality assurance.

A highly motivated individual, I have learned to manage my time for maximum efficiency. In fact, I earned an Associate of Science degree in Manufacturing Technology in my leisure time while excelling in demanding positions which often required variable hours.

I am known for my reliability and diligence. Throughout my years of loyal and faithful service, I have trained and developed many production personnel and supervisory staff who became highly skilled employees.

My wife and I are in the process of permanently relocating to California, and I believe my skills and talents would complement your company's goals. I am a hard worker who can provide outstanding references, and I would welcome the opportunity to be trained to do things your way. Although I have enjoyed my professional challenges in the manufacturing industry, I am eager and ready for a second career which involves extensive customer contact and public relations responsibilities. I am certain that my strong interpersonal skills and highly dedicated nature could be valuable assets to you.

My lovely wife and I hope to have the opportunity to meet with you soon in person, and I would appreciate your contacting me to suggest a time when we could discuss your needs. Thank you in advance for your time.

Yours sincerely,

Nathan Bowles

NATHAN BOWLES

1110½ Hay Street, Fayetteville, NC 28305   •   preppub@aol.com   •   (910) 483-6611

OBJECTIVE   To benefit an organization that can use a dedicated professional with superior communication and motivational skills who offers a strong desire to enhance a company's bottom line through my public relations, customer service, and sales abilities.

EDUCATION   Earned an **Associate of Science degree in Manufacturing Technology,** Akron State University, Akron, OH, 1990.
Studied Microsoft Excel and Works, Akron Technical Community College, March, 2002.
Completed extensive training related to quality assurance, safety, hazardous materials, management, production operations, customer service, personnel administration, and sales provided by my employer.

EXPERIENCE   **MACHINE OPERATOR & SUPERVISOR.** General Motors, Akron, OH (1975-present).
For a division of one of the largest auto makers, have worked a key member of teams achieving ambitious production quotas in a high-tech facility which utilizes state-of-the-art computerized equipment.

Machine Operation:
- Operated force machines; checked for precision tolerances; performed hormonic readings; and handled force grinding of equipment.
- Became an expert in operating and maintaining state-of-the-art manufacturing equipment.
- Operated six machines with four stand-alone computers.
- Maintained constant vigilance in all areas related to quality assurance.
- Was commended for my excellent communication skills and my ability to maintain open lines of communication between management and workers.

Supervision:
- Supervised between 22-52 people involved in the daily production of auto parts.
- Maintained production records while developing an attitude of teamwork among employees; established excellent communications between maintenance and production personnel.
- Was promoted into supervision after working as a Vacation Replacement for supervisors on all three shifts; became respected for my ability to communicate with all ages, races, ethnic groups, and personalities.
- Earned one perfect attendance award for perfect attendance over a five-year period.

Quality Assurance:
Was trained as an inventory management specialist and completed extensive training in all aspects of Total Quality Management (TQM).
- Became skilled in purchasing parts and materials; monitored supply transactions using a specialized computer system.
- Was handpicked to lead a team which made quality control recommendations that were adopted plantwide.

PERSONAL   Am a Red Cross lifetime blood donor. In my spare time, enjoy swimming and reading, especially inspirational materials. Am a positive individual with an upbeat personality. Can provide outstanding personal and professional references. Will travel or relocate.

Date

Exact Name of Person
Exact Title
Exact Name of Company
Address
City, State, Zip

MAINTENANCE SUPERVISOR & OPERATIONS SUPERVISOR

Dear Exact Name of Person (or Dear Sir or Madam if answering a blind ad):

With the enclosed resume, I would like to make you aware of my interest in exploring employment opportunities within your organization and acquaint you with my strong qualifications and diverse experience.

Most recently I have been involved in overseeing instructors teaching manufacturing courses to individuals in formal classroom and in field situations. At this well-known manufacturing management academy, I have supervised 35 instructors in charge of teaching manufacturing courses to more than 3,000 people annually. While managing a $2.5 million budget, I played a key role in making numerous improvements to the curriculum and physical facilities. I oversaw construction of a new dining facility and new residential quarters and spearheaded the transition into new classrooms.

In prior experience, I excelled in management positions in the manufacturing industry. With one textile firm, I began as a Weaving Supervisor and was promoted to Maintenance Supervisor. As a Maintenance Supervisor at Jones & Davis Company, I was responsible for maintenance of spinning, crimping, drawtexturing, and other machines in addition to the polyester plant.

Equally at home in academic environments and in industrial settings, I offer strong problem-solving and decision-making skills, and I am oriented toward making significant bottom-line contributions. I can provide excellent personal and professional references, and I feel confident that I would be described as a disciplined hard worker with strong administrative skills.

If you can use my diverse talents and skills to enhance your organizational effectiveness, please contact me to suggest a time when we might meet to discuss your needs. Thank you in advance for your time.

Sincerely,

Daniel R. Truman

DANIEL R. TRUMAN

1110½ Hay Street, Fayetteville, NC 28305 • preppub@aol.com • (910) 483-6611

OBJECTIVE

I want to contribute to an organization that can use a versatile professional with extensive experience in operations management, personnel supervision, teaching and training, as well as manufacturing and maintenance management.

EDUCATION

College: Completed 192 college credit hours towards a major in Industrial Management, William Carey College and Park College; am pursuing completion of B.S. degree in my spare time.
Professional: Completed extensive management and technical training programs sponsored by the U.S. Army.
Manufacturing: Completed extensive training related to manufacturing operations including training related to loom fixing and worsted manufacturing.

EXPERIENCE

OPERATIONS SUPERVISOR. Senatobia Manufacturing Academy, Senatobia, MS (2000-present). As a member of the management team of a prestigious manufacturing academy, am involved in overseeing instructors responsible for teaching more than 20 courses to hundreds of people yearly attending executive development programs.
- On my own initiative, revised the curriculum of seven courses to assure that they reflected changes in modern manufacturing technology.
- Managed multiple budgets totalling more than $2.5 million.

BRANCH CHIEF. Senatobia Manufacturing Academy, adjunct campus in Tallahassee, FL (1998-00). Was promoted from Course Director to Branch Chief with the responsibility for supervising 35 instructors in charge of teaching leadership and management courses as well as specialized technical courses to more than 3,000 people annually.
- Managed a budget of $2.5 million annually.
- Oversaw the construction of a new dining facility and new residential quarters, and was involved in the early construction phase of new classroom facilities.

Military experience: ASSISTANT SCHOOL SUPERINTENDENT. U.S. Army, Camp Shelby, MS (1992-97). Was handpicked as Assistant Superintendent for an elite management college known as The NCO Academy which provides executive-level training to the military's top middle managers; was praised in a formal evaluation for "enthusiasm and dedication" while supervising a staff of instructors.

Prior to joining the U.S. Army, excelled in supervisory positions in manufacturing:
MAINTENANCE SUPERVISOR & WEAVING SUPERVISOR. Worden Converters, Mann, NC (1990-91). Began as a Weaving Supervisor and was promoted to Maintenance Supervisor for a plant with weaving and twisting departments, shop, and grounds.
- Wrote job and safety procedures; purchased parts and equipment, and performed troubleshooting of plant maintenance problems; supervised maintenance of electrical substation and air conditioning equipment.
- Worked with sales personnel to determine costs on parts and inventory.
- Was extensively involved in cost analysis of plant products and operations.

SUPERVISOR. Jones & Davis Company, Mann, NC (1988-90). Began as a Supervisor and was promoted to Maintenance Supervisor; was responsible for maintenance of machines in spinning, crimping, textile spinning, drawtexturing, and polyester plant.

PERSONAL

Motivated self-starter. Excellent problem solver and motivator. Outstanding references.

Date

TO: James Smith
FROM: Operations Manager
BY FAX TO: (910) 483-6611

MANAGER, INVENTORY CONTROL

Dear Mr. Smith:

I would like to acquaint you with my extensive experience and knowledge of manufacturing and distribution center operations as well as my strong supervisory, communication, and motivational skills.

In the vast manufacturing environment of the corporate giant Low-Mart, I have excelled in a critical supervisory role which places me in charge of shipping critical items to customers after they are manufactured. I have consistently received high marks on performance evaluations and have been honored with nine Salute awards in the last six months. In addition to my regular duties, I train and supervise new employees in the use of forklifts and other heavy power equipment.

As you will see from my resume, I have six years of previous management experience with Prompt Change, Inc., where I supervised eight mechanics. By utilizing my excellent motivational and communication skills, I was able to retrain marginal employees and effectively manage the operations of this fast-paced business. I am certain that with my proven leadership skills, I can make an even greater contribution to Low-Mart's success at the Albany Distribution Center.

I look forward to hearing from you so that we can schedule a convenient time to discuss the company's needs and how I might meet them. Thank you in advance for your time and consideration.

Sincerely,

Randolph D. Morris

RANDOLPH D. MORRIS

1110½ Hay Street, Fayetteville, NC 28305 • preppub@aol.com • (910) 483-6611

OBJECTIVE

To further contribute to Low-Mart in a position of increased responsibility by offering my proven supervisory and motivational skills, as well as my thorough knowledge of Low-Mart operations and procedures to the company as a Distribution Manager.

HONORS

From January 2000 to present, received a total of nine Distribution Salute awards for excellence in job performance at the Distribution Center.
In April of 2001, I was recognized for one year of perfect attendance at the Distribution Center.

LICENSES

I am licensed in the operation of the following heavy power equipment: Stand Up, Pallet Truck, Slip Lift/Clamp, Stock Picker, Reach, and Forklift

EXPERIENCE

MANUFACTURING ORDER FILLER, NON-CONVEYABLE MERCHANDISE. Low-Mart Manufacturing Center, Albany, NY (2000-present). After receiving finished goods from the Quality Assurance Division, fill orders for items too large to be moved on conveyors.

- Train and supervise new employees in the operation of forklifts and other heavy power equipment.
- Consistently excel on performance evaluations.
- Assure a safe work environment for employees in this area of the Distribution Center; achieved a perfect safety record.
- Was selected to serve on numerous quality assurance task forces; worked closely with manufacturing machinists to troubleshoot and resolve chronic defects.
- Perform computerized inventory control and coordinate with the Quality Assurance Division to assure accuracy.
- Monitor changing status of inbound and outgoing merchandise, checking for missed pulls.
- Cross-trained in Distribution, Staple Stock Receiving, and Order-filling.

Other Qualifications: In addition to the above-mentioned skills, I also offer training or experience in the following areas:

Customer Service	Assistant Manager/Manager	Trainer
Inventory Control	Shipping/Non-con Damages	Door Runner
Label Control	P.F.C. Encoder	Jam Runner
Non-con Replenishment and Putaway Driver		Non-con Preloader

MANAGER. Prompt Change, Inc., Utica, NY (1990-99). Supervised eight mechanics at this privately owned location offering quick-service oil changes and chassis lubrication.

- Trained new employees in assigned job tasks, as well as company policies and procedures.
- Applied my excellent organizational skills, completing daily closeout reports and performing the cash register till balancing at end of day.
- Used my excellent motivational skills and my ability to speak Spanish to retrain a Puerto Rican employee who had been considered marginal prior to my training him; he subsequently became an outstanding manager.

LANGUAGES

In additional to excellent communication English skills, speak, read, and write Spanish fluently.

PERSONAL

Am an excellent motivator and communicator with proven supervisory and training skills. Excellent personal and professional references are available upon request.

Exact Name of Person
Exact Title of Person
Name of Company
Exact Address of Company
City, state, zip

**MANUFACTURING
MANIFEST CLERK**

Dear Exact Name of Person:

With the enclosed resume, I would like to make you aware of my manufacturing industry background as well as my interest in exploring employment opportunities with your organization.

For more than 15 years, I have been involved in various aspects of the manufacturing process with one of the country's leading manufacturers of industrial products. In my current position, I assume responsibility for the on-time delivery of manufactured products to many of the company's key customers.

In prior positions with the company, I was trained in a variety of manufacturing processes while receiving extensive training in quality assurance. On numerous occasions I played a key role in identifying solutions for stubborn manufacturing problems. My manufacturing background has aided me greatly in my current involvement in distribution and customer service.

I look forward to hearing from you so that we can schedule a convenient time to discuss the company's needs and how I might meet them. Thank you in advance for your time and consideration.

Sincerely,

Judith Coleman

JUDITH L. COLEMAN

1110½ Hay Street, Fayetteville, NC 28305　　•　　preppub@aol.com　　•　　(910) 483-6611

OBJECTIVE

To further benefit Good's Mart through my versatile experience and reputation as a detail-oriented professional with excellent data entry, computer operation, and clerical skills, as well as expert knowledge of Good's Mart systems, policies, and procedures.

COMPUTERS

Highly computer literate, am familiar with Windows 98, Microsoft Word and Access, and several proprietary UNIX-based distribution programs developed specifically for Good's Mart.

EXPERIENCE

With Good's Mart Distribution and Returns Centers, have advanced in the following "track record" of increasing responsibilities:

2000-present: **MANUFACTURING MANIFEST COORDINATOR.** Good's Mart Center, Beadle, ID. Known as a self-motivated and hard-working young professional, work independently in this fast-paced manufacturing environment as the only person in the receiving office during my shift.

- Key numerous invoices received into the computer, using information from pre-notes and other sources to create computer-generated manifests for all incoming shipments.
- Schedule arrival times and set appointments for inbound deliveries.
- Assist drivers coming into the loading docks with preparation of paperwork and release drivers once their shipments are unloaded.
- Process pre-notes by fax and by telephone, keying purchase order numbers, load weights, and approximate arrival times for each inbound shipment into the computer.
- Perform inbound processing of shipments arriving, entering data into the log book.
- Prepare a packet for each arriving shipment to keep management and associates informed as to which loading docks hold new shipments waiting to be unloaded.

1999: **RETURN-TO-VENDOR CLERK.** Good's Mart Center, Beadle, ID. Worked closely with many different shipping companies, arranging pickup of overstock, damaged, or shipped in error merchandise.

- Processed shipments using special shipping procedures for vendors which required that all returns be shipped through UPS.

1997-1998: **SHIPPING CLERK.** Good's Mart Returns Center, Atlanta, GA. Handled all return-to-vendor shipments of damaged merchandise; adhered to special handling according to procedures required by UPS and the vendor.

- Trained all new UPS clerks on proper handling procedures for damaged merchandise.

1996-1997: **SHRINK WRAP ASSOCIATE.** Good's Mart Returns Center, Atlanta, GA. Performed final preparation before finished pallets were loaded onto outbound trailers; wrapped merchandise stacked on pallets in cellophane shrink wrap in order to ensure safe transit. Assigned tracking numbers to each pallet; recorded pallet information and tracking numbers in the log book to facilitate greater accountability.

1995-1996: **PAINT & HAZMAT ASSOCIATE.** Good's Mart Returns Center, Atlanta, GA. Ensured that all hazardous and volatile materials were packaged, labeled, and loaded properly so that no dangerous chemical interactions would take place during transit.

- Affixed a Materials Safety Data Sheet (MSDS) to each outbound pallet and ensured that trailers loaded with hazardous materials were labeled with DOT-approved signage.
- Maintained a thorough working knowledge of all OHSA Materials Safety Data Sheets.

PERSONAL

Excellent personal and professional references are available upon request.

Career Change

Date

Exact Name of Person
Title or Position
Name of Company
Address (number and street)
Address (city, state, and zip)

MANUFACTURING ACCOUNT REPRESENTATIVE

As you can see, this cover letter is written so that the individual can seek employment not only in the manufacturing arena but also in other fields.

Dear Exact Name of Person (or Dear Sir or Madam if answering a blind ad):

I would appreciate an opportunity to talk with you soon about how I could contribute to your organization through my knowledge related to manufacturing, accounts management, customer service, and public relations.

Most recently I have worked full-time as an Account Representative while going to school at nights and on the weekends to earn my MBA, which I received in May 2002. I was handling key accounts worth more than $2 million annually for my employer and was being groomed for rapid promotion into a higher management position.

I resigned from my position, however, in order to relocate to Talbot permanently because I recently married. My husband owns and manages his own business in the Talbot area. I am seeking an employer who can use a highly motivated individual with very strong communication, sales, customer service, and public relations skills. Because I earned both my undergraduate and graduate degrees while excelling in demanding professional positions, I have acquired excellent organizational and time management skills which permit me to maximize my own productivity.

If you can use a self-starter who could rapidly become a valuable part of your organization, I hope you will contact me to suggest a time when we might meet to discuss your needs and how I might serve them. I can provide excellent personal and professional references.

Yours sincerely,

Susan B. Martin

SUSAN BEATRICE MARTIN

1110½ Hay Street, Fayetteville, NC 28305　•　preppub@aol.com　•　(910) 483-6611

OBJECTIVE　To offer my strong accounts management, sales, marketing, and customer service skills to an organization that would benefit from my strong bottom-line orientation and results-oriented style of developing relationships, establishing trust, and maximizing profitability.

EDUCATION　**M.B.A.,** Francis Marion University, Florence, SC, May 2002.
The School of Business is accredited by The American Assembly of Collegiate Schools of Business (AACSB).
B.B.A., Francis Marion University, Florence, SC, 1997.
- Received a partial athletic tennis scholarship, and was a valued member of the varsity tennis team.

EXPERIENCE　**ACCOUNT REPRESENTATIVE.** Wilde Manufacturing, Inc., Florence, SC (2000-2002). For a manufacturing company which produces both custom and stock file folders, was assigned to handle sales and customer service for the company's second largest customer, the Government Printing Office.
- Handled accounts which amounted to a total dollar volume of $2 million in 2002; increased the dollar volume of account sales in 2001 over 2000, and was above my targeted 2002 sales goals when I married and resigned in order to relocate to Talbot, where my husband owns and manages a business.
- Worked full-time in this job while simultaneously completing a rigorous MBA program; became skilled at managing my time for maximum efficiency.
- Serviced federal government accounts from the first phone call to following up on the shipment of orders;
- Performed cost estimating; prepared bids on onetime as well as yearly federal contracts; handled purchasing, invoicing, as well as the advertising and sales pertaining to my accounts.
- Became skilled at designing specialty products tailored to unique customer needs; was frequently commended by customers for my excellent communication skills and ability to translate their ideas into practical product designs.
- Was honored by my selection to serve on the corporation's Safety Committee, and contributed many ideas which officials regarded as resourceful and practical.
- Was being groomed for rapid advancement into the management structure of this corporation because of my proven ability to handle multiple priorities with precision.

ADMISSIONS ASSISTANT. Francis Marion University, Florence, SC (1995-99). Was recruited by the university where I earned my degree to play a key role in the admissions process; handled a wide range of administrative and public relations responsibilities.
- Prepared and evaluated files pertaining to prospective students, freshmen, transfer students, and international students; conducted student tours.
- Generated weekly reports containing valuable statistical data used in analysis and strategic decision making; handled the weekly cash deposits of the admissions office.
- Prepared correspondence and reports including key reports distributed to the president and vice president of the university.

Other experience: Pharmacy Technician. Bartlett's Drug Store, Florence, SC (1990-94). Assisted pharmacists in filling prescriptions, handling short-order drug orders, and responding to customer needs.

PERSONAL　Can provide outstanding personal and professional references.

Date

Exact Name of Person
Exact Title
Exact Name of Company
Address
City, State, Zip

Dear Exact Name of Person (or Dear Sir or Madam if answering a blind ad):

With the enclosed resume, I would like to make you aware of my extensive background related to industrial production and troubleshooting, equipment repair and maintenance, and forklift operations. I am interested in exploring employment opportunities with your company.

Since receiving my honorable discharge from the U.S. Army, I have worked for seven years for Allen Manufacturing, where I became Second Shift Operations Leader. While at Allen, I have built motor control centers using schematics and diagrams and I have become skilled at testing, troubleshooting, and inspecting motor control centers prior to shipment of the product to customers. I have been extensively trained in Material Safety Data Sheets (MSDS) and in effective quality assurance techniques.

I offer a proven ability to excel in any type of training. I received my General Manufacturing (Electro-Mechanical) certification from Bemidji Technical College, and I also completed a Forklift Safety and Operator Course from BTC. I am experienced at operating forklifts of all sizes and types including 4K, 6K, and 10K. Known for my safety-conscious attitude, I became certified as a Medical First Responder by Allen Manufacturing and I am adult CPR certified. While in military service, I received extensive training in hazardous materials handling, quality assurance, and equipment repair.

If my background and skills interest you, I hope you will contact me to suggest a time when we could meet in person to discuss your needs. I can provide outstanding references. Thank you in advance for your time.

Yours sincerely,

Dean B. Joyce

DEAN B. JOYCE

1110½ Hay Street, Fayetteville, NC 28305 • preppub@aol.com • (910) 483-6611

OBJECTIVE
I want to offer my strong mechanical and troubleshooting skills to an organization that can use a hard worker with extensive experience in equipment repair and maintenance along with specialized expertise related to working with hazardous materials, Material Safety Data Sheets (MSDS), and operating forklifts of all sizes.

FORKLIFTS
Experience in operating forklifts of all types and sizes: 4K, 6K, and 10K. Operate pallet jacks, cranes, and other industrial equipment.

EDUCATION
Adult CPR Certified, **Standard First Aid, American Red Cross, 2000; was previously certified as a** Medical First Responder **by Allen Manufacturing.**
Completed **Forklift Safety and Operator Course,** Bemidji Technical College, 1997.
Received **General Manufacturing Certification/Electro-Mechanical Certification,** Bemidji Technical College, 1995.
Trained in **Material Safety Data Sheets (MSDS),** Weber Industries and Allen Manufacturing, 1995-2001.
Extensively trained in hazardous materials (HAZMAT), quality assurance, equipment repair and maintenance, and personnel supervision, U.S. Army, 1989-93.

EXPERIENCE
MANUFACTURING TECHNICIAN & SECOND SHIFT OPERATIONS LEADER. Allen Manufacturing, Minneapolis, MN (1995-present). Advanced within the Allen organization to become the head of the Second Shift Operations. Resigned from this position in order to travel out of state for several weeks to care for my ailing parents.
- Built motor control centers using schematics and diagrams. Became skilled at wiring and testing motor control centers. Performed troubleshooting and quality control inspections prior to shipment of the product to customers.
- As Shipping and Receiving Attendant, kept records of all goods shipped and received.
- Was responsible for all outgoing shipments on the second shift.
- Inventoried plant material; ordered and received material to ensure plant had proper parts and materials. Disbursed material throughout plant for overall plant use.
- Utilized forklift trucks to move material in and around the plant; loaded and unloaded freight trucks, and became known for my strong emphasis on safety.
- As **Medical First Responder,** gave minor and major first aid to injured plant employees.

LIGHT INDUSTRIAL WORKER (Temporary Contract). Weber Industries, Minneapolis, MN (1994-95). Worked on a short-term temporary contract basis through Quality Temporary Service; assisted Weber in the aftermath of a spill at the company's waste treatment plant which had flowed into the Manville River.
- Utilized my background in working with hazardous materials and quality assurance during Weber's "Operation Water Log."
- Played a key role in helping waste water treatment personnel transfer waste water into tanker trucks. Observed strict OSHA and EPA requirements.

CREW MEMBER. U.S. Army, Ft. Bragg, NC (1991-94). As a Cannon Crew Member, performed preventive maintenance on weapons and weapons systems. Served during Desert Storm, and advanced to the rank of E-4 ahead of my peers. Held a Secret security clearance.

PERSONAL
Highly energetic, highly motivated individual who enjoys working with others to achieve top-notch results in productivity, quality, and customer satisfaction.

Date

Attn: Box 555
c/o Savannah Publishing Co.
P.O. Box 496
Savannah, GA

**MASTER MECHANIC
UTILITIES**

Dear Sir or Madam:

Please accept the enclosed resume as an indication of my interest in being considered for the position of Chemical Plant Technician which you recently advertised in the Richmond Times-Dispatch.

I am confident that I offer a background which would qualify me for this job. I am a high school graduate with mechanical aptitude who is willing to work rotating shifts and overtime. As you will see, I completed the one-year Plumbing and Pipefitting course at Savannah Technical Community College, one year of studies in Electronics, and am licensed as a Plumbing Contractor by the State of Georgia. I have supplemented my college programs with additional courses, such as the Chestron Mechanical Seal course, leak and spill control school, and hazardous communications/confined space safety program.

For the past ten years, I have been employed by Fabrics, Inc., in Savannah where I have earned promotion to Master Mechanic – Utilities after advancing from Utilities Mechanic to Preventive Maintenance Coordinator before receiving this latest advancement in 1999.

Earlier with Gardner, Inc., in Lafitte, GA, I also advanced quickly and worked as a Quality Control Inspector before earning promotion to Filter Plant Operator. Through the years I have attended numerous seminars to develop knowledge of areas such as quality improvement, HVAC, and steam trap operations.

I offer the type of dedication to quality which you seek and could quickly become an asset to your organization. I hope you will contact me to suggest a time when we might meet to discuss your needs and how I could contribute to your organization as a Chemical Plant Technician.

Sincerely,

Dewey J. Keats

DEWEY J. KEATS

1110½ Hay Street, Fayetteville, NC 28305 • preppub@aol.com • (910) 483-6611

OBJECTIVE   To contribute my technical and mechanical skills for the benefit of a company seeking an energetic and highly dependable employee.

EDUCATION   Completed the one-year Plumbing and Pipefitting course, Savannah Technical Community College (STCC), GA, and one year of studies in Electronics; while attending STCC, placed on the **President's List** and was a member, **National Vocational-Technical Honor Society.**

TRAINING & CERTIFICATIONS   Attended training programs and courses which have included:

Hazardous Communication/Confined Space Safety   Yarley Steam Trap seminar
Leak and Spill Control School   HVAC seminar
Chestron Mechanical Seal course   Iventech Bearing seminar
Licensed Plumbing Contractor License for the state of Georgia (P-I Unlimited).

EXPERIENCE   **Am advancing in the following track record with Fabrics, Inc., Savannah, GA:**
MASTER MECHANIC – UTILITIES. (2000-present). Supervise and assist utility mechanics in performing maintenance and repairs, ensuring that all shifts are able to operate without interruptions and that production is not adversely affected due to equipment failures.
- Maintain up-to-date and thorough records of all equipment repairs.
- Control various inventories; order replacement parts and pipe work for utility lines as well as specialty items which include boiler treatment and chemical analysis testing reagents and treatment chemicals for the chiller, cooling towers, and air washer units.
- Design and produce guidelines for utility start-up and shutdown procedures.
- Update material data safety sheets; conduct fire prevention inspections; issue confined space entry permits using TMX-210 Atmospheric Monitor/Tester; repair and overhaul Merrow and Union sewing machinery.

PREVENTIVE MAINTENANCE COORDINATOR. (1998-99). Developed PM programs and procedures, supervised mechanics, personally participated in PM activities for plant utility and production equipment, and documented production equipment repairs.
- Rebuilt gear reducers, pneumatic valves and actuators, centrifugal pumps, Spence valves, condensate pumps, and mechanical pumps.
- Diagnosed problems with heat exchangers, pneumatic systems, and hydraulic systems and fabricated parts needed to improvise repairs until necessary parts could arrive.

UTILITIES MECHANIC. (1993-98). Operated and maintained all plant utility systems, boilers, chillers, cooling tower, air washer, air compressors, and related equipment.
- Performed and logged daily chemical analysis tests and determined the amount of chemical used to keep systems running as efficiently as possible.
- Checked and maintained operating equipment.
- Performed maintenance throughout the plant including plumbing/pipefitting, changing sprockets, seals, bearings, rollers, gear boxes, motors, pumps; repaired mechanical failures.

Advanced with Gardner, Inc, Lafitte, GA (1988-92):
FILTER PLANT OPERATOR. (1990-92). Performed various water analysis tests and added chemicals necessary to keep water within state board of health standards.
QUALITY CONTROL INSPECTOR. (1988-89). Inspected, sized, and graded carpet according to style; supervised and trained packaging personnel.

PERSONAL   Received certificate for perfect attendance for the last three years despite heavy overtime.

MEDIA AND PRINTING COORDINATOR

Dear Sir or Madam:

With the enclosed resume, I would like to express my interest in exploring employment opportunities with your organization and make you aware of my versatile experience related to print production, media planning and buying, as well as sales and customer service.

With a reputation as a well-organized individual capable of managing multiple priorities, I most recently excelled in a track record of achievement with a communication company in Decatur, IL. After previously working for the company as a Customer Service Representative, I was again recruited by this employer and offered the position of Production Coordinator for the Education Division, which served the high-end needs of universities and colleges. In that capacity I coordinated print production of catalogs, brochures, viewbooks, and other publications, and I excelled in all aspects of customer service and client relations. In 2000, when the company was experiencing financial turmoil due to lagging sales, my employer asked me to move from production management into sales. After taking over the accounts of three experienced sales professionals, I quickly increased sales volume in the region to three times the level achieved by my predecessors. I was widely credited with salvaging lost accounts and restoring client confidence in the company. Although I was held in the highest regard and can provide excellent references at the appropriate time, I recently resigned my position in order to relocate permanently to Wisconsin to be near family.

You will see that I offer considerable experience in sales and marketing. In one previous job as a Group Leader and Production Coordinator for Adams Lithography, I trained and supervised three employees while playing a key role in implementing a new concept of cross-functional work teams. In that job, I worked closely with sales/marketing to develop and implement marketing plans while coordinating production of print materials for the Hotel Division. On my own initiative, I developed procedures which streamlined the division's work flow.

If you can use a hard worker with a proven ability to manage multiple priorities and produce top quality work under tight deadlines, I hope you will contact me to suggest a time when we might meet to discuss your needs. I would certainly enjoy the opportunity to talk with you in person.

Sincerely yours,

Diane L. Shade

DIANE L. SHADE

1110½ Hay Street, Fayetteville, NC 28305 • preppub@aol.com • (910) 483-6611

OBJECTIVE

To contribute to an organization that can use a versatile professional who is experienced in producing top-quality results under tight deadlines while applying my expertise in media planning/buying, print manufacturing and production, sales, and customer service.

EDUCATION

Extensive professional training related to printing management, team building and team management, quality improvement, the printing process, media planning and buying, and the advertising process.

COMPUTERS

Proficient with Quark, Photoshop, Illustrator, Pagemaker, Microsoft Word, and other software; knowledgeable of scanning, digital pre-press, and film output.

EXPERIENCE

Was recruited by *Photo Communications,* Decatur, IL in 1996, and then excelled in the following track record of accomplishment in both the sales and production management areas; recently resigned my position in order to relocate to WI:
2000-2002: SALES REPRESENTATIVE. At a time when the company was experiencing financial difficulties because of its poor sales performance, I was asked to move into sales; was the production coordinator *and* the first woman in the company's history ever to be placed in a sales job, and I tripled sales for the company in my first nine months.
- Salvaged lost accounts and then expanded revenue from those accounts.
- Demonstrated my ability to establish and maintain effective long-term relationships.
- Was commended for salvaging the company's reputation with numerous clients.

1996-00: PRODUCTION COORDINATOR. Was recruited by this former employer to coordinate its Education Division accounts comprised of universities and colleges; expertly coordinated multiple simultaneous priorities with as many as 40 major projects in progress.
- Coordinated print production of catalogs, brochures, viewbooks, and other print jobs.
- Became widely respected for my creativity, and many of the projects I managed won awards from the Print Industry Association of Illinois (PIAI).
- It was truly an honor to be recruited for this management job in the Education Division, because the job required a professional who could produce the highest quality work under extremely tight deadlines.

GROUP LEADER & PRODUCTION COORDINATOR. Adams Lithography, Cole, IL (1994-96). Trained and supervised three employees, and played a key role in implementing a new concept of cross-functional work teams as Group Leader; was commended for my ability to motivate and inspire others.
- Worked closely with sales/marketing to develop and implement marketing plans.
- Coordinated production of print materials for the Hotel Division; on my own initiative, developed procedures which streamlined the division's work flow.

CUSTOMER SERVICE REPRESENTATIVE. Photo Communications, Decatur, IL (1992-94). Played a key role in developing a new Hotel Division, and then coordinated the production of print materials; maintained communication between client and sales.

CUSTOMER SERVICE REPRESENTATIVE. Brown & White Color Lab, Columbus, GA (1990-91). Initiated, organized, and implemented the company's first telemarketing program while providing technical services to professional photographers.

PERSONAL

Offer highly refined customer service, sales, and marketing skills.

CAREER CHANGE

Date

Exact Name of Person
Exact Title
Exact Name of Company
Address
City, State, Zip

OFFICE MANAGER IN A MANUFACTURING ENVIRONMENT

A recent downturn in the manufacturing sector has forced this employee into a job hunt. She would enjoy finding a situation in another manufacturing environment, but her resume and cover letter are written so that she can explore options in numerous industries.

Dear Exact Name of Person (or Dear Sir or Madam if answering a blind ad):

With the enclosed resume, I would like to acquaint you with my exceptional organizational, communication, and computer skills as well as my background in purchasing and inventory control; customer service; manufacturing; and employee training and supervision.

As you will see, I have excelled in a variety of positions at the same facility with Bond Manufacturing. In my last position, I oversaw control and disbursement of the company's travel reimbursement fund as well as the purchasing of office supplies and company shirts. In this capacity, I reduced supply expenditures by 50% without compromising the effectiveness of the department. I also read and analyzed engineering diagrams and entered the data into an IBM AS-400 computer system and updated information.

In previous positions as Coordinator of Administrative Services and Computer Terminal Operator, I further honed my computer skills, mastering Microsoft Word, Excel, PowerPoint and Outlook, and the FoxBase engineering program, as well as gaining mainframe computer experience on IBM System 36, System 38, and AS-400 computers. I also provided customer service for seven Bond Manufacturing facilities, and was heavily involved in purchasing, processing invoices and receipts and reconciling discrepant orders and invoices.

Although I was highly regarded by this employer and can provide excellent personal and professional references at the appropriate time, a recent downturn in business has forced Bond Manufacturing to reduce its work force, displacing myself and many of my co-workers. My extensive knowledge of computer hardware and software, as well as my background in manufacturing and inventory control, would make me a valuable addition to your organization.

I have an excellent reputation and could quickly become a valuable asset to your organization. If my skills and personal qualities could be of value to you, I hope you will contact me to suggest a time when we might discuss your needs.

Sincerely,

Vicky Anne Clair

VICKY ANNE CLAIR

1110½ Hay Street, Fayetteville, NC 28305　　•　　preppub@aol.com　　•　　(910) 483-6611

OBJECTIVE　　To benefit an organization that can use a self-motivated and experienced office manager, administrative assistant, and data entry professional with exceptional computer skills along with a background in purchasing and inventory control; customer service; and manufacturing.

EDUCATION　　Division System Specialist Program, Bond Manufacturing training program, 1998.
Continuous Flow Workshop, Bond Manufacturing training program, 1997.
Completed courses in Customer Service (1990) and Basic First Aid (1994), Boise Technical Community College, Boise, ID.

COMPUTERS　　*Am proficient in the following computer software:*
- *Commercial and Office:* Microsoft Word, Excel, PowerPoint, and Outlook
- *Manufacturing and Mainframe:* Skilled in the operation of the IBM AS-400, IBM S/36, and IBM S/38 computer systems; FoxBase engineering software and EDI ordering system.

EXPERIENCE　　*With Bond Manufacturing, have been promoted to positions of increasing responsibility in this busy OEM manufacturing facility.*
2000-2002: ADMINISTRATIVE ASSISTANT. Performed a variety of clerical and administrative duties for this busy manufacturing facility.
- Assisted and instructed employees on the operation of the various components of the Microsoft Office suite, including Word, Excel, PowerPoint, and Outlook.
- Read engineering drawings and entered data into an IBM AS-400 computer.
- Released customer orders for manufacture and shipment.
- Oversaw the maintenance and distribution of the travel reimbursement fund; booked all travel and entertainment arrangements for employees and their guests.
- Purchased office supplies and company shirts; reduced office supply expenditures by 50%.
- Performed routine maintenance on copiers and fax machines.
- Responsible for troubleshooting and correction of order processing problems.

1996-2000: COORDINATOR OF ADMINISTRATIVE SERVICES. Was promoted to this position from computer terminal operator; utilized my organizational and problem-solving skills to ensure that administration support was provided to the facility in an efficient and effective manner.
- Processed engineered customer orders and released them for manufacture.
- Supervised and trained all temporary employees assigned to the department.
- Assisted the scheduler with the purchase of production materials.
- Read engineered drawings and entered pertinent data into an IBM AS-400 or IBM System 38 computer system.
- Learned the FoxBase engineering program, as well as Microsoft Word, Excel, and PowerPoint.
- Filled in for customer service representatives and engineers as needed.

1990-1996: COMPUTER TERMINAL OPERATOR. In addition to administrative and clerical tasks, I was responsible for purchasing and served as customer service representative for seven service centers.
- Entered purchase orders and receipts into IBM System/36 and System/38 computers.
- Expedited and purchased production materials and purchased hardware.

PERSONAL　　Outstanding personal and professional references are available upon request.

CAREER CHANGE

Date

Exact Name of Person
Exact Title
Exact Name of Company
Address
City, State, Zip

PACKAGING ASSOCIATE   Dear Exact Name of Person (or Dear Sir or Madam if answering a blind ad):

With the enclosed resume, I would like to make you aware of my interest in exploring employment opportunities with your organization.

While excelling in a track record of outstanding performance with major manufacturing firms, I gained skills and knowledge which are transferable to a wide variety of work environments. For example, as a packaging associate, I continuously discovered new methods of safely achieving high productivity goals. I have become accustomed to working effectively on teams dedicated to reaching the highest goals related to customer service, quality control, and profitability.

"Doing things right the first time" was a philosophy which became ingrained in me as I worked diligently in manufacturing environments. I received numerous awards and certificates for my attention to detail and high production levels. I am well known for my sunny disposition and good attitude.

Although I am held in the highest regard by my current employer and can provide outstanding references at the appropriate time, I am selectively exploring opportunities outside the manufacturing sector. I would appreciate your keeping my interest in your company in confidence at this time, and I would very much enjoy hearing from you if you feel that my skills and knowledge could be helpful to you.

Sincerely,

Joan Victoria Butler

JOAN VICTORIA BUTLER

1110½ Hay Street, Fayetteville, NC 28305 • preppub@aol.com • (910) 483-6611

OBJECTIVE   I want to contribute to an organization that can use a hard-working young professional with excellent office knowledge, strong customer service and public relations skills, as well as a proven ability to rapidly master new technologies.

EDUCATION   Pursuing Bachelor's degree in Information Systems Programming, Fayden Community College, Fayden, OK; am completing course work in my spare time while excelling in my full-time job.
- Courses completed have included Introduction to Business, Introduction to Computers, Speech and Communications, Financial Accounting, and Economics.

COMPUTERS   Knowledgeable of Windows 95 and 98, Microsoft Word, Excel, PowerPoint, Word Perfect. Offer a proven ability to rapidly master new software and operating systems.

EXPERIENCE   **PACKAGING ASSOCIATE.** Starshine, Inc., Varrow, OK (2000-present). Have excelled in this job which involves assembling sleeve kits consisting of sleeves, channels, clips, UDS tape, and instruction sheets to provide weatherproofing to exposed electrical wiring on light poles as well as for underground wiring.
- Have worked in Seal Caps and Sleeve Kits.
- Have become knowledgeable of the Starshine facility, and would like to contribute to the plant's efficiency and productivity by working in an office support position.
- Have been frequently commended for my sunny disposition, good attitude, and desire to maximize productivity in all I do.

Advanced in a track record of promotion with Electro, Inc., Fayden, OK (1997-00).
1998-99: PACKAGING ASSOCIATE. Was promoted to a position which involved removing finished product from the line, testing it, rejecting defective machines, installing brushes, trimming molding, and putting battery, charges, and instruction sheets in boxes.
- Achieved extremely high production levels and was known for my attention to detail.

1997-98: PRODUCTION WORKER. Started with Electro, Inc. on the production line. Assembled appliances; built, tested, installed, and wired motors and switches.
- Utilized diagnostic tester to analyze the appliance; removed defective motors and returned deficient products to the motor installer for a new motor.
- Was called upon to work in various areas of the plant as production needs required; became known for my cheerful willingness to work wherever I was needed.

CASHIER. Sub Shop, Dunn, OK (1996). Became skilled in all aspects of customer service while working with the public; took orders, handled money accurately, and prepared orders.

PACKAGING ASSOCIATE. Gower's, Dunn, OK (1995-96). Folded apparel, counted items, and then sorted finished products by size and color according to specific customer orders; packaged orders for shipping.

SALES ASSOCIATE. Murray's Department Store, Dunn, OK (1994-95). While still attending high school, became skilled in customer service and learned how to troubleshoot computer and cash register problems; performed shipping and receiving functions, assisted with inventory control, and assumed a key role in periodic and annual inventory audits.

PERSONAL   Am an individual who is always trying to better myself. Always give "110%" to my employer.

Exact Name of Person
Title or Position
Name of Company
Address (number and street)
Address (city, state, and zip)

PLANT MANAGER Dear Exact Name of Person: (or Sir or Madam if answering a blind ad.)

With the enclosed resume, I would like to make you aware of my interest in joining your management team in some capacity in which you could utilize my proven skills in increasing profit, cutting costs, restructuring operations for greater efficiency, and improving market share.

I have excelled in management positions with the General Electric Corporation and then with Baylor Industries, a $7 billion company which acquired General Electric's $1.1 billion electrical control and motor business. In one job as a Plant Manager, I transformed an unprofitable plant into a profitable one and then grew sales from $52 to $82 million. In another position as a Plant Manager, I increased sales 25% annually, from $83 million to $148 million in 1996, while managing 800 employees, eight assembly sites, and $4.5 million in annual capital investments. In earlier jobs as a Product Line Manager with General Electric, I introduced new product lines and modified the way the company did business through its sales channels, customer base structure, investment strategy, pricing structure, and other areas.

In a previous position, I was recruited to direct operations of a home improvements company with two manufacturing plants and a distribution warehouse. Through my leadership, we boosted revenue and the company was acquired by Capel Industries.

If your company can utilize a strong and insightful leader, I would enjoy the opportunity to talk with you in person about your needs and how I might serve them. I offer a reputation as a visionary thinker, aggressive cost cutter, creative strategist, and resourceful opportunity finder. I believe a company must continuously analyze the ways it does business in order to assure maximum efficiency. For example, as a Plant Manager, I profitably outsourced shipping, logistics, mail, document management, and network maintenance functions previously performed internally, and we made highly profitable quality and productivity improvements. I have a strong customer orientation which was derived from my earliest jobs in technical sales and product line management.

If my executive abilities interest you, please contact me. I can provide outstanding references, and I am willing to relocate anywhere in the U.S.

Sincerely,

Milo Germano

MILO GERMANO

1110½ Hay Street, Fayetteville, NC 28305 • preppub@aol.com • (910) 483-6611

OBJECTIVE

To contribute to the profitability of an organization that can use a creative and resourceful executive who has introduced new product lines, restructured operations for greater productivity, and managed internal change in order to cut costs, improve quality, and increase market share.

EXPERIENCE

Excelled in this "track record" of promotion within the General Electric Corporation, and then within Baylor Industries, a $7 billion company which acquired General Electric's $1.1 billion electrical control and distribution business:

PLANT MANAGER. Baylor Industries, Sheraton, GA (2001-present). Directed the plant during its period of greatest growth; **sales increased by 25% annually, from $83 million in 1994 to $148 million in 1996.** Managed 800 employees, eight sites assembling electrical motor control products, $4.5 million in annual capital investments, and an expense budget of $85 million.

- Introduced two new major product lines representing $115 million in sales.
- Implemented multiple marketing expert systems which reduced cycle times 50% while improving total quality; also introduced JIT II.
- Planned and implemented the consolidation of businesses from five locations to one without the loss of any major customers.
- Profitably invested $6 million in quality and productivity improvements which included advanced robotics, computer, phone, and other productivity equipment.
- Profitably outsourced shipping, logistics, mail, document management, and network maintenance functions previously performed internally.
- Reduced inventory by $2 million (25%) through Kanban, cycle-time improvements, fewer suppliers, and product rationalization; gained ISO 9002 certification.

PLANT MANAGER. General Electric Corporation, Dawson, GA (1992-00). Transformed an unprofitable business into a profitable one in my first year of managing this troubled plant; then **grew sales from $52 million to $82 million** over six years while growing market share by 19% and increasing price realization to become #2 in the market.

PRODUCT LINE MANAGER. General Electric Corporation, Philadelphia, PA (1989-91). Introduced product lines representing $40 million in investment and developed strategies including product migration and rationalization to increase market share.

- Changed customer base from OEM to dealer, which increased operating profit 20%; also shifted the sales channel from corporate direct to independent manufacturer's representatives, which reduced selling expenses by $500,000.

DIRECTOR OF MANUFACTURING. Tyson Home Improvements, Winston, SC (1980-88). Was recruited by this home improvement products company with two manufacturing plants and a distribution warehouse; **boosted revenues from $48 million in 1985 to $64 million in 1988.**

- In large measure due to the results achieved through my leadership, the company became an acquisition target and was acquired by Capel, Inc.; assisted in the transition of the company to new management and was offered a top management role, but I decided not to remain with Capel, Inc.
- Cut costs by $1 million; reduced management head count 30%; shrank inventories while simultaneously improving customer satisfaction; established controls to avoid the chronic inventory shortages which had plagued the company.
- Introduced JIT and Kanban while promoting a union-free, multi-racial environment.

EDUCATION

B.S. in Industrial Engineering, Virginia Tech, Blacksburg, VA.
Postgraduate courses in management, marketing, finance, and accounting at George Washington University, University of Dallas, University of Virginia, and Michigan State.

Exact Name of Person
Exact Title
Exact Name of Company
Address
City, State, Zip

PLY CUTTER OPERATOR

When you relocate to a new area, you sometimes have to be "open" to the possibility of finding a different type of work than your previous job. This job hunter has written his cover letter so that it is very versatile, even though his resume is clearly that of an experienced manufacturing professional.

Dear Exact Name of Person (or Dear Sir or Madam if answering a blind ad):

With the enclosed resume, I would like to make you aware of my interest in exploring employment opportunities with your organization. My wife and I have recently relocated permanently to your area because we have decided that we wish to live near our extended family and aging parents.

As you will see from my resume, I recently worked as a Ply Cutter in a manufacturing environment in New Jersey. I became known for my dedication to the highest standards of safety as I established and maintained an outstanding safety record of no accidents and no incidents while operating numerous machines over a 12-year period.

On several occasions, I was chosen to train other employees. For example, I was handpicked to teach a 16-week training program for new employees in the safe and proper operation of bias cutting equipment. I offer very strong written and oral communication skills.

I believe my attitude of attention to detail as well as my highly productive work style would be assets in any type of company. I am a highly resourceful and creative individual who is skilled in the operation of a variety of equipment, and I would relish the opportunity to apply my mechanical skills and technical problem-solving abilities to benefit your organization.

If you can use a highly motivated worker who can provide outstanding references, I hope you will contact me to suggest a time when we might meet to discuss your needs.

Sincerely,

David Paul Robinson

DAVID PAUL ROBINSON

1110½ Hay Street, Fayetteville, NC 28305　　•　　preppub@aol.com　　•　　(910) 483-6611

OBJECTIVE　　To benefit an organization that can use an experienced professional who offers extensive knowledge and experience in the component preparation phase of industrial manufacturing operations as well as a background in training and supervision.

TECHNICAL SKILLS　　Skilled in the operation of all powered material-handling equipment, including standard forklifts, stand-up and gas-operated lift trucks, and others. Extensive knowledge and experience in the operation and maintenance of manual and automatic bias cutters, as well as every type of component preparation equipment used in tire building.

EXPERIENCE　　*With Myer's Manufacturing Company, 1990-2002, built a reputation as a knowledgeable, hard-working professional who could be counted on to assume additional responsibility. Rotated into and out of various positions, contributing my thorough knowledge of component preparation and equipment operation and maintenance:*

1998-2002: **BIAS CUTTER/PLY CUTTER OPERATOR.** Lowesville, NJ. Skilled in the operation of manual Bias Cutters, was a key player in overseeing the rollout of the automatic Ply Cutter; was responsible for ensuring the safe and proper operation of millions of dollars worth of industrial manufacturing equipment.

- Serviced and maintained all manual and automatic bias cutting equipment.

1994-1998: **NRM OPERATOR AND SERVICE TECHNICIAN.** Lowesville, NJ. Operated, serviced, and changed material rolls on the NRM unit, cutting material for use in first-stage tire building.

- Performed quality assurance, monitoring finished product to verify that materials were cut properly and met or exceeded required specifications.

1992-94: **EBP SERVICE TECHNICIAN.** Lowesville, NJ. Serviced and changed material rolls on the EBP unit, which treated ply materials to increase strength and hardness.

1990-92: **HOURLY MANAGER and LABOR TRAINER.** Lowesville, NJ. Hand-picked for this position due to my familiarity with Myer's policies and procedures as well as my extensive knowledge of all plant operations related to component preparation; supervised all aspects of component preparation during several periods when the salaried manager was unavailable.

- Supervised and assigned daily tasks to as many as 40 employees, overseeing the productivity and safe operation of all machines in the component preparation area.
- Maintained a perfect safety record during my several periods of employment as Hourly Manager.
- Due to my thorough familiarity with the safe operation and maintenance of all types of bias cutting equipment, was selected to teach a 16-week training program for new employees in the safe and proper operation of bias cutting equipment.

Other experience: OWNER and **GENERAL MANAGER.** Cascade Mobile Home Movers, Lowesville, NJ. Trained and supervised five employees in the moving, installation, and setup of mobile homes throughout an 8-county region of New Jersey.

EDUCATION　　Attended a college-level certification program in Real Estate Appraisal, Lowesville Technical Community College, Lowesville, NJ, 1995.

PERSONAL　　Excellent personal and professional references are available upon request.

Date

Exact Name of Person
Title or Position
Name of Company
Address (number and street)
Address (city, state, and zip)

Dear Exact Name of Person: (or Dear Sir or Madam if answering a blind ad.)

With the enclosed resume, I would like to make you aware of my top management experience and my desire to utilize my background to benefit your company.

As you will see from my resume, I have most recently served as president of a company which we developed into an attractive acquisition candidate and which subsequently attracted the attention of major corporations. When I took over as president in 1990, it had a negative cash flow and was considering Chapter 11. I aggressively reduced costs while negotiating with vendors, and within two years we achieved a positive cash flow. I rose to the position of president after graduating from MIT and excelling in positions as a plant engineer and then plant manager.

Although my engineering background is vast, I believe the key to my success as a top manager is my creativity and ability to anticipate problems before they actually happen. I offer a proven ability to work effectively with people at all organizational levels.

If my considerable skills, experience, and talents interest you, please contact me. Thank you in advance for your professional courtesies.

Sincerely,

Scott G. Kandt

SCOTT G. KANDT

1110½ Hay Street, Fayetteville, NC 28305 • preppub@aol.com • (910) 483-6611

OBJECTIVE

To benefit an organization that can use a highly resourceful manager who offers a proven "track record" of restoring profitability to ailing operations and troubleshooting stubborn productivity and manufacturing problems, as well as designing new processes, tools, and facilities that improve efficiency and output.

EXPERIENCE

ACTING PRESIDENT. Manufacturing Plus, Aiken, SC (1999-present). Since the company was sold, I have continued on a contract basis and have been offered the job as President and CEO, which I have declined; manage plant operations at three plants including maintenance and upkeep of the equipment, buildings, and grounds for this busy manufacturing company.

PRESIDENT. Manufacturing Plus, Aiken, SC (1990-1999). Reported to a board of directors while managing operations of a company which manufactures grinding wheels and ceramic filters; became president in 1990 after excelling in jobs as plant engineer and plant manager.

- After taking over as president of a company which had a negative cash flow, aggressively reduced costs while extending terms with vendors, a strategy which produced a positive cash flow in less than two years.
- Developed operations/production schedules; determined staffing needs, machine and equipment requirements, tooling needs and development methods, and time standards.
- Planned and implemented programs/procedures to ensure compliance with OSHA and EPA regulations regarding plant safety and materials handling.
- Directed research and development projects for new products and equipment.
- Managed the purchasing of raw materials, equipment, supplies, and services, including procurement of capital equipment and negotiation of contracts.
- Developed or refined written procedures in numerous operational areas in order to assure that company procedures "on the ground floor" were consistent with strategic goals for short-term profitability and long-term growth.
- Oversaw every aspect of internal operations and external relationships for a company with $50 million in sales and up to 975 employees.
- As **plant manager from 1984-90,** improved overall output by 15% and, through new equipment which I designed and built, increased one product line by 1000%.
- As **plant engineer from 1981-84,** developed engineering and maintenance controls, developed and built new equipment, and reorganized manufacturing processes with the net result that operating efficiencies improved by 30%.

PRODUCTION MANAGER & PLANT ENGINEERING MAINTENANCE MANAGER. L.P. Floyd, Inc., Florence, SC (1978-81). Began with this company as a Production Foreman and Maintenance Foreman overseeing 45 employees and responsible for a $1.5 million profit center; promoted to oversee a $6 million profit center with up to 150 employees working in a union shop.

EDUCATION

Bachelor of Science in Industrial Engineering, Massachusetts Institute of Technology (MIT), Boston, MA, 1978.
MBA, University of South Carolina, Aiken, SC, 1984.
Executive development course work sponsored by industry groups and associations.

PERSONAL

Can provide outstanding personal and professional references at the appropriate time. Believe that the kind of creativity and vision I possess give me the ability as a CEO to formulate strategy and anticipate problems before they occur. Am known for my integrity, compassion, and desire to work toward perfection. In excellent health.

Date

Exact Name of Person
Exact Title
Exact Name of Company
Address
City, State, Zip

PRINT SHOP MANAGER

Dear Exact Name of Person (or Dear Sir or Madam if answering a blind ad):

With the enclosed resume, I would like to make you aware of my background in print shop management and mail center distribution, as well as my exceptional technical skills related to printing and my desire to utilize these abilities within your organization.

In my current position as a Printer, I produce color and black-and-white materials using a variety of printing equipment including single and dual-head Heidelberg presses, two-color mechanical presses, and the four-color QuickMaster digital press. I am knowledgeable of the proper procedures for handling and disposal of inks, solvents, and other hazardous materials and skilled in various binding techniques and the operation of the Bostitch stitcher.

In earlier positions as a Print Shop Manager and Mail Distribution Manager, supervised three printers and mail handlers while overseeing the production of booklets, leaflets, bulletins, certificates, and other materials. I ensured the timely distribution of those materials to hundreds of locations and customer organizations.

If you can use a motivated, hard-working professional whose leadership and technical skills related to printing operations have been tested in challenging situations worldwide, I hope you will contact me to suggest a time when we might meet. I can assure you in advance that I have an excellent reputation and could quickly become a valuable asset to your operation.

Yours sincerely,

Lawrence Meadow, Jr.

LAWRENCE MEADOW, JR.

1110½ Hay Street, Fayetteville, NC 28305 • preppub@aol.com • (910) 483-6611

OBJECTIVE

I want to contribute to an organization that can use a hard-working young professional with versatile experience related to print shop management, mail handling and distribution, and customer service, as well as employee training and supervision.

EDUCATION

Completed the Printing & Binding Specialist course, Los Angeles Community College, Los Angeles, CA, 1995.
Completed numerous workshops and training programs related to manufacturing.

Graduated from Okeechobee High School, Okeechobee, FL, 1993.

EXPERIENCE

PRINTER. Cryton Printing, Miami, FL (2000-present). Supervised and trained eight employees including printers, binders, and quality assurance personnel utilizing a variety of mechanical and digital presses and binding equipment in this fast-paced military printing facility.
- Operated and maintained printing and binding equipment including a Heidelberg offset press, a QuickMaster digital press, Bostich stitchers, and cutters.
- Produced multi-color printed matter using a two-color mechanical press and a four-color QuickMaster digital press.
- Operated SORZ and SORD two-headed Heidelberg presses.
- Became knowledgeable of the proper procedures used in disposing of solvents, inks, and other HAZMAT materials.
- Initially trained on the two-headed GTO press; operated this equipment during a tour in Bosnia in support of Operation Joint Endeavor.
- Familiar with many different binding techniques, including saddle stitching and side stitching.
- During a special project, was praised for my leadership in setting up a field printing operation in less than four hours.

PRINTER SHOP MANAGER and **MAIL DISTRIBUTION MANAGER.** Difendal Printing, Los Angeles, CA (1995-2000). Supervised two printers and mail handlers involved in the production of leaflets, booklets, bulletins, certificates, and other materials; distributed printed matter to numerous customer organizations.
- Was accountable for equipment, supplies, and postage valued at more than $40,000.
- Learned to operate and perform maintenance on offset duplicators and presses, copy cameras, platemaking equipment, and various types of bindery and film processing equipment; operated offset press.
- Produced and trained others to produce multi-color printed matter.

PRESS LEADER. Kaydal Printing, Inc. (1994-95). Began as a printer and rapidly advanced ahead of my peers to manage eight other printers and binders.
- Operated a Kodak 300 Photocopier as well as other printing equipment.

Other Experience:
CREW MEMBER. Worked on an irrigation crew, preparing water lines to ensure an adequate supply of water to the trees in an orange grove.

HONORS

Numerous certificates of achievement for my exceptional skills in printing management.

PERSONAL

Excellent personal and professional references are available upon request.

CAREER CHANGE

Date

Exact Name of Person
Exact Title
Exact Name of Company
Address
City, State, Zip

PRODUCTION
ENGINEERING
MANAGER

Dear Exact Name of Person (or Dear Sir or Madam if answering a blind ad):

With the enclosed resume, I would like to make you aware of my background in manufacturing, quality assurance, and employee training.

After completing my degree in Chemistry at the University of Michigan at Ann Arbor, I was recruited by Saginaw Industries to work as a Production Engineering Technician and I have advanced to Production Engineering Manager. While steadily progressing to handle increasingly complex responsibilities, I have excelled in every aspect of my job. In 2002 I received the CEO's award for exception performance during a special project.

Although I am considered on the "fast track" and am being groomed for promotion to further supervisory responsibilities, I have decided to selectively explore opportunities in the pharmaceutical industry. I am confident that my chemistry knowledge and product engineering knowledge could be assets to a pharmaceutical firm that values highly motivated individuals who are able to creatively apply their skills and knowledge.

If you can use my personal qualities of reliability and resourcefulness as well as my vast technical knowledge related to manufacturing and quality assurance, I hope you will contact me to suggest a time when we might meet. I can assure you in advance that I have an excellent reputation and could quickly become a valuable asset to your operation.

Yours sincerely,

Jeff Steven Cole

JEFF STEVEN COLE

1110½ Hay Street, Fayetteville, NC 28305　　•　　preppub@aol.com　　•　　(910) 483-6611

OBJECTIVE　　To benefit an organization that can use an experienced professional with exceptional analytical, communication, and organizational skills who offers a background in manufacturing, quality assurance, and training.

TECHNICAL　　Proficient in the operation of testing instruments and equipment, including the following:
SKILLS

BAS-CV-27 Voltammograph	Abbe A300A Refractometer
Dionex Series 2000 Ion Chromatograph	Fisher Joint Melting Point Apparatus
Parr 1341EB Bomb Calorimeter	Bausch & Lomb Spectronic 2000
Buck 200A Atomic Absorption Spectrometer	Milton Ray Spectronic 20
HP 8452A Diode Array Spectrophotometer	HP S890A Gas Chromatograph
BioRad FTS-40 FT Infrared Spectrometer	Infrared & Mass Spectrometer

COMPUTERS　　Experience with computers includes Windows, Word, PowerPoint, and Slide Writer Plus.

EDUCATION　　**Bachelor of Science** in **Chemistry**, University of Michigan at Ann Arbor, MI, 2000.
Co-author of Physical Chemistry Lab Manual.

EXPERIENCE　　**PRODUCTION ENGINEERING MANAGER.** Saginaw Industries, Saginaw, MI (2000-present). Began as a Production Engineering Technician and was promoted to Manager; now oversee quality assurance testing for this local manufacturing facility of the large multinational chemical company.

- Perform testing of various resins, analyzing the reheat, color, size, strength, and clarity; allocate product to specific customers by comparing customer requirements with specifications yielded through testing of finished resins.
- Train operators, managers, lab technicians, and shift supervisors on the operation of the plant's proprietary computer system, SETCIM.
- Instruct operators and shift supervisors in performing all routine analytical testing; taught shift supervisors how to manually enter production data.
- Developed and manage a system for recording all Losses of Production; train operators on use of this system as well as producing a monthly production report.
- Supervise the operation of an In-Line Viscometer, measuring the intrinsic viscosity of the resin.
- Direct daily sampling plans; coordinate the sale or blending of all off-grade resin.
- Introduced three new bottle resins into the carbonated soft drink and specialty container market.
- Commissioned the construction of a new soft drink container; received the 2002 CEO's award.

STOCK CLERK. Central Stores, University of Michigan, Ann Arbor, MI (1994-2000). Worked my way through college in this job; performed a variety of shipping and receiving, delivery, inventory control, and warehousing duties while attending college full-time, completing a rigorous degree program in Chemistry.

Other experience: SERVICE TECHNICIAN. Tire Hut, Ann Arbor, MI. Worked in this family-owned business throughout high school; changed tires, replaced brake pads, repaired or replaced fluid hoses and tubes, installed headlights, windshield wipers, and signal lights.

PERSONAL　　Excellent personal and professional references are available upon request.

Date

PRODUCT DESIGN DIRECTOR

To whom it may concern:

With the enclosed resume, I would like to make you aware of the strong management skills and technical knowledge which I could utilize for the benefit of an ambitious company.

As you will see, I hold a degree in Mechanical Engineering and have recently excelled as Director of Product Design and Development with Leaman Products. While directing worldwide customer and product support, I manage a department of 36 employees and a $5 million operating budget. I have made numerous contributions to the bottom line. I successfully designed and implemented a Design Control System which has resulted in zero instances of nonconformance during three surveillance audits. I also smoothly planned and directed the relocation of the entire corporate engineering staff from Oklahoma to Tennessee, which involved restaffing the entire department. I am known for my exceptionally strong team-building skills.

Although I am held in high regard and can provide excellent references at the appropriate time, I am selectively exploring opportunities in companies which can utilize my technical knowledge as well as my management abilities. I have a keen interest in moving to a higher level of business unit management and profit center management. I am available for relocation.

If you would like to suggest a time when we might talk further by telephone or in person, please contact me to suggest a convenient time and location. I look forward to hearing from you.

Sincerely,

Paul Valium

P.S. I will be in Spain for the next week or so, so don't think I am not interested if you call me and I don't respond immediately!

PAUL VALIUM

1110½ Hay Street, Fayetteville, NC 28305 • preppub@aol.com • (910) 483-6611

OBJECTIVE

To build upon my technical management capabilities by undertaking further responsibilities in business unit management and profit center management.

EDUCATION

Bachelor of Science in **Mechanical Engineering, Manufacturing concentration**, University of Memphis, Memphis, TN, 1990.

Completed numerous advanced training programs sponsored by Leaman Products Company which were designed to refine the executive abilities and manufacturing knowledge of corporate managers.

EXPERIENCE

With Leaman Products Company, have been promoted to positions of increasing responsibility by this international manufacturer of original equipment and after-market air, oil, and fuel filtration devices:

2000-present: **DIRECTOR, PRODUCT DESIGN & DEVELOPMENT.** Memphis, TN. Relocated Corporate Engineering from Tulsa, OK, to Memphis, TN. Restaffed department by recruiting, hiring, training, and developing engineers as well as support staff personnel.

- Oversee all aspects of aftermarket and original equipment manufacturing air, oil, and fuel filtration products, including Product Design, Product Development, Packaging Engineering, and the technical aspects of Filter Testing.
- Manage a department of 36 employees including seven direct reports and 18 degreed engineers as well as a $5 million operating budget.
- Direct worldwide customer and product support, to include significant international travel for the purpose of customer support and business development.
- Successfully designed and implemented a Design Control System which has resulted in zero instances of nonconformance during three surveillance audits.

1994-99: **MANAGER, LIQUID DESIGN ENGINEERING.** Tulsa, OK. Held responsibility over Product Design for all original equipment and aftermarket oil, fuel, and hydraulic filtration products.

- Managed ten degreed engineers at the corporate and various plant locations.

1993-94: **ORIGINAL EQUIPMENT SALES ENGINEER.** Southfield, MI. Relocated to Detroit after Leaman secured 100% of a major automobile company's business, totaling $50 million annually. Provided on-site engineering assistance to develop and implement an approval process that allowed Leaman to convert purchased product into manufactured product.

- Served as Project Manager for all new vehicle platforms to ensure that product development coincided with the customer's vehicle program timing requirements.

1991-1993: **PRODUCT DESIGN ENGINEER.** Memphis, TN. Designed and developed oil filtration products for aftermarket and original equipment.

Highlights of earlier experience:

PRODUCT ENGINEER. Kaydon Corporation, LaGrange, GA (1990-1991). Designed and developed lubrication and hydraulic filter cartridges for off-road Original Equipment Manufacturer (OEM) and industrial applications.

COMPUTERS

Highly computer proficient with software including Word and Excel as well as Autocad.

PERSONAL

Excellent personal and professional references on request.

Exact Name of Person
Exact Title
Exact Name of Company
Address
City, State, Zip

PRODUCT DEVELOPMENT DIRECTOR

Dear Exact Name of Person (or Dear Sir or Madam if answering a blind ad):

With the enclosed resume, I would like to make you aware of my interest in exploring the possibility of joining your executive team in some capacity in which you can utilize my vast experience related to new product development and strategic planning/positioning.

As you will see from my resume, I am currently excelling as Director, New Product Development, for Manning Manufacturing Company. I was recruited by the company in 2002 to take over new product development for its Life and Lube Products ($90 million in sales) and, in May 2002, I was promoted to direct new product development for all company products ($200 million). Although I am held in the highest regard and can provide outstanding references at the appropriate time, I would ask that you not contact my current employer until after we talk. The company I work for is currently up for sale, and I am selectively exploring opportunities in other organizations.

In previous positions since earning my B.S. degree in Mechanical Engineering, I have gained experience in design engineering, process development engineering, machine design engineering, project management, and new product development in multiple industries. I worked for giants in the aircraft industry and made major contributions to new engine proposals and new aircraft production. Subsequently working on the development of consumer products for Nelson Foods, Inc, I was promoted to develop manufacturing processes for new food products. Then with Drakesmith, Inc., I was promoted from Senior Project Manager to New Product Development Group Manager. While at Drakesmith, I transformed a poorly organized group suffering from low output into a highly focused and productive product development team which developed numerous profitable new products.

I offer a proven ability to bring focus and strategic direction to product development teams, and I would welcome the opportunity to meet with you in person to discuss how I might positively impact your bottom line. If you think my considerable skills and experience could benefit you, please contact me to suggest the next step I should take in exploring the possibility of becoming a valuable part of your executive team.

Yours sincerely,

Fred Ward Baker

FRED WARD BAKER

1110½ Hay Street, Fayetteville, NC 28305   •   preppub@aol.com   •   (910) 483-6611

OBJECTIVE   To contribute to the growth and profitability of a company that can use a visionary business leader with expertise related to all aspects of new product development including project management, strategic planning, project justification and prioritization.

EDUCATION   **Bachelor of Science (B.S.) degree in Mechanical Engineering,** Brigham Young University, Provo, UT, 1990. Graduated *cum laude;* 3.72 GPA.
Annually attend the respected executive development program at University of Minnesota's Carlson School of Management, The Masters Forum, 1999-2002.

EXPERIENCE   **DIRECTOR, NEW PRODUCT DEVELOPMENT.** Manning Manufacturing Company, Blair, MN (2000-present). Was recruited by this company to grow its top line through new product development; was promoted in May 2002 from Director of New Product Development for Lifting and Lube Products ($90 million in sales) to Director of New Product Development for all company products ($200 million).
- Oversee a $5 million engineering budget and a staff of 38 managers, engineers, designers, drafters, technicians, and assistants; report to the President.
- Closed down new product development operations in Kentucky and rebuilt the new product development organization in Minnesota; hired 18 managers, engineers, designers, and technicians while also organizing lab facilities and test equipment.
- Played a key role in identifying and arresting faltering financial performance; developed and implemented a disciplined new product development process that included organizing and flowcharting the process, developing work instructions, creating process and authorization forms, and designing a financial model for control.

GROUP MANAGER, NEW PRODUCT DEVELOPMENT. Drakesmith, Inc., Rochester, MN (1998-00). Excelled as a Senior Project Manager from 1998-99 and was promoted in 1999 to New Product Development Group Manager; reported to the VP of Engineering.
- Facilitated the design and development of high-quality innovative industrial fluid-handling products at the lowest cost and in the shortest possible time.

PROCESS DEVELOPMENT ENGINEER. Nelson Foods, Inc., Rochester, MN (1995-98). After making major contributions as a Machine Design Project Engineer from 1995-97, was promoted to develop manufacturing processes for new food products.
- Served as the Process Engineering Representative on new product development teams.
- Defined, tested, and installed new processing equipment; also developed and implemented equipment operating procedures needed to transition new products from the R&D labs to full-scale plant production.

STRUCTURAL INTEGRITY ENGINEER. Jetson Aircraft Engines, Los Angeles, CA (1994-95). Received two Engineering Achievement Awards for my leadership and contributions to the F-120 engine proposal.

DESIGN ENGINEERING LEAD. Aircraft Design, Inc., San Jose, CA (1989-94). Excelled as a Structural Design Engineer from 1989-92 and designed primary aircraft structure for new production F-16 aircraft, and was then promoted to manage all structural design and production support activities related to the F-16 aft fuselage.
- Supervised eight engineers; reviewed aircraft change requests from the customer.

PERSONAL   Excellent references. Highly resourceful leader who excels in managing the creative process.

Date

Exact Name of Person
Title or Position
Name of Company
Address (number and street)
Address (city, state, and zip)

PRODUCT ENGINEERING MANAGER

Dear Exact Name of Person (or Sir or Madam if answering a blind ad):

I would appreciate an opportunity to talk with you soon about how I could contribute to your organization through my versatile experience as an engineer in product engineering, product marketing, and project management.

As you will see from my resume, I have excelled in a track record of accomplishment with Warren since graduating with my B.S. degree in Mechanical Engineering (Industrial concentration).

I started my employment with the company as a Design Engineer in Kershaw, AR, and earned an Engineering Recognition Award. I have developed multiple control designs for use in several industries. I became a Product Marketing Manager and later received a prestigious award for Excellence in Marketing. As a Product Marketing Manager, I played a key role in producing a gross sales increase of $22.6 million over a two-year period.

In 2000 I was specially selected to act as a Product Engineering Manager and relocated to Victorfield, SC, where I have handled a wide range of tasks related to the strategic and tactical transfer of products from an assembly plant in Kershaw to a Custom OEM assembly plant in Victorfield. I have set up the engineering department, standardized product production of $20 million in sales, communicated with outside sales professionals and customers during the phase-in process, and created documentation related to the manufacture and assembly of products. While supervising a team of nine design engineers and two draftspeople in developing new products and planning production methods, we have added $3.4 million in revenue through recent product development programs.

I am approaching your company because I believe my versatile experience in project management, product development, marketing analysis and sales, and engineering design could be of value to you. I can provide outstanding personal and professional references at the appropriate time.

If you can use a superior performer with a strong bottom-line orientation and an ability to think strategically, I hope you will contact me to suggest a time when we might meet to discuss your needs and how I might help you achieve them. Thank you in advance for your time.

Sincerely,

Horace P. Smithson

HORACE P. SMITHSON

1110½ Hay Street, Fayetteville, NC 28305   •   preppub@aol.com   •   (910) 483-6611

OBJECTIVE

To benefit an organization that can use an engineer with a reputation as a creative problem solver along with experience in project management, electrical and mechanical product design, and marketing, quality assurance, documentation/auditing, and profitability management.

EDUCATION

B. S. in Mechanical Engineering, Industrial Concentration, Western Kentucky University, Bowling Green, KY, 1990.

EXPERIENCE

Since earning my B.S., have worked for Warren Company:

2000-present: PRODUCT ENGINEERING MANAGER. Victorfield, SC. Was transferred from Warren's Arkansas location to handle a wide range of tasks related to the strategic and tactical transfer of products from an assembly plant in Kershaw to a Custom OEM assembly plant in Victorfield.

- **Project Management:** Was tasked to develop the phase-in operation plan for a new plant, which involved the detailed plan for product phase-in as well as the transfer of equipment from other sites; this plan determined the timetable for a $6 million inventory transfer and the employment of 185 production personnel.
- **Start-up Management:** Set up the engineering department of a customer OEM assembly plant; standardized product production of $20 million in sales.
- **Product Development and Employee Supervision:** Supervised a team of nine design engineers and two draftspeople in developing new products meeting customer requirements and in planning product production methods. **Recent product development programs have added $3.4 million in revenue.**
- **Customer Communication and Liaison:** Communicated with outside sales personnel as well as the customer base regarding product transfer updates. Coordinated a product phase-in which involved two manufacturing plants, 7 product lines, and thousands of product variations.
- **Documentation:** Created documentation required to manufacture and assemble products including mechanical and electrical drawings, assembly instructions, bill of materials, and agency approvals; developed warranty return policies and procedures and automated order entry procedures.
- **Quality Assurance:** Quality assurance initiatives, procedures, and practices we established have increased first-time yield rates from 76% to 92%.

1997-99: PRODUCT MARKETING MANAGER: Kershaw, AR. Increased assigned product sales volume by 40% while boosting overall net profit by 2%, and was responsible for a gross sales increase of $22.6 million over this period.

- **Market Analysis and Sales:** Identified target industries for sales penetration and identified market areas and potential customers, oversaw field sales personnel's activities in gaining new accounts. Received prestigious *Award for Excellence in Marketing.*
- **Profitability Management:** Monitored profit margin of products; established pricing levels.

1990-97: DESIGN ENGINEER. Kershaw, AR. Formulated product plans for sales presentation, support manufacturing disciplines, and product design. Received a special *Engineering Recognition Award in 1993.* Developed multiple control designs for use in several industries.

PERSONAL

Excellent references. Proficient with AUTOCAD and other software.

Exact Name of Person
Title or Position
Name of Company
Address (no., street)
Address (city, state, zip)

PRODUCTION CONTROL MANAGER

Dear Exact Name of Person (or Dear Sir or Madam if answering a blind ad):

With the enclosed resume, I would like to make you aware of my achievements in manufacturing management and production control and to express my interest in confidentially exploring employment opportunities with your company.

As you will see, I hold an M.B.A. as well as a B.S. degree, and I have completed extensive training related to state-of-the-art systems for quality control, inventory control, materials purchasing, production control, and other areas. Systems which I have helped implement and maintain include QS9000, JIT, SPEDE, KANBAN, FIFO, BPCS, MRO, and others.

In 2000, I was recruited by my current employer for a production planning position, and I developed a Just-in-Time (JIT) system with suppliers while playing a key role in implementing the SPEDE inventory control system and the BPCS production control system. I was then promoted to Production Control Supervisor and helped the company achieve cost savings of more than $400,000. Promoted in 2000 to Production Control Manager, I have played a major role in helping the company respond to a downturn in sales by strategic downsizing and aggressive cost-cutting. In FY 2002, the company is positioned to reap cost savings of $1.8 million. In my current position, I report to the Plant Manager while managing a $4 million annual MRO budget as well as a monthly inventory of $2.2 million. I am meeting or exceeding a wide range of ambitious objectives, including aggressive goals for product delivery and turnaround time. I have also led the Production Control Department through QS9000 accreditation.

Although I am highly regarded in my current position, I am selectively exploring opportunities in companies that can utilize my proven problem-solving and opportunity-finding skills. I have excelled as a member of senior management in responding to economic downturns as well as sharp increases in customer demand, and I am experienced in authoring procedures and systems used to optimize the efficiency of inventory turnover, production control, purchasing, and material handling. If you can use my strategic thinking ability and management experience, I hope you will contact me to suggest a time when we might meet to discuss your needs. Although I can provide outstanding references at the appropriate time, I would like you to hold my expression of interest in your company in confidence until after we talk in person.

Sincerely yours,

Paul L. Abacus

PAUL L. ABACUS

1110½ Hay Street, Fayetteville, NC 28305   •   preppub@aol.com   •   (910) 483-6611

OBJECTIVE

I want to contribute to an organization that can use an accomplished and versatile manager who has excelled in handling senior-level responsibilities for manufacturing and production management while consistently achieving and exceeding aggressive sales and customer satisfaction goals.

EDUCATION

M.B.A., Boston University, Boston, MA, 1997.

B.S. degree, major in Business Administration and minor in Management, Boston University, Boston, MA, 1990.

Completed extensive training sponsored by my employers in ISO/QS9000 Quality Systems documentation, MOPAR Supplier Symposium Training, MIS, and inventory management.

EXPERIENCE

Have excelled in the following track record of promotion to executive-level responsibilities with Quality Products, Boston, MA, 1990-present:

2000-present: PRODUCTION CONTROL MANAGER. After promotion to this position, was a key member of the strategic planning group that planned, implemented, and managed the company's downsizing and strategic repositioning in FY 01; greatly strengthened my strategic thinking and problem-solving abilities while repositioning the company to reap cost savings of $1.8 million for FY 2002.

- Report directly to the Plant Manager; directly supervise 16 individuals while managing a $4 million annual MRO budget as well as a monthly inventory of $2.2 million.
- Oversee functions including forecasting, planning, and scheduling; customer service; inventory turnover; raw materials warehousing; material storage and issuance systems; as well as inbound and outbound traffic.
- Am excelling in this position while being measured according to ambitious objectives related to freight claims, customer delivery performance, inventory turn, premium freight, and other areas.
- Satisfy a sophisticated customer base as well as suppliers to the automotive plants and special sealing products groups.
- Have gained expertise related to the following:

Raw materials purchasing and	Plant MRO purchasing
Bar Code/Inventory Control System (SPEDE)	MRO/PM System (MP2)
MRP/Production Control System (BPCS)	

- **Accomplishments:** Led the Production Control division through QS9000 accreditation. During the 2000 downsizing due to a sales volume decline, managed the department so that it achieved sales-per-employee goals. Implemented systems and procedures to error-proof the shipping and receiving processes; implemented a FIFO system for stock rotation. Worked with material suppliers to create Just-In-Time (JIT) and KANBAN systems.

1990-00: PRODUCTION CONTROL SUPERVISOR. Achieved cost savings of $198,000 for FY 98 and $224,000 for FY 99 while authoring procedures for Production Control and Shipping/Receiving.

- Transformed stockroom layout and controls for FIFO and inventory accuracy.
- Led the Matrix Team which initiated improvements in internal plant communications.
- Managed 10 people while overseeing raw material scheduling and JIT systems as well as shipping and receiving operations including the bar code system for inventory, cycle counting, inventory reporting and accuracy, material handling, and consignments.

PERSONAL

Can provide outstanding personal and professional references.

Date

Exact Name of Person
Exact Title
Exact Name of Company
Address
City, State, Zip

PRODUCTION FOREMAN   Dear Exact Name of Person (or Dear Sir or Madam if answering a blind ad):

With the enclosed resume, I would like to express my interest in offering my background and accomplishments to a facility that can benefit from my knowledge and experience related to food processing sanitation and manufacturing operations.

As you will see from my enclosed resume, I am presently a Production Foreman and the Sanitation Department Manager at Fresh Air Farms in Ames, IA. In my approximately two years with Fresh Air Farms I have been credited with reducing the rates of absenteeism and turnover for the Sanitation Department through my leadership and the example I set. Because I am fully bilingual in Spanish and English, I am able to communicate with the company's many non-English speaking employees and assist them in learning procedures and becoming a part of a productive team. I have received training in hazardous materials handling as well as in First Aid and CPR.

With a reputation as an intelligent, articulate, and creative professional, I have excelled in motivating and instructing others in prior jobs in fast food management and as a Foreign Language Instructor of Spanish. Throughout my career I have been singled out for praise by senior personnel for my ability to achieve results with limited resources, increase productivity and efficiency, and motivate others to learn and work together as a team while exceeding expected goals.

If you can use an experienced manager with specialized knowledge and training in sanitation and production operations, I hope you will call me soon to discuss how I might contribute to your organization. Thank you for your consideration of my qualifications and skills.

Sincerely,

Norman Storm

NORMAN STORM

1110½ Hay Street, Fayetteville, NC 28305 • preppub@aol.com • (910) 483-6611

OBJECTIVE   To offer my specialized knowledge, experience, and qualifications in sanitation management within the food production industry to a facility which can benefit from my exceptional motivational, planning, and leadership abilities as well as from my language skills.

EDUCATION   Studied Accounting, Oklahoma University, Norman, OK.
& TRAINING   Graduated from Cascia Hall Preparatory School for Boys, Tulsa, OK.
Received company-sponsored training which has included:
   Situational Leadership II, Ken Blanchard Company, 2000
   Hazardous Material Handling, Ames Community College, 2000
Completed American Heart Association programs: First Aid, CPR, and Heart Saver Plus, 2000.

LANGUAGE   Am fully bilingual in English and Spanish and have used my language skills to translate
SKILLS   employee handbooks and other written materials for the benefit of personnel.

EXPERIENCE   **PRODUCTION FOREMAN** and **SANITATION DEPARTMENT MANAGER.** Fresh Air Farms, Ames, IA (2000-present). As foreman for shift deboning operations at this poultry processing plant, oversee daily operation of eight production lines for deboning and five lines for wing disjointing while also gaining experience in overseeing all operations of the sanitation department.
- Through my emphasis on safety, have reduced the number of reportable accidents an impressive 68% for the most recent one-year period.
- Provide leadership while emphasizing safety, quality control, and reaching production levels.
- Am setting an example of professionalism and dedication to quality standards which has resulted in reducing the absenteeism rate to 2.1% and rate of turnover to 1.5%.

OPERATIONS AND TRAINING MANAGER. Jerry's Chicken and Biscuits, Cherryville, IA (1997-00). Worked closely with a co-manager while overseeing daily activities with an emphasis on training and supervising employees in order to ensure fast, courteous service and accuracy.
- Applied my Spanish language skills and ability to communicate clearly in writing in a special project translating the employee handbook and sexual harassment policy pamphlet.

OPERATIONS MANAGER. Karl's Fried Chicken, Norman, OK (1990-96). Gained knowledge of management responsibilities such as training and supervision of employees and of fiscal management while advancing from co-manager to store manager.

Became known as a proficient FOREIGN LANGUAGE INSTRUCTOR in part-time jobs:
Central Texas College. Trained linguists assigned to a military intelligence unit within the 82nd Airborne Division; developed instructional materials. Achieved excellent results in a six-week refresher course which saw 75% of my students improve overall test scores and obtain expected standards as a direct results of my skills.
Cherryville Technical Community College. Provided instruction in Spanish to members of a military intelligence unit.

PERSONAL   Am detail oriented and extremely capable of performing multiple simultaneous tasks. Enjoy the challenge of motivating and leading others to achieve goals and exceed expected standards.

PRODUCTION MANAGER

Dear Sir or Madam:

With the enclosed resume, I would like to make you aware of my interest in exploring employment opportunities with your organization. Although I am held in the highest regard by my current employer and can provide outstanding references at the appropriate time, I would like to ask that you keep my interest in your company confidential until after we speak.

As you will see from my resume, I have worked for only two employers since graduating from Lincoln High School. In a simultaneous part-time job, I also worked as a Welding Instructor teaching night classes at San Diego Technical Community College for seven years. With a reputation as a loyal and reliable individual, I have not missed a day of work or been late any day in the past five years.

I was recruited for my current position in 1997 by a Louisiana company which wanted to set up a shop in San Diego to service the West Coast. I began as a Lead Installer and was promoted to Production Manager. I have hired, trained, and managed detailers, truck builders, parts personnel, and mechanics, and I have provided extensive training to employees in welding, installation, and fabrication as well as quality assurance and safety.

In my subsequent position, which was my first job after high school, I began as a Welder and Fabricator and advanced to handle maintenance management responsibilities. I trained and managed 45 people who included crane operators, welders, truck drivers, bailer operators, forklift drivers, diesel truck mechanics, and others. On one occasion I disassembled a 500-ton Harris Shear in Pennsylvania and then reassembled it in California. I am experienced in maintaining, repairing, and operating a wide variety of industrial equipment including hydraulic and cable cranes, front end loaders, semi tractor-trailers, and other equipment.

I am interested in joining a company that can utilize my manufacturing expertise and extensive knowledge related to safety and quality assurance. If you can use my considerable skills, I hope you will contact me to suggest the next step I should take in exploring employment opportunities with your company. I can provide excellent references from all previous employers.

Sincerely,

Edward V. James

EDWARD V. JAMES

1110½ Hay Street, Fayetteville, NC 28305 • preppub@aol.com • (910) 483-6611

___

OBJECTIVE

I want to contribute to an organization that can use a hard-working maintenance professional who offers vast experience in industrial maintenance, quality assurance, safety, and production management.

EDUCATION

Completed **Welding Program**, San Diego Technical Community College, San Diego, CA., 1988.
- Learned mig, tig, arc welding and subsequently became a **College Welding Instructor.**
Completed numerous training programs and schools related to **hydraulics;** completed **NAPA School**, 1999, on **advanced mechanics, engineering, and hydraulics.**
Completed **Harris, Bailer & Shear School**, Cordele, GA, 1988; studied areas including:
  Electricity, hydraulics, wiring, and pneumatics
  Operation, repair, and maintenance of forklifts, loaders, hydraulic cranes, cable cranes, shears, and bailers.

EXPERIENCE

PRODUCTION MANAGER. West Coast Upfittings, San Diego, CA (1997-present). In the past five years, have not missed a day of work nor have I have been late any day; strive to set an example of reliability and dependability for the 24 employees I manage.
- Was recruited by the 60-year-old parent company, headquartered in Baton Rouge, LA, to help set up its San Diego shop, which now handles the company's West Coast operations.
- Hired, trained, and manage 20 detailers, truck builders, and parts personnel; trained mechanics in welding.
- Began as a **Lead Installer** and was promoted to Production Manager after a year; report to the General Manager; as a Lead Installer, cut and stretched truck chassis, rewired and relocated electrical lines, fabricated and designed new accessories, read blueprints, installed air line and gas lines, and handled extensive maintenance work.
- Schedule work; inspect work and am the in-house quality assurance expert; handle shipping/receiving as well as dispatching of trucks made to customer order.

MANUFACTURING MANAGER. Salteen & Son Salvage, San Bernadino, CA (1990-97). In my first job after graduating from high school, began as a **Welder** and **Fabricator** and was rapidly promoted to manufacturing management responsibilities; trained and managed 45 people who included crane operators, welders, truck drivers, bailer operators, forklift drivers, diesel truck mechanics, and others.
- On one occasion, disassembled a 500-ton Harris Shear in PA and reassembled it in CA.
- Operated all the company's equipment including hydraulic and cable cranes; drove a semi-tractor trailer, front end loader, and all other heavy equipment.
- Was the trusted "right arm" to the owners, and handled a variety of management responsibilities. Maintained an outstanding safety record.

WELDING INSTRUCTOR. San Diego Technical Community College, San Diego, CA (1988-97). After graduating from SDTCC, I was recruited to teach the community college's night classes in the welding program; taught at night while working full-time at the jobs above.

SKILLS

Offer a wide range of industrial skills related to these and many other areas: Welding: Mig, tig, and arc, hydraulics, plumbing, production machines, OSHA policies, respirator training fabrication, reading blueprints and schematics.

PERSONAL

Honest, loyal, and dedicated with a positive attitude. Attention to detail. Safety conscious.

Exact Name of Person
Title or Position
Name of Company
Address (no., street)
Address (city, state, zip)

**PRODUCTION
MANAGER**

Dear Exact Name of Person: (or Dear Sir or Madam if answering a blind ad)

I would appreciate an opportunity to talk with you soon about how I could contribute to your organization through my strong management and communication skills as well as my leadership ability and organizational know-how.

As you will see from my resume, in 2000 I began in a management trainee program with Raytheon Industries and advanced into a supervisory position as Production Manager in less time than any management trainee in my plant. Although I am considered within Raytheon to be on the "fast track" and am being groomed for rapid promotion into corporate management, I have a great desire to put down roots in the South Carolina area, where both my wife and I are from. As you will also see from my resume, I graduated from The Citadel and was elected to serve on the Honor Court in my senior year.

While working at Raytheon, I have had an opportunity to demonstrate my supervisory ability and have managed people in various jobs within the plant. I am widely respected for my knack for solving stubborn technical problems, and I have recently improved the speed and efficiency of a particular yarn for a major customer through taking a new approach to an old problem.

You would find me in person to be a dedicated and hard-working individual who prides myself on giving my best effort to my employer. I believe I could become a valuable asset to your organization, and it would be my desire to make a difference to your strategic posture and operating efficiency. I can provide outstanding personal and professional references upon request.

I hope you will welcome my call soon to arrange a brief meeting at your convenience to discuss your current and future needs and how I might serve them. Thank you in advance for your time.

Sincerely yours,

Rick Nunez

RICK NUNEZ

1110½ Hay Street, Fayetteville, NC 28305 • preppub@aol.com • (910) 483-6611

OBJECTIVE

To contribute to an organization that can use a resourceful young professional who offers a proven ability to troubleshoot and solve problems in industrial environments along with exceptionally strong communication skills, leadership ability, and organizational know-how.

EDUCATION

B.A. degree in **Economics and Business**, The Citadel, 1996.
- Was elected by my peers in my senior year to serve on the **Honor Court**, the judicial body which administers the Honor System.

EXECUTIVE TRAINING

Completed several months of technical and professional training sponsored by Raytheon Industries and University of Virginia in these areas:

Spun yarn manufacturing	Industrial engineering
Production management	Quantitative analysis
Employee supervision	Systematic decision making

COMPUTERS

Am proficient in the use of Word, Access, Lotus 1-2-3, Word, and Excel.
Am thoroughly knowledgeable of Uster Sliverdata, an on-line production and quality monitoring system in spinning production.

EXPERIENCE

PRODUCTION MANAGER. Raytheon Industries, Virginia Beach, VA (2000-present). Was specially recruited for this management position by Raytheon Industries, and am being groomed for rapid promotion to key corporate management positions; while excelling in Raytheon's rigorous management trainee program, advanced to a supervisory position more rapidly than any trainee in my plant.
- Through the formal training program, have gained knowledge about every phase of the manufacturing process.
- Acquired "hands-on" experience in a variety of supervisory jobs throughout the plant as the regular and off-shift manager of operational areas ranging from raw material coordination to finished product distribution.
- Supervised between 10 and 35 employees in nearly every aspect of plant operation.
- On my own initiative, combined what I learned in formal training with my natural creativity in devising a way of improving speed and efficiency of a particular yarn for a major customer.
- Have been commended for my ability to rapidly master complex technical concepts and for my ability to apply my training in solving stubborn production problems.
- Have become not only well versed in the details of production management but also knowledgeable about the "big picture" of the textile industry and sister industries in the global market.

SUPPLY MANAGER & MILITARY OFFICER. U.S. Army, Ft. Lee, VA (1996-99). After graduating from The Citadel, was commissioned as a second lieutenant, and then completed a six-month course pertaining to these areas:

supply management	service operations management
subsistence ordering	petroleum supply management

- Became knowledgeable about the "nuts and bolts" of the supply process, from the procurement process to the disposal of environmentally hazardous materials.

TECHNICAL ASSISTANT. Ivy Hill Golf Club, Forest, VA (Summers, 1992-96). Learned supervisory skills at an early age while supervising three adults performing maintenance.

PERSONAL

Have been told that I am on Raytheon's "fast track" and have a bright future in the company. Feel confident in my ability to transfer my management skills, creative problem-solving ability, and technical training to any industry. Excellent references.

Exact Name of Person
Title or Position
Name of Company
Address (no., street)
Address (city, state, zip)

**PRODUCTION
MANAGER**

Dear Exact Name of Person: (or Dear Sir or Madam if answering a blind ad)

I would appreciate an opportunity to talk with you soon about how I could contribute to your organization through my manufacturing background as well as my proven management and supervisory skills.

As you will see from my resume, in 1992 I began as a Product Manager with Raytheon Textiles and then progressed into positions as a Department Manager of increasing larger and more complex operations. I have become well known for my personal initiative. In my current job, I have directed a pilot project which has increased production in a key area of manufacturing by 6%. I pride myself on my ability to develop and implement timesaving and cost-efficient programs and procedures.

I hope you will welcome my call soon to arrange a brief meeting at your convenience to discuss your current and future needs and how I might serve them. Thank you in advance for your time.

Sincerely yours,

Richard Williamson

Alternate last paragraph:
I hope you will call or write me soon to suggest a time convenient for us to meet and discuss your current and future needs and how I might serve them. Thank you in advance for your time.

RICHARD WILLIAMSON

1110½ Hay Street, Fayetteville, NC 28305 • preppub@aol.com • (910) 483-6611

OBJECTIVE	To benefit an organization that can use a manager with a strong manufacturing background and excellent leadership skills as well as the ability to develop and implement timesaving and cost-efficient programs and procedures.
EXPERIENCE	*At Raytheon Textiles, have advanced in the following "track record" of increasing responsibility with this large manufacturer:* **2000-present: DEPARTMENT MANAGER II.** Reston, VA. Due to my success in managing the Spinning and Winding department, was entrusted with the supervision of an additional department (Carding). • Directly manage seven supervisors and 140 employees producing 250,000 pounds of finished product per week. • Develop and manage a quarterly supply budget of $120,000 as well as an $80,000 quarterly projects budget; total budgetary responsibility is $800,000 per year. • Direct a pilot project which has increased spinning frame production by 6%. • Responsible for the maintenance of $7 million in manufacturing equipment. • Coordinated a technical trial involving several departments which resulted in detection of a critical processing defect; correction of the problem would greatly improve quality and runnability. ***1997-00:* DEPARTMENT MANAGER II.** Reston, VA. Promoted to this position; managed the Spinning/Winding department. • Developed a program and coordinated efforts with the Engineering Department which resulted in an annual energy savings of $60,000. • Implemented procedures that resulted in a 3% capacity increase. ***1994-97:* DEPARTMENT MANAGER I.** Merriweather, GA. Promoted to this position from a Product Manager/Supervisor position at the SC plant; managed the Spinning/Winding department. • Managed four supervisors and 80 employees. • Developed new programs for producing tencel and high-twist yarn. • Achieved and maintained 16% improvement in S&E labor cost. ***1992-94:* PRODUCT MANAGER, SUPERVISOR.** Mayfield, SC. Performed texturing process during shift assignment. • Produced two-thirds of the written documentation for implementing I.S.O. procedures including all of the Manufacturing and Quality Control sections; our facility was the first Burlington plant to achieve I.S.O. 9002 certification. With the United States Marine Corps, achieved the rank of Captain and proudly served in the Persian Gulf War: **OFFICER. U.S.M.C.** Cherry Point, NC (1988-1992). • As a HAWK missile Platoon Commander, managed 70 personnel and $45 million worth of advanced equipment. • Effectively presented a new training program involving senior agencies that was adopted in preparation for Operation Desert Storm. • Received numerous prestigious awards and medals for exemplary service.
EDUCATION	Bachelor of Arts degree in Political Science, South Carolina State University, 1988. Numerous professional development courses related to manufacturing, leadership, and management as well as military training.
PERSONAL	Have excellent communication skills. Excellent references available.

Date

Exact Name of Person
Exact Title
Exact Name of Company
Address
City, State, Zip

Dear Exact Name of Person (or Dear Sir or Madam if answering a blind ad):

With the enclosed resume, I would like to make you aware of my recent background in management as well as my previous experience in sales.

As you will see from my resume, I am currently excelling as a Production Manager with Senor Carlo Mexican Foods, a company which has rewarded my strong problem-solving and communication skills by promoting me in a rapid track record of advancement. In my current position managing three supervisors and three departments, I indirectly supervise 125 people and am regarded as an articulate communicator with a flair for getting my point across.

With a reputation as an aggressive and goal-oriented individual, I thrive on the challenge of tackling ambitious goals. On my own initiative, I have developed and designed process improvements in two of the departments I manage, and under my direction, equipment troubleshooting guides were created which have significantly aided my junior supervisors in achieving high production goals.

If you can use a dynamic individual and resourceful problem solver who thrives on the challenge of a fast-paced environment, I hope you will contact me to suggest a time when we might meet to discuss your goals and how I might help you achieve them. Thank you in advance for your time.

Sincerely,

Nancy W. Xavier

NANCY W. XAVIER

1110½ Hay Street, Fayetteville, NC 28305   •   preppub@aol.com   •   (910) 483-6611

OBJECTIVE   To benefit an organization that can use an enthusiastic, highly motivated professional with strong communication skills and proven sales ability who offers a reputation as a disciplined hard worker and creative problem solver known for persistence and perseverance.

EDUCATION   Earned **Bachelor of Business Administration**, Florida State University, Tallahassee, FL.
& TRAINING   1992.
Excelled in extensive management and technical training through Senor Carlo Foods.

EXPERIENCE   *With Senor Carlo Mexican Foods, a large national food service manufacturer in Tampa, FL, have advanced in the following "track record" of promotion while earning a reputation as a dynamic individual and resourceful problem-solver who thrives on the challenge of a fast-paced environment:*

PRODUCTION MANAGER. (2000-present). Report to the plant manager; was promoted to this position from Shift Superintendent; manage all aspects of first-shift production operations and direct the work of three supervisors and two processing departments.
- Interview, hire, and train new personnel; motivate, discipline, and counsel up to 125 employees.
- Consistently achieve or exceed objectives in all areas of production management; meet ambitious production quotas and keep turnover, absenteeism, and safety issues within prescribed goals.
- On my own initiative, designed and implemented process improvements in the corn and flour departments; under my direction, troubleshooting guides were created for Iapak, Corn, and Die-Cut equipment to aid supervisors and operators in solving problems.
- Have become known for my ability to maintain effective working relationships at all levels of the organization; lead by example, encouraging others to mirror my results-oriented approach to problem solving and my strong work ethic.
- Am regarded as an articulate communicator with a flair for getting my point across.

SHIFT SUPERINTENDENT. (1995-00). Oversaw first-shift production in the flour and corn departments, providing supervisory oversight to five supervisors and 150 team members and coordinating with other shifts to maintain work flow and ensure that production objectives were met or exceeded.
- On my own initiative, created a new troubleshooting guide for supervisors and operators.
- Established evaluation procedures and reviewed all team members' performance appraisals written by supervisors whom I managed.
- Provided oversight for a training program for production personnel to prevent repetitive motion injuries and reduce inefficiency.
- Increased production yields on small press lines from 125 to 136 in a three-month period.
- Approved all work orders and requisitioned equipment for production.

DEPARTMENT SUPERVISOR. (1993-95). Managed all phases of first shift production on the taco lines, tostado line, and chip line, supervising more than 50 team members.
- Trained operators and team leaders; prepared performance evaluations on all employees and became known for my excellent writing and counseling skills.
- Conducted research and development testing to monitor customer reaction to new products.
- Implemented and conducted monthly safety meetings; ensured compliance with policies.

PERSONAL   Excellent personal and professional references are available upon request. Aggressive, goal-oriented individual who thrives on tackling ambitious goals.

Exact Name of Person
Exact Title
Exact Name of Company
Address
City, State, Zip

**PRODUCTION
SUPERVISOR,
ATHLETIC FOOTWARE
COMPANY**

Dear Exact Name of Person (or Dear Sir or Madam if answering a blind ad):

   With the enclosed resume, I would like to make you aware of my background of excellence in the management of human, fiscal, and material resources, and to acquaint you with the strong leadership, staff development, communication, and organizational skills which I could put to work for your company.

   As you will see from my resume, I have been excelling in a track record of accomplishment with one of the world's largest manufacturers of athletic footwear, where I began as a Production Associate while still attending college and advanced through the ranks into upper management. While serving in various leadership roles in this large production facility, I have supervised as many as 200 employees, managed large operating budgets, and provided oversight to inventory control, safety, and quality assurance programs. In one position as a Business Unit Manager, I essentially operated a separate "factory" within the plant, managing production, packing, shipping, receiving, quality assurance, and maintenance functions. I also developed material resources, capital equipment, and budgetary requirements for the Business Unit, determining the most profitable and efficient use of funds equaling one-quarter of the facility's total operating budget.

   Although I was highly regarded by my current employer and can provide excellent personal and professional references at the appropriate time, I have decided to seek other opportunities with organizations that can use my strong leadership and training skills. I feel that my extensive management and staff development experience would be a valuable asset to any organization, and I look forward to the opportunity to meet with you to discuss the contributions that I could make to your company's operation.

   I hope you will welcome my call soon when I try to arrange a brief meeting to discuss your goals and how my background might serve your needs. Thank you in advance for your time and consideration.

                                        Yours sincerely,

                                        Patrick G. Donald

PATRICK G. DONALD

1110½ Hay Street, Fayetteville, NC 28305 • preppub@aol.com • (910) 483-6611

OBJECTIVE

To benefit an organization that can use a skilled motivator and experienced professional with exceptional communication, organizational, and supervisory skills who offers a background of excellence in the management of human, fiscal, and material resources.

EDUCATION

Completed nearly two years of college-level course work toward a **Bachelor of Science in Manufacturing Management,** Springfield Community College, Springfield, IL.

Have supplemented my formal education with a number of leadership, technical training, and staff development courses sponsored by my employer, including:
- Supervisor Training Program, 80 hours, Robeson Community College.
- TC² Textile Training School (Modular Training), 40 hours, TC², Hot Springs, AR.
- Gaz-Way (Gazelle Team-building course), 8 hours, Gazelle, Inc., Hot Springs, AR.
- Creative Problem Solving (PCS), 40 hours, Gazelle, Inc., Philadelphia, PA.

COMPUTERS

Familiar with many computer operating systems and software, including Windows, Microsoft Word, Excel, and UNIX as well as Gazelle's proprietary systems.

EXPERIENCE

With Gazelle, Inc., was promoted to positions of increasing responsibility by this large international athletic shoe manufacturer; played a key role in meeting production goals:

2000-present: **PRODUCTION SUPERVISOR.** Hot Springs, AR. Supervised as many as 78 employees while overseeing all production line activities; accepted this position after the company was reorganized, eliminating the individual business units. Trained new production department personnel in all aspects of equipment operation, quality assurance, and safety, as well as company policies, regulations, and procedures.

1997-1999: **BUSINESS UNIT MANAGER.** Hot Springs, AR. Was promoted to lead my own business unit (essentially a separate "factory" within the plant) on the basis of my strong performance as a Production Department Manager.
- Supervised 120 employees, directing the activities of the production, packing, shipping, receiving, quality assurance, and maintenance departments of my business unit.
- Developed budgetary, material resources, and capital equipment requirements for each department under my management; determined the most efficient use of funds while overseeing the disbursement of one-quarter of the facility's operating budget.
- Trained employees in each of the above departments; set individual production goals to ensure that the Business Unit met or exceeded corporate goals.

1992-1997: **DEPARTMENT MANAGER.** Hot Springs, AR. Managed second shift operations, supervising four Production Managers and directing the work of up to 200 employees; conducted periodic performance evaluations to monitor the performance of Coordinators. Oversaw implementation of the quality assurance program for the department, and monitored its performance; prepared quality assurance reports.

1985-1992: **PRODUCTION ASSOCIATE.** Springfield, IL. Supervised and trained as many as 35 employees while overseeing second shift production line operations; oversaw the implementation of the safety program. Set individual production goals and conducted periodic performance appraisals to monitor employee performance and ensure that departmental and corporate objectives were met or exceeded.

PERSONAL

Excellent personal and professional references are available upon request.

Exact Name of Person
Exact Title
Exact Name of Company
Address
City, State, Zip

**PRODUCTION TEAM
LEADER**

Dear Exact Name of Person (or Dear Sir or Madam if answering a blind ad):

With the enclosed resume, I would like to make you aware of my interest in offering my managerial and supervisory abilities as well as my Spanish language skills to an organization that can use an articulate and dedicated professional.

As you will see from my resume, I am presently advancing in a track record of promotion with Deluxe Meat Company. Although I am held in high regard by this company and am being groomed for advancement to higher levels of responsibility, I am at a point in my career where I wish to explore other employment opportunities.

Originally hired by this company as an Interpreter, I was involved in translating documents and signs into Spanish for a largely Spanish-speaking work force. I was promoted to a Production Team Leader's job when a new automated system was put into operation and then to manage a 15-person custodial crew of all non-English-speaking employees. Most recently I was asked to take on a new challenge – three previous managers had been unable to accomplish adequate production levels in the Barn Room. I am accomplishing excellent results managing three Spanish-speaking helpers in this area. Other aspects of this job include the processing of large amounts of paperwork and working closely with a USDA medical doctor while inspecting and providing quality control to ensure compliance with all applicable USDA requirements for food processing operations.

I served my country with distinction in the U.S. Army, and my military experience was for the most part in field artillery units where I advanced to supervisory roles. During one period, I was assigned as an Instructor and taught Army Reserve and National Guard personnel in both languages.

If you can use an excellent communicator with high degrees of enthusiasm, energy, and drive, I hope you will contact me soon to suggest a time we might meet to discuss how I could contribute to your organization.

Sincerely,

Regis Sanchez

REGIS SANCHEZ

1110½ Hay Street, Fayetteville, NC 28305   •   preppub@aol.com   •   (910) 483-6611

OBJECTIVE   To offer well-developed managerial abilities and a broad base of experience in quality control and inspection, office administration, and production control to an organization that can benefit from my Spanish language skills and effectiveness as a manager.

EDUCATION & TRAINING   Completed a six-month Electronics Course; am preparing to get my Electrician's License. Earned an Associate's degree in Electronic Communication, Huertas Junior College, PR, 1987; completed an Electricity Program at Miguel Such Vocational School, PR; was trained as an Electrician.

Was born and lived in the Bronx, NY, until age 15 when my parents relocated to Puerto Rico; graduated from Horace G. Benites High School, PR.

Received U.S. Army training in professional leadership development.

LANGUAGES   Fluently read, speak, and write Spanish and offer experience as an interpreter.

EXPERIENCE   **Am advancing in a track record of accomplishments and being groomed for higher levels of responsibility with Deluxe Meat Company, Dixon, MT:**
TEAM LEADER, BARN ROOM. (2001-present). Handpicked for a job in which three previous managers had been unable to accomplish adequate production levels, manage three Spanish-speaking helpers in a holding area for cows and bulls.
- Received training in quality control and inspection techniques and now complete visual inspections of the live animals and dressed carcasses.
- Interact on an daily basis with the USDA medical doctor on site while ensuring compliance with all applicable USDA regulations.
- Am succeeding in resolving numerous problems caused by the language barrier while completing and processing a wide range of paperwork including all Workman's Compensation and accident reports.
- Assist in other areas of the plant as an interpreter for entry-level personnel.
- Recruited for a part-time job as a **Translator** and **Sales Representative** for Dave's Auto in MacBee, MT, to assist Spanish-speaking customers in completing paperwork.

TEAM LEADER, CUSTODIAL CREW. (2000). Managed a work crew of 15 Spanish-speaking employees while ensuring the total cleanliness of all areas of the plant.

PRODUCTION TEAM LEADER. (1999). Oversaw two employees in a new area when the company began the operation of an Automated Machine System (AMS) room.
- Worked on a mainframe computer used for diagnosing equipment problems.

INTERPRETER. (1997-98). Originally hired to translate documents and signs for a largely non-English-speaking work force, assisted in Workman's Compensation situations.

Developed managerial skills while serving in the U.S. Army:
TEAM SUPERVISOR. Ft. Bragg, NC, and Korea (1995-97). Supervised as many as ten employees in field artillery units while also controlling supply and equipment inventories.

INSTRUCTOR. Puerto Rico (1992-95). Provided instruction in both English and Spanish while teaching field artillery skills to Army Reserve and National Guard personnel.

PERSONAL   Am single and available for relocation. Held a Secret clearance.

CAREER CHANGE

Date

Exact Name of Person
Exact Title
Exact Name of Company
Address
City, State, Zip

PRODUCTION TECHNICIAN

This young professional communicates clearly in her cover letter that she has been recently downsized from a manufacturing firm. She inspires confidence in potential employers by communicating that she has shown personal initiative by enrolling in community college courses to refine her skills in other areas.

Dear Exact Name of Person (or Dear Sir or Madam if answering a blind ad):

I would appreciate an opportunity to talk with you soon about how I could contribute to your organization through my strong communication and organizational skills, self-motivation, and "can do" attitude.

Most recently I have been involved in production-level manufacturing jobs, first at Jones Manufacturing and most recently at Crosby Manufacturing. In this position, I was credited with making contributions which allowed the company to achieve its goal of "zero defects" in on-time shipping, and was a member of a department which successfully qualified for ISO 9000 certification.

While I was highly regarded by this employer, and can provide excellent references at the appropriate time, recent downturns in business have forced the company to reduce its workforce, displacing myself and many of my co-workers. I have taken this opportunity to supplement my strong clerical and secretarial skills with a Bank Teller training course from Carson City Community College, and I feel that my positive personality, education, and work experience would be well suited to a banking environment.

Prior to my current situation, I worked in a clerical/ secretarial capacity for Classic Hair Coifs in Wilson, NV. I essentially performed the functions of an office manager or administrative assistant, scheduling appointments, ordering supplies, operating a multi-line phone system, and handling all correspondence.

If your organization could benefit from a motivated, detail-oriented young professional with exceptional organizational, customer service, and communication skills, I hope you will contact me to suggest a time when we can meet to discuss your needs and how I might meet them. I assure you in advance that I have an excellent reputation, and would quickly become a strong asset to your company

Sincerely,

Karen Marie Steardon

KAREN MARIE STEARDON

1110½ Hay Street, Fayetteville, NC 28305 • preppub@aol.com • (910) 483-6611

OBJECTIVE   To benefit an organization that can use a motivated self-starter with excellent organizational and communication skills as well as a strong background in clerical/secretarial work, wiring, and electrical assembly.

EDUCATION   Bank Teller Training course, Carson City Community College, Carson City, NV, July 1998.
General Manufacturing (GMC) course, Reno Technical Community College, Reno, NV, 1996.
Zinger-Miller Course, Reno Technical Community College, Reno, NV, 1996.

SPECIAL SKILLS   In addition to my formal education, I offer the following skills and am familiar with the operation of the following equipment and/or software:

Typing – 55 WPM   Operate multi-line phone system
Operate 10-key calculator   Operate photocopier
Windows   Microsoft Word

EXPERIENCE   **PRODUCTION TECHNICIAN.** Crosby Manufacturing, Las Vegas, NV (2000-present). Performed a variety of electrical assembly and wiring tasks in this fast-paced factory environment.
- Read wiring diagrams, schematics, and engineering order specifications to ensure units were completed according to requirements and proper standards.
- Assembled, wired, and performed troubleshooting on motor control units for industrial and commercial grade air compressors.
- Learned testing and troubleshooting of a wide variety of motor control units from different manufacturers.
- Was credited with making contributions which allowed the company to reach its goal of "zero defects" in on-time shipping.
- Member of a department which successfully qualified for ISO 9000 certification.

PRODUCTION WORKER. Jones Manufacturing, Las Vegas, NV (1997-1998). During my time at Jones, I worked on an assembly line building power tools; wired jig saws and mounted the set screw to close the case.

OFFICE MANAGER. Classic Hair Coifs, Wilson, NV (1997). Performed various clerical, secretarial, and cash handling duties in this busy salon.
- Answered multi-line phone system, taking messages and directing calls.
- Operated a 10-key calculator to figure the customer's total; took payments and wrote receipts.
- Scheduled appointments for hair designers.
- Took inventory; ordered, purchased, and picked up supplies.
- Typed letters, memos, flyers, and other correspondence.

Other experience: SALES CLERK/ASSISTANT. Salvation Army, Las Vegas, NV (1997 & 1998). Worked with the Salvation Army part-time over the 1997 & 1998 Christmas seasons.
- Assembled and decorated Christmas trees that were donated to the warehouse so that they could be sold at the Thrift Stores.
- Collected donations at the main office.

PERSONAL   Excellent personal and professional references are available upon request.

Exact Name of Person
Exact Title
Exact Name of Company
Address
City, State, Zip

PRODUCTION MANAGER   Dear Exact Name of Person (or Dear Sir or Madam if answering a blind ad):

With the enclosed resume, I would like to make you aware of my interest in exploring employment opportunities with your organization.

As you will see from my resume, I handle numerous simultaneous responsibilities as the Production Superintendent for a food packing company. In a prior position in the agricultural industry, I supervised the breeding and farrowing of farm animals. In my earliest positions in food manufacturing, I began as a Production Worker on the transfer line and then became an Assistant Supervisor.

Although I am held in high regard by my current employer and am being groomed to assume additional management responsibilities, I am selectively exploring opportunities with quality organizations in the food manufacturing industry. I can provide outstanding references.

Sincerely,

Kenny Jacque Davis

KENNY JACQUE DAVIS

1110½ Hay Street, Fayetteville, NC 28305 • preppub@aol.com • (910) 483-6611

OBJECTIVE

To benefit an industrial organization that can use a resourceful problem solver who offers extensive experience in production operations and who is known for strong communication, technical, and supervisory skills as well as expert planning and organizational abilities.

EDUCATION

B.S., Manufacturing Technology, Turner State University, Turner City, MI, 1993.

COMPUTER KNOWLEDGE

Am proficient in solving industrial problems by applying knowledge of the following: Windows, Microsoft Word, Microsoft Excel, Microsoft Access, Lotus 1-2-3, and Fortran

TECHNICAL TRAINING

Completed courses in subject areas which include Quality Assurance, Production Engineering, Motion & Time Study, Fluids Technology, Statics, and Dynamics.
* Gained expert skills in testing the strength of wood, metal, and plastic materials.

EXPERIENCE

PRODUCTION SUPERINTENDENT. Kamfield Packing Company, Detroit, MI (2000-present). Began as Production Supervisor; was quickly promoted to Superintendent, assisting the Plant Manager while overseeing an operation ensuring that casings are properly pulled and cleaned by employees, then finished production is packed and shipped.
* *Production scheduling*: Coordinate production work in the casing department, managing up to 50 employees; schedule staff according to production to control labor hours.
* *Data analysis*: Perform analysis of data related to production schedules and productivity in order to make effective decisions regarding manpower and resource requirements.
* *Quality control*: Plan and implement quality assurance measures.
* *Government regulations*: Ensure compliance with all applicable OSHA and USDA regulations and guidelines in order to prevent loss of production.
* *Maintenance*: Perform routine maintenance and repairs on the production line, to include repairing rollers, removing and replacing defective motors, and installing belts.

SUPERVISOR. Johnson's Foods, Laurel, MI (1998-99). Supervised the breeding and farrowing of 2,400 sows, including direct mating and artificial insemination; managed breeding, farrowing, and finishing for 1,200 sows.

Was promoted into production supervision after mastering production line tasks and demonstrating the communication skills and leadership ability, Fine Turkeys, Sands, MI (1993-98).
ASSISTANT SUPERVISOR. Consistently achieved or exceeded production goals while overseeing five different departments in the plant, each employing 35 to 40 workers, including the chiller department, breast line, drums line, thigh line, and transfer line.
* Analyzed data and rendered decisions regarding manpower and resource requirements.
* Implemented quality assurance/quality control measures.
* Managed multiple projects, overseeing activities ranging from line preparation, to weighing and shipping, to machine maintenance.

PRODUCTION WORKER. Working on the transfer line, applied my creativity and problem-solving skills to ensure that goods processed were of high quality in the most cost-effective manner; learned to cut turkeys, run turkeys through a leg processor, and pack parts.
* Was handpicked for promotion to the job above after mastering all nine jobs on the production line; was commended for my ability to communicate with workers.

PERSONAL

A motivated self-starter, have attended approximately 30 hours of continuing education courses on the principles of supervision and being an effective leader.

Exact Name of Person
Title or Position
Name of Company
Address (number and street)
Address (city, state, and zip)

**PURCHASING
MANAGER**

Dear Exact Name of Person: (or Dear Sir or Madam if answering a blind ad)

I would appreciate an opportunity to talk with you soon about how I could contribute to your organization through my extensive background in purchasing parts and services for a manufacturing firm.

You will see from my enclosed resume that I have been with Goodyear Consumer Products, Inc., in St. Louis, MO, for several years. Although I enjoy this position and have advanced with the company from a Materials Buyer position to Purchasing Manager, I am interested in confidentially exploring opportunities within your company.

Because of my ability to reduce costs and negotiate product contracts with a wide variety of vendors, I have received numerous awards and honors recognizing my purchasing expertise and management ability. I believe that you would find me to be an enthusiastic and outgoing professional who offers strong organizational abilities and attention to detail.

I hope you will welcome my call soon to arrange a brief meeting at your convenience to discuss your current and future needs and how I might serve them. Thank you in advance for your time.

Sincerely yours.

Deana Hardwick

Alternate last paragraph:
I hope you will call or write me soon to suggest a time convenient for us to meet and discuss your current and future needs and how I might serve them. Thank you in advance for your time.

DEANA HARDWICK

1110½ Hay Street, Fayetteville, NC 28305 • preppub@aol.com • (910) 483-6611

OBJECTIVE	To offer my extensive background in purchasing and my aggressive bottom-line orientation to an organization that can use a positive and enthusiastic professional known for attention to detail as well as expertise in all aspects of purchasing both parts and services.
EXPERIENCE	**PURCHASING MANAGER & MATERIALS BUYER.** Goodyear Consumer Products, Inc., St. Louis, MO (2000-present). Began as a Materials Buyer and was promoted to Purchasing Manager in charge of a five-person department; provide oversight of the purchasing of a wide range of products valued at $6 million annually.

- Received a letter of appreciation from the company president in recognition of my accomplishments and contributions including my ability to continually reduce costs, January 2001.
- Wrote the standard operating procedures (SOPs) used by all purchasing department personnel, not only at the St. Louis central office but also at the 12 field offices.
- Oversee MRO (Maintenance, Repair, and Operating) purchasing contracts for plant services at 16 plants; negotiate contracts valued at $25 million annually.
- Negotiated a contract for additional commodities including labels and instruction books.
- Have acquired expertise in commodity buying including the purchasing of all electrical and electronic parts, fasteners, screw machine, and imported parts including finished goods.
- Chaired a task force which developed a new line of ceiling fans: the project was successfully completed ahead of schedule and within corporate budget guidelines and restrictions.
- On my own initiative, established a new buyer training program which has led to numerous efficiencies; set up a complete how-to system and oversaw the implementation of a new automated system used for tracking inventory and purchasing.

Highlights of previous experience:

- Refined skills as a Clerk/Typist and Secretary for a Human Relations/Equal Opportunity Office and the Director of Personnel and Community Affairs for an Army post in Germany.
- Earned several letters and certificates of commendation and a Sustained Performance Award in recognition of my professionalism and accomplishments as a government employee.
- Became familiar with the functions of a purchasing office as a Departmental Secretary, Goodyear Industries, Inc., St. Louis, MO.
- Gained experience in jobs as a Office Clerk/Claims Handler/Dispatcher for a trucking company and Real Estate Salesperson.

EDUCATION	Associate's degree in **Industrial Management Technology,** St. Louis Technical Community College, MO, 1996. Completed 60 credit hours in **Personnel Management** through a correspondence course. Attended Bohecker's Business College, Ravenna, OH: received training in the field of executive secretarial duties.
PERSONAL	Active in church activities, have served as vice president and secretary of the women's organization; served on the finance committee. Am a friendly and enthusiastic individual.

Date

Ms. Jane Allen
Management Consultants & Executive Recruiters
Beacon Hill
Boston, MA 06713

QUALITY ASSURANCE MANAGER

Dear Ms. Allen:

I would like to make you aware of my interest in a Quality Assurance position within a corporation which can utilize my strong executive skills as well as my proven ability to apply my technical expertise in resourceful ways that improve the bottom line while strengthening customer satisfaction.

As you will see from my resume, I have progressed in a track record of advancement with the Kaysey Corporation, one of the world's leading consumer products manufacturing companies. In my current job, I manage a 29-person QA department in a plant which employs 1,925 people and manufactures personal care products totaling $550 million. While managing a departmental budget of nearly $2.5 million, I have transitioned the plant from a regular production assembly line operation into a team-managed operation in which teams of employees are responsible for individual products. This has shifted QA from a "police" role to a consulting and monitoring role. I have also developed, implemented and managed a Cost-of-Quality Program which achieved cost savings of $750,000 by identifying and eliminating unnecessary processes.

In my previous job at Quality Assurance Manager at the company's plant in Lawrence, KS, I developed and implemented a Quality Demerit System which the company now uses corporate-wide. The Quality Demerit System transformed four manufacturing plants from a quality level of 67% defect-free product to the consumer to 98.2% defect-free. The targeted goal for 2003 is 99.0% defect-free product.

I offer extensive expertise related to blow molding and injection molding. Both in my current and previous job, I managed Quality Assurance related to blow molding and injection molding. In the plant, we achieved a 10% improvement in lots accepted when using Mil. Std. 105E to determine acceptable quality levels (AQLs).

You would find me in person to be a congenial individual who prides myself on my ability to establish and maintain effective working relationships. I can provide outstanding personal and professional references at the appropriate time. I hope you will contact me to suggest a time when we might meet to discuss your needs as well as my skills, experience, and qualifications.

Sincerely,

Hugh Visco

HUGH VISCO

1110½ Hay Street, Fayetteville, NC 28305 • preppub@aol.com • (910) 483-6611

OBJECTIVE	To benefit an organization that can use a knowledgeable quality assurance executive with a proven ability to lower costs, improve customer satisfaction, reduce defects, and strengthen employee accountability.
EXPERIENCE	*1991-present: Have excelled in the following track record of promotion with Kaysey Corporation, a $1 billion a year Fortune 500 company which recently became a part of Consumer Products USA, a $4 billion corporation.* **QUALITY ASSURANCE MANAGER. (2000-present).** Champaign, IL. Manage a 29-person department which includes five QA Supervisors and a Laboratory Manager in a plant which employs 1,925 people and manufactures personal care products totaling $550 million.

* Developed, implemented, and managed a Cost-of-Quality Program which identified and eliminated non-value-added process activities; this process produced a 1999 cost saving of $750,000.
* Implemented analytical and microbiological testing of raw materials and bulk products which instituted QA at the earliest possible point in the process.
* Through aggressive training, have transformed my Quality Assurance Department into the one acknowledged as the best within the corporation.
* Manage a departmental budget of $2.5 million; developed and implemented initiatives which stimulated cost efficiencies and improved worker participation in all facets of QA.
* Transitioned this plant from a regular production assembly line operation into a team-managed operation in which teams are responsible for individual products. This has shifted QA from a "police" role to a consulting role.
* Implemented Employee Information Boards for each team which shows vital information including the top five defects, wastage, and efficiency measures.
* Developed some flexible work schedules which improved customer service.

QUALITY ASSURANCE MANAGER. (1995-99). Lawrence, KS. In a plant that employed 2,500 people, managed and directed plant quality efforts through process evaluations, quality measurements, and cycle time reductions; supervised 42 people and managed a budget of $1.9 million.

* Instituted educational and training programs that improved line efficiencies by 30% and produced cost savings of at least $200,000.
* Developed and implemented a Quality Demerit System which the company now uses corporate-wide; the Quality Demerit System transformed four manufacturing plants from a quality level of 67% defect-free product to the consumer to 98.2% defect-free.

INSPECTION SUPERVISOR. (1991-94). Wichita, KS. Developed, managed, and directed the vendor certification program with the result that the customer service level was raised to 99%.

* Led efforts to enhance the Just-In-Time (JIT) process which saved millions of dollars in operating costs and lowered inventory carrying costs.

EDUCATION	Completing MBA in my spare time at Newton University; degree to be awarded 2003. B.A. with Major in Psychology, Southern Illinois University, Carbondale, IL, 1991. Numerous executive development courses including training in QA ISO 9001.
AFFILIATIONS	Member, American Management Society; American Society of Quality Control; and Southern Aerosol Technical Association.
PERSONAL	Can provide outstanding personal and professional references.

CAREER CHANGE

Date

Exact Name of Person
Exact Title
Exact Name of Company
Address
City, State, Zip

QUALITY ENGINEER

Dear Exact Name of Person (or Dear Sir or Madam if answering a blind ad):

Can you use a quality assurance professional with extensive experience related to the manufacturing process?

With a B.S. in Mathematics and an M.S. in Industrial Engineering, I have applied my textbook knowledge in highly resourceful ways in manufacturing environments. In my current position as Quality Engineer Supervisor, I handle extensive troubleshooting and problem-solving responsibilities as I assist eight manufacturing facilities in identifying and resolving quality issues. In my prior position I developed and managed the quality system for the company's communication products, and I provided training to personnel in ISO 9001.

Although I am excelling in my current position and can provide outstanding references at the appropriate time, I have decided to explore opportunities outside the telecommunications industry. I am confident that my strong analytical and problem-solving abilities could make a positive impact on your bottom line.

I hope you will contact me to suggest a time when we might meet to discuss your needs, and I certainly appreciate in advance your time and professional courtesies.

Sincerely,

Rachel Breece

RACHEL BREECE

1110½ Hay Street, Fayetteville, NC 28305   •   preppub@aol.com   •   (910) 483-6611

OBJECTIVE

To contribute proven analytical, problem-solving, and communication abilities to an organization that can use a detail-oriented professional with excellent technical skills.

EDUCATION

M. S. in **Industrial Engineering**, North Dakota A&T State University, Dawson, Bismark, ND, 1998.
- Was honored with membership in Alpha Pi Mu Industrial Engineering Honor Society.

B. S. in **Mathematics**, University of North Dakota at Bismark, ND, 1993.

Handpicked as a mathematics tutor to student-athletes and an assistant to mathematics professors.

EXPERIENCE

Advanced with BCD Incorporated, Winston, ND (1999-present):

2002-present: QUALITY ENGINEER SUPERVISOR. Promoted to manage and supervise three engineers, two technicians and 13 process auditors/receiving inspection employees while assisting plant personnel with quality issues related to **manufacturing facilities,** customer complaints, cost requirements, and delivery.
- Assist eight manufacturing facilities with identifying and closing gaps utilizing the Business Excellence Process which focuses on the customer.

1999-02: QUALITY ENGINEER IV, III, AND II. Developed, managed, and maintained the quality system for Communication products; provided training to all personnel in ISO 9001 requirements and quality specifications while serving as Lead Assessor.
- Developed and implemented quality systems involving FMEAs, Control Plans, and Design Reviews to improve manufacturing processes for new products.
- Extensively involved in preventive and corrective actions taken during manufacturing processes; performed capability studies.
- Approved and trained others in approving tooling changes and assisted with improvements in process engineering and error-proofing projects.

Became skilled in all aspects of quality assurance while advancing with Kaylee Hosiery:

QUALITY CONTROL MANAGER. Kaylee Hosiery, Hartsville, SD (1997-99) and Rockingham, ND (1996-97). Managed and implemented quality standards for manufacturing, packaging, and shipping of products in two hosiery facilities: a manufacturing facility with approximately 400 employees and a distribution center with more than 700 employees. Trained and supervised 23 quality control personnel.
- Worked closely with other manufacturing facilities and managers to correct problems with incoming products; helped operators and mechanics with process improvements.
- Implemented a customer awareness program within the plant and with area retailers.
- Initiated process improvements and error-proofing activities in both plants through time studies and process analyses.

Other experience: **QUALITY CONTROL SUPERVISOR.** CATLING Telecommunications Cable Systems Group, Roanoke, VA (1993-96). Managed the quality of single-mode optical fiber for telephone cables while attending graduate school; utilized the Team Concept to ensure fiber met quality standards set by Bell Laboratories.

SPECIAL TRAINING

Certified by Lloyd's as a Lead Assessor for ISO 9001. Highly knowledgeable of the Deming Concepts, which figured heavily in my Master's thesis, as well as implementation of Total Quality Management and Team Building Concepts.

Date

Exact Name of Person
Title or Position
Name of Company
Address (number and street)
Address (city, state, and zip)

**REGIONAL
MANAGER**

Dear Exact Name of Person: (or Sir or Madam if answering a blind ad)

With the enclosed resume, I would like to make you aware of my interest in the possibility of putting my strong management, production operations, and sales background to work for your company. Please treat my enquiry as highly confidential at this point. Although I can provide outstanding personal and professional references at the appropriate time, I do not wish my current employer to be aware of my interest in your company.

As you will see from my enclosed resume, I have been in the multi-purpose concrete applications business my entire working life. I began in entry-level positions with a small concrete business in northern Iowa and was promoted to Plant Manager and Sales Manager. Then I joined Smith & Son, Inc. where I tripled production and transformed that company into an attractive acquisition candidate which caught the attention of Bullworth Concrete. When Bullworth Concrete Company bought Smith & Son in 1992, I became a Division Manager and in 2000 was promoted to Regional Manager.

In my current position I manage operations at 10 divisions while supervising three Division Managers and overseeing activities of 85 people at 10 locations. I also supervise four sales and customer service professionals while preparing budgets for each of the 10 divisions.

If you can use a versatile professional with a thorough understanding of all facets of the concrete applications business, I hope you will contact me to suggest a time when we might meet. Should you have ambitious goals in either the production management or sales area, I feel certain that my extensive industry knowledge and contacts could be useful.

Sincerely,

Harvey Herron

HARVEY HERRON

1110½ Hay Street, Fayetteville, NC 28305 • preppub@aol.com • (910) 483-6611

OBJECTIVE

To benefit an organization that can use an experienced manager with exceptional organizational skills who offers a background in managing multi-plant operations and expertise in multi-purpose concrete applications.

EDUCATION

Business Administration studies, Faison Technical College, Faison, IA, 1974.
Completed numerous seminars including AGC Seminars, Capital Associated Industries Seminars; also completed extensive training related to EPA, DOT Procedures Applications, and other areas.

CERTIFICATIONS

ACI Certified; NRMCA Sales Certified

AFFILIATIONS

Member, Homebuilders Association
Former President, Iowa Concrete Association, Faison Chapter

EXPERIENCE

With Bullworth Concrete Company, have been promoted to positions of increasing responsibility by this multi-purpose concrete company while playing a key role in annual sales increases of more than 10%:
2000-present: **REGIONAL MANAGER.** Faison, IA. Was promoted to this position from Division Manager for this region with multimillion-dollar annual sales; am continuing to provide valuable leadership in producing outstanding sales and profits after helping the company achieve its record year in 2001.
- Manage operations at 10 divisions while supervising three Division Managers and overseeing activities of 85 people at 10 locations.
- Supervise four Customer Service and Sales Representatives.
- Prepare annual budgets for each of the 10 division locations.
- Am accountable for production of 250,000 yards of concrete annually.

1992-99: **DIVISION MANAGER.** Bladen, IA. While overseeing three divisions, provided supervisory oversight of 30 people while directing production, maintenance, safety, and sales activities related to the production of 55,000 cubic yards of concrete annually for such applications as bridges, waste water treatment plants, as well as commercial and industrial buildings.

Joined Bullworth Concrete Company when Bullworth bought Smith and Son, Inc., a northern Iowa company which I had transformed into an attractive acquisition candidate while excelling in the following history of promotion:
1983-92: Was **GENERAL MANAGER** at Smith and Son, Inc., during these years while tripling production from 12,000 cubic yards to 36,000 cubic yards annually; managed ten truck operations.
- Directed operation of central shop for the entire company.

PLANT MANAGER & SALES MANAGER. Granger Concrete, Walton, IA (1974-83). Started with this company as a truck driver and learned the business from the ground up; was promoted to Plant Manager and then to Sales Manager, and made major contributions to the company in both roles.
- Trained and managed two sales people.
- Sold and managed production of 36,000 cubic yards of concrete annually.
- Managed operations with 12 drivers at two sites.
- Before promotion into the management ranks, worked as a Loader Operator and Mechanic in addition to Truck Driver; these early experiences gave me first-hand knowledge of how the concrete industry works on the ground floor of operations.

PERSONAL

Excellent personal and professional references. Outstanding reputation.

Exact Name
Exact Title
Exact Name of Company
Exact Address
City, State, Zip

**SALES
REPRESENTATIVE**

Dear Exact Name:

With the enclosed resume, I would like to introduce myself and the substantial sales and marketing background I could put to work for you.

As you will see, I offer a proven track record of outstanding results in producing a profit, improving the profit margin, developing new accounts, increasing market share, satisfying customers, and expanding territories. In my current position, I have led a four-person team which has increased sales of a plant's manufactured products by 15% instead of the expected 5%. In a previous job, I developed a new territory while training and managing an eight-person sales staff. I am known for my ability to contribute significantly to the company's bottom line through my results in delivering a hefty profit margin.

I am respected for my ability to creatively and resourcefully apply my considerable knowledge, and I am always on the lookout for new ways to refine my own selling techniques. I am confident of my ability to produce a highly motivated team of sales professionals.

If you can use my talents and knowledge, please contact me and I will make myself available for a meeting with you to discuss your needs and how I might help you. I can provide outstanding personal and professional references.

Sincerely,

Rodney Lewis

RODNEY LEWIS

1110½ Hay Street, Fayetteville, NC 28305 • preppub@aol.com • (910) 483-6611

OBJECTIVE	To become a valuable member of an organization that can use an outgoing and highly motivated sales professional who offers a proven ability to produce a profit, improve the profit margin, develop new accounts, satisfy customers, and motivate employees.
EDUCATION	Received Bachelor of Arts degree in **Psychology**, University of Miami, Miami, FL, 1986. Have excelled in numerous sales and sales management training programs sponsored by major industrial suppliers. • Pride myself on my ability to creatively and aggressively apply any and all sales training. • Have especially benefited from advanced training related to product marketing, cold calling and other sales skills, and techniques for increasing sales, profits, and motivation.
EXPERIENCE	**MANUFACTURING SALES MANAGER.** Braxton & Co., Chicago, IL and Toronto, Canada (2001-present). Was recruited to join a four-person sales team responsible for increasing by 5% the sales of a plant in Toronto which was affiliated with a company with total annual sales of $368 million. • Greatly exceeded management expectations and our targeted goals; increased sales by 15% instead of the projected 5%. • Retrained sales personnel in Canada in all aspects of their jobs; significantly improved their ability to prospect for new commercial and retail accounts and refined their ability to close the sale. • Personally established numerous new commercial accounts and dramatically expanded the territory which the company had been servicing. **SALES MANAGER.** TrueTest Supply Network, Macon, GA (1994-2001). Was recruited by key marketing officials in the parent company for this job which has involved developing a new territory as well as hiring and supervising an eight-person sales staff. • In addition to my management responsibilities, am actively involved in sales; call on colleges, major retailers, hospitals, military accounts, and large industrial facilities. • Sell virtually any product needed for the daily operations; provide products ranging from cleaning supplies to televisions, VCRs, refrigerators, nuts and bolts, and light bulbs. • Have trained and organized the eight-person sales team so that it is now a sales machine known for outstanding product knowledge, customer service, and resourcefulness. • Taught my sales peers how to improve profit in each sale by at least 5%. • Have learned how to "work smart" in order to increase sales and sales calls by 32%. • Trained sales personnel to establish aggressive goals and then helped them learn the practical tools which would help them achieve those goals. • Am contributing significantly to the company's bottom line through my ability to deliver a 40% profit margin. **SALES CONSULTANT & SALES REPRESENTATIVE.** Smoot Consulting, Dallas, TX (1986-93). Worked for one of the country's leading sales/marketing consulting firms; acted as a management consultant under contract with numerous companies that wanted expert help in expanding their territories, boosting sales, and improving profitability. Called on and established new retail and commercial accounts.
PERSONAL	Am skilled at dealing with people and earning their confidence. Hard working, dependable, honest. Am always seeking new opportunities to improve my sales presentation skills. Known for my ability to creatively apply the knowledge I already have. Will relocate.

Date

Exact Name of Person
Exact Title
Exact Name of Company
Address
City, State, Zip

SENIOR FACILITIES ENGINEER

Dear Exact Name of Person (or Dear Sir or Madam if answering a blind ad):

I would appreciate an opportunity to talk with you soon about how I could contribute to your organization through my distinguished background of accomplishments and experience in the management of maintenance, construction, and renovation projects.

As you will see from my enclosed resume, I offer a strong history of reducing costs, bringing projects in on time, and handling the complexities of large-scale domestic and offshore construction and renovation projects. In my most recent position as Senior Facilities Engineer for Murphy Products in Hayward, CA, I oversaw all phases of physical plant expansion and renovation projects for this 1,400-employee manufacturing plant.

Earlier as the Manager for Facilities Engineering for Kool Knit Products in Inglewood, CA, I provided expertise during a period of major growth and expansion for this consumer goods manufacturer with 65 sites. I managed construction projects of up to 100,000 square feet in Puerto Rico, Honduras, and Costa Rica to include developing methods for reducing property insurance costs while guaranteeing the quality and timeliness of renovation and building activities. In a prior position as a Senior Facilities Engineer, I managed a $3.5 million asbestos abatement program, developed maintenance management training programs, reduced maintenance expenses, and managed multiple plant projects.

If you can use a positive, results-oriented manager who enjoys challenges and meets deadlines and pressure with control and enthusiasm, I hope you will contact me to suggest a time when we might meet to discuss your needs. I can assure you in advance that I have an excellent reputation and could quickly become a valuable asset to your company.

Sincerely,

Allen M. Sellers

ALLEN M. SELLERS

1110½ Hay Street, Fayetteville, NC 28305　　•　　preppub@aol.com　　•　　(910) 483-6611

OBJECTIVE	To offer a strong background of distinguished accomplishments in the areas of equipment and facilities construction, maintenance, and renovation to an organization that can benefit from my management experience in project engineering and maintenance.
EDUCATION	**B.S., Manufacturing Management**, Northrop University, Inglewood, CA, 1985.
EXPERIENCE	*Have built a reputation as a hard-charging and innovative management professional:*

SENIOR FACILITIES ENGINEER and **MAINTENANCE MANAGER.** Murphy Products, Hayward, CA (2000-present). Was promoted in 2000 to oversee all phases of improvements to the physical plant.

- Administered ongoing renovations to an 800,000-square-foot nonunion plant with 1,400 employees producing automotive air and oil filters.
- Enhanced my familiarity with EPA regulations, fire protection, and safety while reducing property insurance costs and increasing employee safety through renovations to the fire and emergency alarm systems.
- Negotiated fees and made spot purchases which reduced expenses for utilities.
- Assisted in the completion and start up of a 500,000-square-foot distribution center.
- As Maintenance Manager, was interim manager of the electrical and environmental departments and organized the maintenance department.
- Developed and implemented long-range plans for plant HVAC, lighting, and roofing installations.

ACCOUNT REPRESENTATIVE. Personnel Recruiters, Chason, CA (1994-00). Recruited management personnel for textile and apparel companies.

MANAGER FOR FACILITIES ENGINEERING. Kool Knit Products, Inglewood, CA (1985-94). Was promoted in 1987 to manage three engineers and oversee the construction and renovation of facilities for this rapidly growing and expanding organization after approximately eight years as Senior Facilities Engineer.

- Made vital contributions which allowed the company to expand to 65 plants; as manager for construction projects in the Caribbean and Central America, oversaw a $10 million operational budget for the company in 1991.
- Developed innovative ideas which resulted in a $240,000 cost reduction for property insurance for the 65 facilities.
- Supervised engineers involved in construction, renovation, environmental, and maintenance projects in both domestic and offshore facilities.
- As Senior Facilities Engineer from 1985-90, provided oversight for capital projects related to plant and equipment improvements, including developing and implementing fire protection programs, production improvements, EPA compliance, and expansions.
- Managed a $3.5 million asbestos abatement program for domestic and offshore facilities.
- Reduced plant maintenance budgets by $200,000; developed maintenance management and training programs.

Highlights of other experience: Built a reputation for being able to handle deadlines and bring projects in on time in positions which included Director of Maintenance, Engineering, and Construction; Plant Industrial Engineer; and Division Material Handling Engineer.

PERSONAL	Am available for relocation according to employer needs. Determined to excel.

Date

Dear Sir or Madam:

With the enclosed resume, I would like to express my interest in seeking employment with your organization and make you aware of my skills and experience related to your needs.

As you will see from my resume, I have gained experience in both manufacturing and retail environments. In my current job with the A.C. Holden Company, I am a machine operator. Previously employed by Premium Knitwear, the Holden Company hired me immediately upon the strong recommendation of my supervisor when Premium closed its plant and moved its manufacturing operations to Central America.

Prior to working in manufacturing companies as a machine operator and service technician, I worked as a manager and assistant manager in the convenience store business. I began as a Cashier and was promoted into management to handle responsibility for training and developing other employees, controlling inventory, preparing daily report and operating summaries, making deposits, and coordinating with vendors. I earned a reputation as a dependable hard worker known for honesty and attention to detail in handling finances.

If you can use a loyal and dedicated employee, I hope you will call or write me soon to suggest a time when we might meet to discuss your needs. I can provide excellent references and could make myself available for a personal meeting at your convenience. Thank you in advance for your time.

Sincerely,

Joseph Allgood

JOSEPH ALLGOOD

1110½ Hay Street, Fayetteville, NC 28305 • preppub@aol.com • (910) 483-6611

OBJECTIVE

To become a valuable member of an organization that can use a dependable and honest employee who offers a proven ability to work individually, as part of team, or in a managerial role serving customers, achieving high levels of productivity, and maximizing efficiency.

EDUCATION

Graduated from Prospect High School, Swannee, LA.
Completed managerial and technical training sponsored by my employers.

EXPERIENCE

MACHINE OPERATOR. A.C. Holden Company, Dixie, LA (2000-present). Was immediately hired by the Holden Company upon the strong recommendation of my former supervisor at Premium Knitwear, Inc. after Premier ceased operations.
- Rapidly mastered the operations of a complex, multimillion-dollar machine.

SERVICE TECHNICIAN. Premium Knitwear, Inc., Dixie, LA (1994-00). Was in charge of servicing about 50 sewing machine operators with sleeves, thread, and t-shirts.
- Planned ahead to ensure adequate stock levels so that maximum productivity could be maintained.
- Became known for a helpful attitude and excellent problem-solving skills.
- After the NAFTA Agreement was signed, Premium Knitwear decided to cease manufacturing in the U.S. and move its operations to Central America.

MANAGER. X & Z Enterprises, Dixie, LA (1986-93). Began as a Cashier and was promoted into management in this convenience store business.
- Eventually assumed the responsibility for training and developing new managers.
- At the Amoco Convenience Store and Gas Station, was in charge of stocking, operating the cash register, preparing the daily report and operating summaries, overseeing time cards, and making deposits.
- Was frequently commended for my attention to detail and for my honesty in handling finances.

LIBRARY ASSISTANT. Coleridge Elementary School, Sewanee, LA (1982-85). Assisted the librarian in shelving books and checking books in and out.

ASSISTANT MANAGER. Star Convenience Store, Sewanee, LA (1981-82). Began as a store clerk and was rapidly promoted into management.

TEACHER AIDE. Coleridge Elementary School, Sewanee, LA (1975-80). Assisted the teacher with group classes and in all support activities.

PERSONAL

Dependable hard worker. Can provide excellent references.

Date

Exact Name of Person
Exact Title
Exact Name of Company
Address
City, State, Zip

Dear Exact Name of Person (or Dear Sir or Madam if answering a blind ad):

I would appreciate an opportunity to talk with you soon about how I could contribute to your organization through my background in the logistics field as well as through my skills and knowledge related to all phases of manufacturing management, shipping and receiving, warehouse operations, and supply management.

As you will see from my enclosed resume, I excelled as a Manufacturing Management Coordinator for one of the country's leading manufacturers. At the Central Manufacturing Facility in Atlanta, I supervised the manufacturing of millions of dollars worth of products which were then distributed to customer locations throughout the world. Among my accomplishments in this position were providing supervision and guidance for up to ten people, training as many as 30 people in manufacturing policies and procedures, and applying computer skills while processing support documentation for these multimillion-dollar inventories. I was selected to receive special training in hazardous materials handling, storage, and transportation and then earned certification as a trainer in this specialized area.

Although I was excelling in that job, I resigned in order to relocate to Hope, KS, where my wife accepted the position of controller with a local company. I am currently working under a short-term temporary basis with a local retailer.

If you can use an experienced manufacturing supervisor and manager who offers a reputation as an articulate and enthusiastic professional who can be counted on to find a way to achieve results and exceed goals, I hope you will contact me to suggest a time when we might meet to discuss your needs. I can assure you in advance that I could rapidly become an asset to your organization.

Sincerely,

Michael Privette

MICHAEL PRIVETTE

1110½ Hay Street, Fayetteville, NC 28305   •   preppub@aol.com   •   (910) 483-6611

OBJECTIVE

To contribute through the application of my knowledge and experience in manufacturing management as well as shipping and receiving procedures for the benefit of an organization that can use an enthusiastic, articulate, and results-oriented young professional.

EDUCATION & TRAINING

Completed one semester of course work at United University, Elm Creek, KS.
Excelled in training including a logistical operations/traffic management coordination course and hazardous materials/federal hazardous communications training.
Completed Environmental Awareness Course, Elm Creek Technical Community College, KS.

SPECIAL SKILLS

Computers: Windows 95, MS Word, Excel, WordPerfect, and proprietary systems specific to the logistics industry at Value Mart and the U.S. Army
Material-handling equipment: Forklifts ranging in capacity from 2,000 to 15,000 lbs. used to load and unload aircraft, trains, and trucks; pallet jacks; fixed and movable conveyer belts
Other: computer database entry using bar code scanners, readers, and printers; ensuring compliance with government laws and regulations including OSHA and HAZMAT

EXPERIENCE

FREIGHT PROCESSING SPECIALIST. Value Mart Distribution Center, Hope, KS (2002-present). Ensure the timely and correct processing of freight being delivered by trucks to a regional distribution center.

- Am increasing my knowledge of the freight processing policies and procedures unique to this major retailer.
- Have been called on to train other personnel based on my demonstrated knowledge and strong communication skills.

Gained a strong experience base in manufacturing logistics while working with one of the country's leading manufacturers, Gordon Products, Inc.
MANUFACTURING MANAGEMENT COORDINATOR. Atlanta, GA (1999-02). Handled multiple duties while building a reputation as a reliable professional who was always available to help train other personnel during the manufacturing process.

- Gained experience in working with a wide variety of materials, to include hazardous materials.
- Supervised as many as ten people to include evaluating their job performance, preparing written monthly counseling statements.
- Trained approximately 30 people in logistics policies and procedures.
- Accepted and processed millions of dollars worth of supplies, equipment, and vehicles which were then distributed to customer units throughout the installation.
- Received special training in the storage, handling, and transportation of hazardous materials and was certified to train others in these areas.
- Earned a Certificate of Excellence for professionalism and dedication.

SHIPPING AND HANDLING SPECIALIST. San Francisco, CA (1995-99). Became recognized as a thoroughly reliable and knowledgeable young professional while learning shipping and handling procedures, material handling equipment uses, and computer applications unique to the logistics industry in my first military assignment.

- Was awarded a certificate of achievement for processing more than 10,000 pieces of freight during a large-scale project.

PERSONAL

Am known for my exceptional organizational and planning skills. Available for relocation.

Date

Mr. John Smith
Quality Shipping
4250 Jonestown Road SE
Atlanta, GA 30315

Dear Mr. Smith:

I would appreciate an opportunity to talk with you soon about how I could benefit Quality Shipping as a Branch Terminal Manager/Account Manager through my strong background in the transportation industry.

Known for my expertise in increasing sales and revenue while reducing costs, you will see by my enclosed resume that I have in-depth experience gained while working for the regional carrier McDonald Transportation. In my 14 years with this company I advanced to management roles after beginning in a ground-floor position as a Driver and Freight Handler. I am also a skilled accounts representative and enjoy the challenge of selling transportation services. I have become very adept at selling transportation services based mostly on quality and service rather than on price.

Throughout my career with McDonald Transportation, I consistently made changes which resulted in increased sales and revenue while reducing costs and eliminating unnecessary expenses. For instance, in my most recent position as Branch Terminal Manager at the Raleigh, NC, terminal I was credited with bringing about a 35% increase in sales and revenue, a 15% reduction in operating costs, and an increase in on-time rates from 89% to a near-perfect 98%.

Selected to attend corporate training courses in quality management, sales, and front-line supervisory techniques, I was appointed to Quality Improvement Teams and was elected as team chairman one year.

I am certain that you would find in me a talented manager who communicates effectively with others at all levels and is experienced in making sound decisions under pressure. With an excellent reputation within the transportation industry, I am a flexible and versatile individual who would consider serving your needs in a variety of capacities and functional areas. I can provide very strong references.

I hope you will welcome my call soon to arrange a brief meeting at your convenience to discuss your current and future needs and how I might serve them. Thank you in advance for your time.

Sincerely yours,

William Velasquez

WILLIAM VELASQUEZ

1110½ Hay Street, Fayetteville, NC 28305 • preppub@aol.com • (910) 483-6611

OBJECTIVE	To offer my reputation as a thoroughly knowledgeable professional with special abilities related to terminal operations, sales, quality management, and customer service gained while advancing to increasingly higher managerial levels within the trucking industry.
QUALITY MANAGEMENT	Appointed to Quality Improvement Teams in Georgia, North Carolina, and Florida; was elected as chairman in 1995. Believe in total quality results, top to bottom.
EXPERIENCE	*Built a track record of promotion while becoming known for my expertise in increasing sales and reducing operational costs with McDonald Transportation, an interstate trucking company operating predominately in the southeastern U.S.:*

BRANCH TERMINAL MANAGER. Raleigh, NC (2000-present). Continued to find ways to increase revenue and efficiency while managing all aspects of daily terminal operations ranging from staffing and training, to managing a sales territory, to supervising the terminal's account manager.
- Displayed a talent for introducing changes which increased annual sales/revenue 35%.
- Brought about a 15% reduction in operating costs while increasing on-time delivery rates to an almost-perfect 98% rate from the previous 89%.

TERMINAL MANAGER. Greensboro, NC (1994-99). Reduced operating costs 10% over a two-year period while directing total terminal operations including staffing and training employees in every section of the business; supervised two account managers.
- Increased annual sales and revenue 30% each year.

ACCOUNT MANAGER and **BRANCH TERMINAL MANAGER.** Baxley, GA (1992-94). Wore "two hats" as a combination Account Manager and Branch Terminal Manager; earned rapid promotion because of my success in sales and in hiring/supervising 15 people.
- During only nine months in this job, made improvements resulting in a 30% growth in sales and revenue as well as an 18% decrease in operating costs.

SALES REPRESENTATIVE. Miami, FL (1991-92). Refined sales and customer service skills as the account manager for approximately 50% of the customer base for a company which provides sales and service within 80-100 miles of each local terminal.
- Maintained a strong repeat customer base while bringing about a 41% increase in sales,

DISPATCHER/OPERATIONS MANAGER. Orlando, FL (1988-91). Learned to remain in control under pressure and constant deadlines while scheduling deliveries and pick ups and dispatching trucks throughout the area.
- Applied my problem-solving skills by decreasing the number of missed pick ups 70%, thereby increasing customer satisfaction and boosting the bottom line.

SHIPPING SUPERVISOR. Orlando, FL (1987-88). Supervised ten dock workers; established truck routes; ensured shipments were on time with no errors or damage.
- Improved procedures so that the number of damage claims was greatly reduced while also reorganizing routes so that work loads increased and costs decreased.

TRAINING	Was selected to attend numerous corporate-sponsored professional development programs and seminars related to these and other areas:

Front-line supervisory practices	Sales and closing techniques
Breaking down work processes	Making quality improvements

PERSONAL	Offer an outstanding reputation within the transportation industry and can provide excellent references. Am skilled in competing based on quality and service, not just on price.

Exact Name of Person
Title or Position
Name of Company
Address (No., street)
Address (city, state, zip)

SHIPPING MANAGER Dear Exact Name of Person: (or Dear Sir or Madam if answering a blind ad)

I would appreciate an opportunity to talk with you soon about how I could contribute to your organization through my experience in all aspects of traffic and transportation management. I offer extensive knowledge of LTL, TL, Intermodal, rate negotiations, pool shipments, and cost analysis to determine the most economical method of shipping.

As you will see from my resume, I am currently site freight coordinator for a Fortune 500 company, and I have continuously found new ways to reduce costs and improve efficiency while managing all inbound and outbound shipping. On my own initiative, I have recovered $10,000 in claims annually while saving the company at least 40% of a $10 million LTL budget. In addition to continuous cost cutting, I have installed a new bar code system in the finished goods shipping area and have installed a new wrapping system.

In previous jobs supervising terminal operations, I opened up new terminals, closed down existing operations which were unprofitable, and gained hands-on experience in increasing efficiency in every terminal area.

With a reputation as a savvy negotiator, I can provide excellent personal and professional references. I am held in high regard by my current employer.

I hope you will call or write me soon to suggest a time convenient for us to meet and discuss your current and future needs and how I might serve them. Thank you in advance for you time.

Sincerely yours,

Pedro Palacios

Alternate last paragraph:
I hope you will welcome my call soon to arrange a brief meeting at your convenience to discuss your current and future needs and how I might serve them. Thank you in advance for your time.

PEDRO PALACIOS

1110½ Hay Street, Fayetteville, NC 28305 • preppub@aol.com • (910) 483-6611

OBJECTIVE   To contribute to an organization that can use a skilled traffic management professional who offers a proven ability to reduce costs, install new systems, optimize scheduling, negotiate rates, anticipate difficulties, solve problems, and keep customers happy.

EXPERIENCE   **SITE FREIGHT COORDINATOR**. DuPont Corporation, Wilmington, DE (1989-present). For this Fortune 500 company, have continuously found new ways to cut costs and improve service while managing all inbound transportation as well as outbound shipping totaling in excess of one million dollars in finished goods daily; supervise ten people.

- Saved the company at least 40% of a $10 million LTL budget by resourcefully combining my technical knowledge with my creative cost-cutting skills.
- Recovered $10,000 annually in claims; prepare all cargo claims documents for corporate office and oversee all procedures for proper claims documentation.
- Installed a bar code system in Finished Goods Shipping, and also installed a new wrapping system.
- Reduced overtime by 90% while simultaneously cross-training some employees and improving overall morale.
- Became familiar with Total Quality Processes while analyzing transit times to ensure consistent and timely Just-In-Time delivery schedules.
- Am a member of the B & D corporate committee for North American rate negotiations; negotiate rates with various carriers on special moves.
- Justify capital appropriation requests for funding special projects; audit all freight bills and process them for payment.
- Prepare all documents for export shipments to Canada; also advise about the shipment of hazardous materials and maintain proper documentation placards and labels.
- Coordinate all site printing of product information and warranty cards.
- Am responsible for site switcher and equipment such as leased trailers.
- Have earned a reputation as a savvy negotiator with an ability to predict future variables that will affect traffic costs.

SUPERVISOR. International Freightways, Inc., Atlanta, GA (1986-88). Supervised up to 12 drivers while managing second-shift operations and controlling inbound and outbound freight at this terminal operation.

- Increased efficiency in every operational area; improved the load factor, reduced dock hours, and ensured more timely deliveries.

INVENTORY SPECIALIST. La-Z-Boy East, Inc., Florence, SC (1984-86). Learned the assembly process of this name-brand furniture manufacturer while managing replenishment of subassemblies for daily production.

Highlights of other experience:
- As Terminal Manager for Spartan Express, opened a new terminal in South Carolina; determined the pricing structure, handled sales, and then managed this new operation which enjoyed rapid growth.
- Gained experience in closing down a terminal determined to be in a poor location.
- As Operations Manager for a break bulk operation, supervised up to 12 people in a dock center while managing the sorting/segregating of shipments from origin to destination.

EDUCATION   Studied business management and liberal arts, Ohio State and LaSalle University. Completed extensive executive development courses in the field of transportation and traffic management sponsored by University of Toledo and Texas Technical University

Date

Exact Name of Person
Exact Title
Exact Name of Company
Address
City, State, Zip

**SHIPPING AND
RECEIVING MANAGER**

Dear Exact Name of Person (or Dear Sir or Madam if answering a blind ad):

With the enclosed resume, I would like to make you aware of my interest in exploring employment opportunities with your organization and introduce you to my background and credentials related to manufacturing and supply chain management.

As you will see from my resume, I served my country with distinction and was the recipient of numerous medals and honors praising my management abilities and technical expertise related to supply management. In my most recent position as Chief of Manufacturing Operations, I organized the provision of all types of supplies and services for hundreds of people involved in worldwide projects. In my previous position, I was handpicked as Supply Branch Chief and Senior Logistics Consultant. In that capacity, I provided oversight for supply management systems of 75 different organizations and led them in activities which included reducing shrinkage, improving ordering and shipping time, and resourcefully utilizing excess equipment. As the "resident expert instructor" on automated systems for supply chain management, I established a new automated system for tracking the ordering, storage, and inventory control of perishable and non-perishable items.

While becoming an expert on supply management, I have gained a reputation as an individual of "unquestionable integrity and loyalty." I have managed dozens of people, controlled budgets of more than $400,000, and accounted for millions of dollars in assets. I have managed the supply chain for all types of supplies including perishable and grocery products, engineering and repair parts, telecommunications items, vehicle parts and automotive equipment, as well as computers and office supplies. In every job I have held, I have made major contributions to productivity. For example, as Logistics Branch Manager for an organization in Turkey supporting NATO activities, I reduced a spare parts backlog from 635 parts to less than 44 monthly.

I have received the highest evaluations of my ability to communicate effectively with others, and I have trained hundreds of individuals in automated inventory control systems and supply management. If you can use my considerable expertise related to shipping and receiving, expediting and dispatching, logistics and transportation operations, as well as manufacturing management, I hope you will contact me to suggest a time when we might meet to discuss your needs.

Yours sincerely,

Mark Wordsworth

MARK WORDSWORTH

1110½ Hay Street, Fayetteville, NC 28305   •   preppub@aol.com   •   (910) 483-6611

OBJECTIVE

I want to contribute to an organization that can use an experienced manager who offers expertise related to shipping and receiving, expediting and logistics management, supply chain management, as well as inventory control and warehouse operations management.

EDUCATION

College: **Associates Degree in General Studies,** Central Texas College, 1999.
Professional and Technical Training: Graduated from these professional courses taught at the highly respected U.S. Army Quartermaster School for logistics and supply managers: Materiel Control and Accounting, Food Service and Grocery Supply Management, Property Book Accounting, Automated Systems Management (SAILS, SARRS), Advanced Logistics Supervision, Retail Supply Chain Management and Re-Supply, Total Quality Management.

COMPUTERS

Proficient with automated systems for supply chain management.

EXPERIENCE

CHIEF OF MANUFACTURING OPERATIONS. U.S. Army, Ft.Campbell, KY (1999-present). Was recommended for promotion to the highest enlisted rank (Sergeant Major) based on my outstanding performance in managing the manufacturing of parachute equipment supporting a 1,500-person organization.

- In one project, provided transportation, maintenance, food, water, fuel, laundry, and bath support for 1,600 people working in a rugged setting in Nicaragua for three months.
- Supervised 15 people while providing oversight for the ordering and storage of perishable and nonperishable materials in multiple warehouses.
- Trained more than 200 personnel in operating automated inventory control systems.
- Continuously emphasized safety and quality control, which resulted in zero accidents.

SUPPLY BRANCH CHIEF & SENIOR LOGISTICS CONSULTANT. U.S. Army, Ft. Shafter, HI (1996-99). Was handpicked for this position which involved providing oversight for supply management systems of 75 separate organizations; inspected their internal systems and procedures and provided expert technical direction.

- Established a new automated system used to track the ordering, storage, and inventory control of perishable and nonperishable items.
- Decreased shrinkage and waste through highly improved automated procedures.
- In one organization, led personnel in identifying and recycling more than $6 million in excess equipment; in another organization, led personnel to establish 100% accountability of $4 million in equipment and property.

Highlights of prior U.S. Army management and supply experience:
LOGISTICS BRANCH MANAGER. Turkey. Received the prestigious Joint Service Commendation Medal for my leadership and technical expertise on behalf of NATO.

- Reduced a spare parts backlog from 635 parts to less than 44 monthly while coordinating logistical support for mobile and fixed communications systems.
- Instituted a logistical accounting system to monitor repair parts and supply transactions. Ensured the provision of critical repair parts during the Gulf War.
- Accounted for $40 million in communications equipment.

ACCOUNTING AND CONTROL SPECIALIST. Korea. Received and stored map products.

PERSONAL

In formal performance evaluations, was often praised for "unquestionable integrity and loyalty." Have learned how to motivate others to reach for the highest goals in terms of personal productivity.

CAREER CHANGE

Date

Exact Name of Person
Title or Position
Name of Company
Exact Address
City, State, Zip

Dear Exact Name of Person (or Sir or Madam if answering a blind ad):

SHIPPING MANAGER

This talented individual seeks to apply his strong background in shipping and receiving in a manufacturing environment.

With the enclosed resume, I would like to make you aware of my background as an experienced shipping professional with strong leadership and communication skills who offers a results-oriented management style and a history of excellence in the training, motivation, and supervision of distribution center personnel.

With Super-Mart distribution centers, I started as a Floor Associate in the shipping department, and have rapidly advanced to positions of increasing responsibility. Currently, while serving as Shipping Manager at the Iowa City distribution center, I supervise up to 55 employees, including two desk clerks, five yard drivers, and more than 35 shipping associates. I interview, hire, and train all new employees as well as conduct annual employee performance appraisals. Earlier, as a Shipping Supervisor in Syracuse, NY, I provided direct supervision to as many as 45 shipping associates. I developed a load quality auditing system which tracked the performance of each associate, providing personal accountability and raising quality standards for shipping department personnel. In my earliest position with the company, I quickly mastered the essential methods and practices of shipping in a high-volume distribution center environment.

As you will see, I have completed nearly two years of college-level course work toward a Bachelor of Science degree in Criminal Justice. In addition, I have excelled in leadership and management courses sponsored by Super-Mart.

If you can use an experienced shipping manager whose proven leadership and communications skills have been tested in challenging, high-volume distribution environments, I hope you will contact me to suggest a time when we might meet to discuss your needs. I assure you that my integrity is beyond reproach; I have an outstanding reputation, and would quickly become an asset to your organization.

Sincerely,

Bruce E. Jewel

BRUCE E. JEWEL

1110½ Hay Street, Fayetteville, NC 28305 • preppub@aol.com • (910) 483-6611

OBJECTIVE

To benefit an organization that can use an experienced shipping manager with exceptional leadership ability and strong communication skills as well as a track record of success in the training, motivation, and supervision of distribution center personnel.

EXPERIENCE

With Super-Mart Distribution Centers, have advanced in the following "track record" of increasing responsibilities:

2000-present: **SHIPPING MANAGER.** Iowa City, IA. Promoted to manage the Shipping Department for this large regional distribution center which ships nearly $4 million worth of merchandise daily after ably serving the company as a Shipping Supervisor.

- Supervise up to 55 associates, including two supervisors, five yard drivers, and more than 35 shipping associates.
- Interview, hire, and train supervisors and employees; conduct annual performance appraisals for all associates under my supervision.
- Monitor all phases of the shipping process, ensuring that the department meets production quotas without exceeding hours and overtime guidelines.
- Calculate minimum labor hours required to process shipments on a daily basis; transfer, reschedule, or cancel shipping department personnel accordingly to control labor costs.
- Prepare and maintain all monthly operational paperwork, to include overtime reports, shipping quality and accuracy reports, safety reports, and productivity reports.
- Calculate and produce profit and loss forecasts.

1998-2000: **SHIPPING SUPERVISOR.** Syracuse, NY. Advanced to this position after demonstrating leadership and exceptional job performance as a Floor Associate in the Shipping Department; supervised the shipping operation for a regional distribution center which processed nearly $5 million worth of outbound freight each day.

- Managed up to 45 employees, ensuring that all freight was loaded accurately.
- Interviewed, hired, trained new personnel for the shipping department.
- Calculated labor hour usage per volume of merchandise shipped, and reported these figures on the Team Performance Report (TPR).
- Tracked time and attendance for all employees under my supervision.
- Developed a load quality auditing system which tracked associate performance, providing personal accountability; raised quality standards for the shipping department.

1997-1998: **FLOOR ASSOCIATE.** Syracuse, NY. In my earliest position with Super-Mart, quickly mastered systems, procedures, and shipping methods while working in the Shipping Department of this busy regional distribution center.

- Utilized the systems monitor computer to ensure that freight was loaded on the right pallet and all pallets were loaded in the correct trailer.
- Loaded shipments on outbound trailers, maintaining the highest possible standards of load quality and positioning freight for maximum safe load levels.

Highlights of earlier experience: Proudly served my country as a Land Surveyor in the U.S. Army and Military Policemen in the Army National Guard.

EDUCATION

Finished nearly two years of college-level course work toward a Bachelor of Science degree in Criminal Justice, Herkimer Community College, Herkimer, NY.

PERSONAL

Excellent personal and professional references are available upon request.

CAREER CHANGE

Date

Mr. John Smith
Plant Manager
Edwards Foods
500 Edwards Avenue
Dallas, TX 33490

**SHIPPING
SUPERVISOR**

This individual has an
unusual career change in
mind. He wants to return to
work for a former employer
in the food manufacturing
industry.

Dear Mr. Smith:

With the enclosed resume, I would like to make you aware of my interest in
employment with Edwards Foods in some supervisory capacity in which I could be of
value to the organization.

I began with Edwards Foods as a Production Supervisor in the flour and corn
department and earned promotion to Shipping Supervisor, where I excelled in all
aspects of my job and was held in high regard until my voluntary resignation to pursue
other opportunities. It is my strong desire to rejoin the company, and I feel my versatile
management skills and technical knowledge could be of value to you.

As you will see from my resume, I have excelled most recently in positions in the
security field and am currently working for Taylor Security, Inc. I can provide excellent
references.

Thank you for your consideration.

Yours sincerely,

Matthew Kipling

MATTHEW KIPLING

1110½ Hay Street, Fayetteville, NC 28305   •   preppub@aol.com   •   (910) 483-6611

OBJECTIVE   Seeking a position within an organization where more than 30 years of experience, education, skills, and abilities in logistics, administration, management, or training would be of value.

EXPERIENCE   **SECURITY OFFICER.** Taylor Security, Inc., Santee, AZ (2001-present). Assure security pertaining to commercial shipments, property, and personnel; maintain vigilance to prevent pilfering and vandalism; advise the security officer on industrial needs.

SECURITY OFFICER/COUNSELOR. Sherman Senior High School, Santee, AZ (2000). Acted as principal advisor to the principal, staff, and students for Lee County High School Safety Operation within the school campus; monitored all parking lots; observed incoming and outgoing traffic; intensively managed and monitored students to ensure school's policies were followed as related to safety, equipment, and personal property in the parking lot.

SALESMAN. Allen Pest Control, Paradise, AZ (1997-99). Certified Termite and Pest Control Representative; visited potential customers' homes to inspect problem areas and acted as the principal advisor in determining what pest problem they were encountering within the home; developed a pest control program that would treat the problem; implemented numerous pest control plans which created a cleaner environment and protected their investment.

SHIPPING SUPERVISOR. Edwards Foods, Paradise, AZ (1995-97). Began as a Production Supervisor in the flour and corn department and earned promotion to Shipping Supervisor in charge of a nine-person team responsible for shipping $40,000 per truck of finished products out to customers; ensured inventory accountability, billing, lading, stacking trucks, tracking, and performing quality assurance controls.
- Determined small package, Less Than Truck Load (LTL), and truck load shipping arrangements in addition to selecting the appropriate carrier.
- Greatly reduced employee turnover by personally selecting team members who demonstrated the skills and potential to perform productively.
- As Production Supervisor, excelled in supervising all three shifts; conducted monthly quality issue and safety meetings to reinforce the importance of quality and safety.
- Participated in the Corrective Action Committee assembled to discuss ideas and methods to help resolve problems with foreign materials in the finished product.
- Selected to represent the Shift Quality Improvement Team as Team Leader where we were focusing on eliminating waste, cutting unnecessary cost, and decreasing downtime.

Highlights of military experience, U.S. Army, various locations: Earned promotion to increasing responsibility through my success including the following:
Administration: Established, implemented, and monitored effective organizational policies for organizations ranging in size from 50 to 22,000.
- Responsible for initiating and maintaining morale, safety, and welfare programs for personnel to reduce accidents while maintaining work force strength.

EDUCATION   **Undergraduate Training**:
El Paso Community College, El Paso, TX: **Marketing**
Paradise State University, Paradise, AZ: **Effective Writing**

PERSONAL   Excellent references on request. Stable married individual.

CAREER CHANGE

Date

Exact Name of Person
Exact Title
Exact Name of Company
Address
City, State, Zip

SHOP FOREMAN   Dear Exact Name of Person (or Dear Sir or Madam if answering a blind ad):

I would appreciate an opportunity to talk with you soon concerning how I could contribute to your organization through my technical expertise and management experience.

As you will see from my resume, I am currently excelling as a Shop Foreman in a bottling company, and I can provide excellent references from my current employer.

However, I am eager to return to a manufacturing environment. After earning my associate's degree in Automotive Manufacturing Technology, I went to work for one of the leading manufacturers of automotive parts, and I set new production records while training and managing workers on a production line. I am eager to return to a manufacturing environment because I welcome the opportunity to be measured according to the highest standards of quality, safety, and productivity.

If you can use a results-oriented manager with a strong background in manufacturing management, I hope you will suggest a time when we might meet to discuss your needs. I can assure you in advance that I have an excellent reputation and could quickly become a valuable asset to your company.

Sincerely,

Scott Charles Harris

SCOTT CHARLES HARRIS

1110½ Hay Street, Fayetteville, NC 28305　　•　　preppub@aol.com　　•　　(910) 483-6611

OBJECTIVE　　To contribute a background of experience in automotive shop supervision and operations to an organization that can use a highly skilled and dedicated professional.

EDUCATION & TRAINING　　Associate's degree in **Automotive Manufacturing Technology**, City Colleges of Chicago, 1989. Completed corporate-sponsored training programs which included:

　　Powered industrial lift truck training (materials handling and storage), 1998

　　Heavy equipment operator training, 1998

　　Allison transmission systems analysis, troubleshooting, and onboard diagnosis, 1997

　　Brake clinic sponsored by Wilson Heavy Duty Systems, 1994

　　Automated supply systems, 1989 and 1990

CERTIFICATIONS　　N.C. Class A Commercial and U.S. Government Heavy Motor Vehicle Operator's Licenses.

EXPERIENCE　　**SHOP FOREMAN.** PremiumBottling Company, Juniper, GA (2000-present). Promoted to this supervisory role after excelling as a Diesel Mechanic, oversee operations in a shop which maintains and repairs 125 vehicles – purchase parts, assign and schedule work, and deal with outside contractors for any work which must be subcontracted.

- Brought about major cost reductions through fleet upgrading and equipment standardization, and effective management of time; reduced the staff from five to two.
- Prepared cost justifications and purchased all new shop equipment.
- Performed scheduled preventive maintenance as well as applying skills in welding and in sheet metal and aluminum fabrication and repair.
- As a Diesel Mechanic, worked on commercial and industrial vehicles with gasoline, diesel, or multifuel engines to complete major and minor overhauls and repairs using specialized testing equipment.

Gained supervisory and mechanical experience with a leading automobile parts manufacturer, Bentley Manufacturing:

PRODUCTION LINE MANAGER. Caison, IL (1995-00). Supervised sixty employees on a production line which produced quality automobile parts for high-end vehicles.

- Was credited with increasing productivity 18% in just three months.
- Promoted on the basis of my performance as the senior mechanic in 1992-93, received the corporate Gold Award for my accomplishments as supervisor of a special production line during the war in the Middle East; controlled a $30,000 tool set while ensuring proper maintenance and equipment control for a contact maintenance team.

ASSISTANT SHOP FOREMAN. Caison, IL (1992-94). Developed and polished supervisory and mechanical knowledge while supervising mechanics performing preventive maintenance, scheduled services, and preparations for transfer to higher-level maintenance facilities for an inventory of 85 vehicles and pieces of equipment.

- Supervised and personally constructed special parts for communications vans.

ASSISTANT MAINTENANCE MANAGER and **TRAINING SUPERVISOR.** Caison, IL (1991-92). Supervised six maintenance personnel while controlling a $3 million inventory of recovery equipment and performing preventive maintenance checks and services. Set up a driver training program for more than 250 people.

PERSONAL　　Extensive training in manufacturing management and quality assurance. Can handle pressure and deadlines.

SENIOR SERVICE REPRESENTATIVE

Dear Sir or Madam:

With the enclosed resume, I would like to make you aware of my background as an experienced customer service professional and order management supervisor with highly polished skills related to supervising employees as well as solving complex customer problems.

As you will see from my resume, I have excelled in a track record of advancement with a Fortune 500 company, and I have been involved in resolving customer problems related to the ordering, manufacturing, and shipment of industrial products including motor controls. I began with the company in an entry-level position after briefly serving my country in the U.S. Navy, and I was quickly promoted to a role which involved production planning. I then supervised a 20-person department involved in the assembly, wiring, and shipment of half a million dollars in industrial products monthly.

As my career within Roberts Manufacturing progressed, I was promoted to senior positions which involved managing orders and handling customer service. Because of my understanding of product manufacturing and engineering as well as my highly effective communication skills, I excelled in coordinating the often-complex process of customer ordering and order fulfillment. I established and maintained cordial relationships with customers worldwide while expertly performing liaison with all functional areas involved in filling the customer's order including sales, engineering, manufacturing, and quality control.

In my most recent position I significantly reduced costs for Roberts through my ability to handle product warranty inquiries and claims. In 2002, I reduced by 50% the cost of product warranty claims compared to 2001, and I have greatly reduced the company's response time to product warranty inquiries. I am proud that the Pocatello facility now responds to 90% of inquiries within 24 hours.

If you can use a versatile and experienced professional who offers extensive knowledge of manufacturing, production, and sales functions, I hope you will contact me to suggest a time when we might meet to discuss your needs. I would be committed to helping your company achieve the highest customer satisfaction levels.

Sincerely,

Ned Lawrence Arabia

NED LAWRENCE ARABIA

1110½ Hay Street, Fayetteville, NC 28305   •   preppub@aol.com   •   (910) 483-6611

OBJECTIVE

I want to contribute to an organization that can use a dedicated professional with experience in product line engineering, and manufacturing and customer service supervision.

EDUCATION

Bachelor of Science in **Marketing**, Pocatello State University, Pocatello, ID, 1982. Associate's degree in **Business Administration**, Pocatello Community College, Pocatello, ID. Extensive company-sponsored professional training related to **customer service, statistical process control, manufacturing supervision, production planning**, other areas.

EXPERIENCE

After a distinguished career with **Roberts Manufacturing**, *have taken an early retirement in order to pursue other opportunities; advanced in the following track record of promotion at this company's Pocatello, ID location:*

1999-present: **PRODUCT WARRANTY COORDINATOR & SENIOR CUSTOMER SERVICE REPRESENTATIVE.** For a state-of-the-art manufacturing facility, handled product warranty inquiries and claims; determined correct action after extensive problem analysis which involved coordinating local and field engineering personnel.
- In 2002, reduced by 50% the cost of product warranty claims compared to 2001.
- Improved the department's response time so that 90% of inquiries are responded to within 24 hours.

1997-99: **SENIOR CUSTOMER SERVICE REPRESENTATIVE.** In a very fast-paced job, coordinated the shipping of expedited orders and obtained outsourced material while also maintaining the manufacturing schedule for a department of 50 people; coordinated scheduling with field personnel and performed liaison with customer service on orders.

1990-97: **SENIOR ORDER MANAGEMENT REPRESENTATIVE.** Worked closely with engineering, manufacturing, and materials departments to optimize scheduling for customers; processed changes to orders including pricing changes. Coordinated customer visits for the review of engineering work and the inspection of equipment.

1987-90: **MANAGER OF ORDER MANAGEMENT.** Managed three people while supervising a department which performed scheduling of manufacturing; acted as the Customer Service Representative for field inquiries and interfaced with engineering, marketing, and manufacturing in achieving the highest quality product and turnaround time for customers.

1985-87: **ASSOCIATE PRODUCT LINE ENGINEER.** Utilized technical catalogs for quoting prices and delivery times of aftermarket parts and assemblies; provided customer service once the orders were received from the field sales organization.

1982-85: **MANUFACTURING SUPERVISOR.** Supervised a 20-person department involved in the assembly, wiring, and shipment of $500,000 in parts and assemblies monthly. Supervised hourly employees and became skilled at preparing performance reports.

1982: **ASSOCIATE PRODUCTION PLANNER.** After beginning as a Manufacturing Technician making wiring harnesses from engineering wiring diagrams and schematics, was promoted after 3 months to be in charge of reviewing material and engineering content of orders to be scheduled for manufacturing; scheduled work to ensure level production while managing on-time shipments to customers.

PERSONAL

Serve on the Board of Directors for Junior Achievement of Eastern ID-Pocatello.

Exact Name of Person
Exact Title
Exact Name of Company
Address
City, State, Zip

**SENIOR
MANUFACTURING
ENGINEER**

Dear Exact Name of Person (or Dear Sir or Madam if answering a blind ad):

   With the enclosed resume, I would like to make you aware of my background as an experienced, self-motivated, and educated industrial and manufacturing engineer with excellent communication and organizational skills and a background in manufacturing, quality assurance, and safety.

   In my most recent position as a Senior Manufacturing Engineer at Westfield, I was responsible for the security and maintenance of more than $9 million worth of equipment, and developed and managed a $1.5 million budget for the maintenance department. Through proper process and materials selection, I reduced hazardous waste generated by the plant by 99%. I also oversaw the removal and proper disposal of all hazardous materials from the paint line and paint booth after that operation ceased.

   In previous positions with Westfield, I was responsible for training employees on environmental, health, and safety issues and personally addressing any problems in these areas. Through my initiative, the facility drastically reduced its generation of hazardous waste, which resulted in a downgrading of our Hazardous Waste Generator Status to Conditionally Exempt.

   My innovative ideas were displayed when, as a Senior Manufacturing Engineer, I designed a wiring harness for one of our products, resulting in a $100,000 per year reduction in the manufacturing costs for that item. As Management Systems Supervisor, I managed three departments simultaneously, including the product transfer team that moved nearly $10 million worth of production materials to Chicago from a facility in another state in order to support the addition of a new product to our production line and the expansion of our operation.

   If you can use a highly skilled manufacturing engineer with strong communication and problem-solving skills as well as a background which includes hazardous materials handling and safety, I hope you will contact me soon. I can assure you in advance that I have an outstanding reputation and could rapidly become a valuable addition to your company.

Sincerely,

Christopher T. Abraham

CHRISTOPHER T. ABRAHAM

1110½ Hay Street, Fayetteville, NC 28305 • preppub@aol.com • (910) 483-6611

OBJECTIVE

To benefit an organization that can use an experienced, self-motivated, and educated industrial engineer with excellent communication and organizational skills and a background in manufacturing, quality assurance, and safety.

EDUCATION

Master's degree in **Engineering**, Chicago State University, Chicago, IL, 1997.
Certificate in Business Administration, Keller Graduate School of Management, Chicago, IL, 1982.
Bachelor of Science in **Industrial Engineering**, University of Illinois, Urbana, IL, 1974.

EXPERIENCE

*After a distinguished career with **Westfield, Inc.**, have taken an early retirement in order to pursue other opportunities; advanced in the following track record of promotion:*
SENIOR MANUFACTURING ENGINEER II. Chicago, IL (2000-present). Perform a variety of manufacturing, safety, and maintenance functions, taking on additional responsibilities while still performing the duties of Junior Manufacturing Engineer.

- Supervise 14 employees in the maintenance department and tool room; improved on-time performance of all preventative maintenance tasks from 25% to 98%.
- Through proper process and materials selection, lowered the amount of hazardous waste generated drastically, resulting in a downgrade in our Hazardous Waste Generator Status to Conditionally Exempt, reducing future liability and exempting us from certain regulations.
- Reduced hazardous waste generated by 99%.
- Responsible for the security and maintenance of over $9 million worth of equipment.
- Developed and managed a $1.5 million budget for the maintenance department.
- Managed the International Standards Organization (ISO) equipment calibration system.
- Oversaw removal and proper disposal of all hazardous materials from the paint line and paint booth after operation ceased, reducing future liability and returning the area to productive use.

SENIOR MANUFACTURING ENGINEER. Chicago, IL (1994-2000). In addition to the customary duties of a Senior Manufacturing Engineer, I took on additional responsibility for hazardous waste management, safety training and special projects.

- Addressed all problems related to and developed employee training on environmental, health, and safety issues; administered the Worker's Compensation program.
- Reduced hazardous waste generated by the facility 25% and effected compliance with OSHA guidelines and regulations regarding materials handling.
- Oversaw completion of special projects, including replacing the facility's roof and HVAC.

SENIOR MANUFACTURING ENGINEER. Chicago, IL (1990-1994). Directed the trouble-shooting and resolution of engineering and manufacturing problems to ensure the smooth operation of the production department

- Trained all new employees in my assigned areas of the facility.
- Developed a wiring harness which reduced production costs by $100,000 per year.
- Directed the preparation of new releases of existing products.

MANAGEMENT SYSTEMS SUPERVISOR. Chicago, IL (1984-1990). Managed three different departments in order to ease the transition to computerization of product engineering; supervised 13 employees in the maintenance and tool room department.

PERSONAL

Outstanding personal and professional references are available upon request.

Exact Name of Person
Title or Position
Name of Company
Address (number and street)
Address (city, state, and zip)

SENIOR POLYMER & ADHESIVES CHEMIST

Dear Exact Name of Person (or Dear Sir or Madam if answering a blind ad):

With the enclosed resume, I present my extensive experience and talent as a Chemical, Polymer, and Adhesive Specialist possessing exceptional technical abilities that have been proven in a wide variety of research laboratories and manufacturing environments.

I am currently excelling as a Senior Polymer & Adhesives Chemist for Appleton, Inc.'s Montgomery Point manufacturing facility, where I formulate a broad range of chemicals and polymer adhesives used for bonding leather, nylon, polyester, cotton, and other fabrics to vulcanized rubber substrates to facilitate the manufacture of new product lines and to improve existing product lines.

In earlier positions, I have made substantial contributions in areas of technical knowledge advancement through applied research which improved efficiencies in existing products and processes, and also resulted in the introduction of newly developed products. I have extensive experience with customer service and technical support, both over the phone and at customer facilities. I am an accomplished problem-solver, innovative thinker, and hands-on, results-oriented individual. I possess extensive experience in project management, research benchwork, pilot scaleup to full production, and formulation design to meet specific end-use requirements. I have a capacity for accuracy and for detail, and I like to make systems and processes operate efficiently and precisely.

Although I am highly regarded by my present employer and can provide excellent personal and professional references at the appropriate time, I am interested in exploring career opportunities in a larger metropolitan area. I am not limiting my job search to one specific type of position; consequently, I welcome opportunities to explore options in any field where my chemical, scientific, technical, business, manufacturing and people skills, knowledge, and experience can be fully utilized.

I can assure you in advance that I have an outstanding reputation and would quickly become a valuable asset to your operation. I am available to discuss employment opportunities at your earliest convenience. I can be reached at (910) 483-6611 after 5 PM Monday through Friday and anytime during the weekends.

Sincerely,

Bradley T. Dickinson

BRADLEY T. DICKINSON

1110½ Hay Street, Fayetteville, NC 28305　　•　　preppub@aol.com　　•　　(910) 483-6611

OBJECTIVE　　To technologically advance an organization seeking a talented Chemical, Polymer, and Adhesive Specialist with exceptional technical and managerial skills who is experienced in research, development, product/process improvement, and manufacturing optimization.

EDUCATION　　**B.S., General Science,** concentrations in Chemistry, Mathematics, Geology, and Life Science, Oregon State University, Corvallis, OR, 1975.

EXPERIENCE　　**SENIOR POLYMER & ADHESIVES CHEMIST.** Appleton, Inc., Montgomery Point, WI (2000-present). Perform a variety of R&D, supervisory, and project management tasks, while developing water-based polymer adhesives for this large footwear manufacturer.
- Develop, manage, and implement multiple projects with emphasis on integrating new products and processes into the existing manufacturing system.
- Develop new latex polymer adhesives for bonding leather, nylon, polyester, cotton, and other fabrics to vulcanized rubber substrates.
- Provide technical guidance to upper management and provide managerial oversight and training to eight employees.

RESEARCH & DEVELOPMENT MANAGER. Smithson Corporation, Covington, MA (1996-1999). Provided project management, supervisory oversight, formulation development, and customer technical support services for this busy custom formulator and compounder of latex polymer products.
- Created latex polymer formulations specifically developed to meet manufacturing customers' specifications, while providing technical service support to a client base that generated in excess of $2 million annually.

SENIOR POLYMER CHEMIST. Jones Laboratories, Whiting, SC (1994-1996). Tasked with streamlining chemical and polymer mixing processes, improving overall quality, and increasing production yields for this large manufacturer of pharmaceutical polymer products.
- Developed process improvements and modifications in chemical and polymer formulations which resulted in a 35% increase in production yield rates.
- Determined the cause of and resolved a serious product defect, forestalling a massive product recall which would have cost the company millions of dollars.

TECHNICAL SERVICE REPRESENTATIVE. Davis Synthetic Rubber & Latex Company, Mt. Troy, OH (1989-1993). Provided technical assistance to manufacturing customers who purchased Davis plantation latex.
- Averted an impending lawsuit which could have cost Davis hundreds of thousands of dollars, by designing and testing evaluations at the customer's facility to demonstrate that the customer's product defects were not a result of defective latex supplied by Davis.

ASSISTANT TECHNICAL MANAGER. Universal Specialties, Inc., Marion, OH (1987-1989). Responsible for chemical inventory control, formulation of polymer products, and ensuring that all needed materials were provided daily to keep production lines running at optimum levels for this facility which produced 3 million specialty advertising balloons daily.
- Created a new line of elastic inks used for printing onto specialty advertising balloons.
- Developed an impermeable barrier coating for the inside of specialty advertising balloons that retained helium for up to 7 days rather than the normal 8 to 12 hours.

PERSONAL　　Excellent personal and professional references are available upon request.

Date

Exact Name of Person
Exact Title
Exact Name of Company
Address
City, State, Zip Code

SENIOR QUALITY ENGINEER

Dear Exact Name of Person (or Dear Sir or Madam, if answering a blind ad):

With the enclosed resume, I would like to acquaint you with my exceptional skills and years of experience as an industrial and quality engineer with a solid background in manufacturing, quality assurance, and project management.

As you will see from my resume, I have worked at the same facility since before Allied Industries took over the operation from Monarch, Inc. In my years at this plant, my loyalty to the company and outstanding problem-solving skills, strong personal initiative, and extensive knowledge of all phases of industrial , manufacturing, and quality engineering have allowed me to progress into positions of increasing responsibility.

As Senior Quality Engineer, I have been responsible for increasing first-pass yield of a complex manual assembly from 3% to 56%, exceeding the company objective six months before the projected deadline to meet that goal. I served on the Certification Committee that achieved ISO 9002 certification for the facility, and I have worked hard to ensure increased productivity by increasing awareness of initial quality, reducing rework and warranty cost by more than 50%.

I have earned a Master of Business Administration degree and also possess a Bachelor of Science in Electrical Engineering. I have also supplemented my degree programs with graduate-level courses on planning, scheduling, and inventory control.

If your organization could benefit from the services of a talented and self-motivated industrial, electrical, or manufacturing engineer, I hope you will contact me. I assure you that I have an excellent reputation as a loyal and dedicated worker, and would quickly become a strong asset to your operation.

Sincerely,

Irving B. Dellon

IRVING B. DELLON

1110½ Hay Street, Fayetteville, NC 28305　　•　　preppub@aol.com　　•　　(910) 483-6611

OBJECTIVE　　To benefit an organization that can use an experienced, self-motivated, and educated quality and industrial engineer with and a background in manufacturing and project management.

EDUCATION　　**MBA in General Management,** Kansas State University, Lawrence, KS, 1997.
Bachelor of Science in Electrical Engineering, 1984.
Graduate-level course on Production planning, scheduling, and inventory control, Kansas State University, Lawrence, KS, 1989.

EXPERIENCE　　**SENIOR QUALITY & MANUFACTURING ENGINEER.** Allied Industries (formerly Monarch, Inc.), Lawrence, KS (1990-present). Started with Monarch, Inc. as a Manufacturing Engineer; became Senior Manufacturing Engineer, a job title that was changed to Senior Quality Engineer after Allied Industries took over the plant in 1995.

- Interacted with Original Equipment Manufacturer (OEM) customers, manufacturing and production departments to deliver high-quality products according to customer specifications.
- Increased first-pass yield of a complex manual assembly and wiring operation from 3% to 56% in a 15-month period. Company objective was to achieve 55% by the end of 2001; achieved this goal by June of 2000.
- Raised productivity by increasing quality awareness; reduced rework and warranty cost by more than 50%.
- Served on the plant's ISO Certification Committee; facility was awarded ISO 9002 certification.
- Created a new layout for the production line to reduce inventory and transfer the manufacturing process into a "just in time" process.
- Completed hazardous waste management projects and waste minimization projects to comply with EPA, SARA, and OSHA regulations; coordinated UL activities and procedures.

Quality Control: Used the following quality control principles in my position as Quality Engineer:
- Apply statistical process control in fabrication, assembly and finishing operations. Design and process FMEA. Quality audits of products and process. Establish and monitor quality control programs. Team leader and facilitator of corrective action and continuous cycle time improvement teams. Plan and implement ISO 9001 and 9002 quality system, periodic audit, and document control. Implement OEM specific Customer requirements.

Manufacturing/Industrial Engineering: Used the following manufacturing and industrial engineering processes and principles in my position as a Manufacturing/Industrial Engineer.
- JIT system of manufacturing, which includes:

Standardization of designs, processes, and equipment	Group technology
Demand flow technology in the assembly process	KANBAN inventory control
Powder paint system evaluation and implementation	CIM/Cell Technology

General Manufacturing/Industrial: Apply the following techniques and principles:
- Implement new products and designs into manufacturing
- Resolve manufacturing problems
- Provide technical support in assembly and fabrication area
- Run computer simulations of new methods and layouts
- Implemented new copper manufacturing cell and welding booth

PERSONAL　　Outstanding personal and professional references are available upon request.

CAREER CHANGE

Date

Exact Name of Person
Exact Title
Exact Name of Company
Address
City, State, Zip

Dear Exact Name of Person (or Dear Sir or Madam if answering a blind ad):

With the enclosed resume, I would like to introduce you to an educated, meticulous professional with excellent communication and organizational skills.

I am currently excelling in a rigorous Mechanical Engineering degree program while working part-time to finance my education. My academic excellence has earned me a position on the Dean's List for the last two semesters, and I will receive my Associate's degree in 2003. I have already completed a number of courses in Computer-Aided Drafting and the operation of related software, including: Technical Drafting 1 and II, AutoCAD 1 and II, CAD/CAM (using AutoCAD R12 and R13), and Drafting Design I (using AutoCAD R13 and R14). I have also taken a course on Pro-Engineer, which is a design and production program used to automate the mechanical development of a product from conceptual design through production.

In previous experience, I worked as a Surgical Technologist, providing operating room support and assistance in surgical procedures from appendectomies to open heart surgery. I gained experience in the use of new instruments, equipment, and procedures as well as in integrating new technologies with the existing equipment and procedures already in use. Prior to my medical career, I served my country in the U.S. Air Force, most recently as an Air Cargo Loading Supervisor and Air Evacuation Medical Specialist. The attention to detail and problem-solving ability required in these positions, as well as my education in Mechanical Engineering, will make me a valuable asset to your organization.

If you can use a self-motivated, meticulous computer-aided drafting professional with excellent communication and organizational skills and a growing knowledge of CAD and related software, I look forward to hearing from you soon to arrange a time when we might meet. I can provide outstanding personal and professional references.

Sincerely,

Natalie Bunce

NATALIE BUNCE

1110½ Hay Street, Fayetteville, NC 28305　•　preppub@aol.com　•　(910) 483-6611

OBJECTIVE　　To benefit an organization that can use an educated, meticulous computer-aided drafting professional with excellent communication and organizational skills who offers a background in medical, surgical, and logistics environments requiring careful attention to detail.

EDUCATION　　Completing an **Associate degree** program in **Mechanical Engineering**, Central Carolina Community College, Sanford, WI; will receive degree 2003.
- Made the Dean's list for the last two semesters.

Have completed the following courses directly related to Computer-Aided Drafting: Technical Drafting I, Technical Drafting II, AutoCAD I, AutoCAD II, CAD/CAM (using AutoCAD R12 and R13), and Drafting Design I (using AutoCAD R13 and R14),.

Graduated from the Surgical Technology Program, Sampson Community College, Madison, WI, 1990.

EXPERIENCE　　**MECHANICAL ENGINEERING STUDENT.** Sanford Community College, Sanford, WI (2001-present). Currently excelling in a rigorous degree program while working part-time to finance my education.
- During my final four semesters of this degree program, I will be embarking upon four-month assignments in four different manufacturing plants.

CASHIER. Etna Snack Mart, Carthage, WI (2000-present). Perform a variety of customer service, cashier, stocking, and shelving duties while completing my college degree.

SURGICAL TECHNICIAN. Cape Hope Medical Center, Madison, WI (1994-2001). Served as a member of the surgical team in this busy hospital environment.
- Assisted the surgeon in the performance of surgical procedures.
- Prepared operating room for surgeries, ensuring that all necessary supplies and equipment were available; broke down surgical cases after procedures were completed.
- Restocked surgeries and prepared case carts for the next day's surgical cases.
- Cleaned, disinfected, and performed sterilization procedures on surgical instruments and equipment.

SURGICAL ASSISTANT. Valley Medical Surgical Clinic, P.A., Franklin, TX (1992-1994). Provided the doctor with support and assistance in the performance of in-office and hospital surgical procedures.
- Coordinated and managed patient scheduling for office and hospital surgical procedures.
- Updated and maintained patient's medical records, ensuring that charts and files were complete and accurate.
- Performed sterilization procedures on surgical instruments and equipment.

Highlights of earlier experience: proudly served my country in the U.S. Air Force.
AIRCRAFT CARGO SUPERVISOR. Charleston AFB, Charleston, SC (1990-1992). Exercised careful planning and attention to detail in calculating the weights and balances of aircraft cargo and/or passengers to be placed on the aircraft; these calculations were used by the flight crew to prepare the aircraft for flight. Oversaw the configuration and set-up of aircraft for Emergency Medical Evacuation.
- Supervised a ground loading crew of eight employees loading and unloading aircraft.

PERSONAL　　Outstanding personal and professional references are available upon request.

Date

Exact Name of Person
Exact Title
Exact Name of Company
Address
City, State, Zip

TELECOMMUNICATIONS SUPERVISOR

Dear Exact Name of Person (or Dear Sir or Madam if answering a blind ad):

With the enclosed resume, I would like to make you aware of my background as an experienced manager who offers a reputation as an articulate communicator, talented leader, and trainer who can be counted on to achieve results while building productive teams.

As you will see, I earned my bachelor's degree from Hoisington State University in Hoisington and was the recipient of a prestigious scholarship. Presently excelling as a Production Supervisor for a textile company, I supervise approximately 30 employees with an emphasis on quality control, high productivity, and morale. I have earned the respect and loyalty of management, supervisory, and subordinate personnel for my professionalism and persistence in demanding high standards for myself and motivating others to set their own goals and standards to higher levels.

Although I am highly regarded by my present employer and can provide excellent personal and professional references at the appropriate time, I am interested in exploring career opportunities in a field where my personality and strong customer service orientation would be more effectively utilized. I would appreciate your keeping my inquiry confidential until after we have had the chance to speak in person.

If you can use an articulate professional who offers excellent communication and organizational skills, as well as experience in management and customer service, I hope you will contact me to suggest a time when we might meet to discuss your needs. I can assure you in advance that I could rapidly become an asset to your organization.

Sincerely,

Simon Peters

SIMON PETERS

1110½ Hay Street, Fayetteville, NC 28305 • preppub@aol.com • (910) 483-6611

OBJECTIVE   To contribute through my managerial skills and experience to an organization that can benefit from my expertise in interpersonal communications, ability to motivate and train others, eye for detail, and talent for planning and carrying out corporate goals.

EDUCATION   B.S. degree, Hoisington State University, Hoisington, WA; concentration in **Textile and Apparel Manufacturing Management,** 1995.
- Was awarded a prestigious Charles Hart Memorial Scholarship.

COMPUTERS   Offer the ability to quickly and easily master new software and operating programs such as the following:

    Microsoft Word, Excel, Access, PowerPoint, Works, Explorer, and Money

Windows	Lotus cc:Mail and Notes
WordPerfect	Netscape Navigator
Norton Antivirus	First Aid
QuattroPro	OS/2 Warp

EXPERIENCE   **PRODUCTION SUPERVISOR.** Bradley Yarn, Bradley, SC (2002-present). Supervise approximately 30 employees with the responsibility for ensuring that productivity and attendance policies and standards are met.
- Provide oversight for the quality control requirements and standards by completing a system of audits and checks of all stages of the production process.
- Train new employees as well as reinforcing the training of existing personnel in order to improve procedures and bring about increases in product quality as well as in staff performance and efficiency levels.
- Was credited with initiating changes which resulted in improving the handling of "off-quality" or inferior products which had reached the packaging stage.
- Am earning the respect of my subordinates, peers, and superiors and the loyalty of my subordinates for my professionalism and effective leadership style.
- Apply my creative abilities while assisting in new product development for the benefit of existing and potential future customers.
- Provide leadership and guidance while answering questions, explaining various stages of the manufacturing process, and discussing objectives with supervisory and managerial personnel.

DEPARTMENTAL SUPERVISOR. Corey Denim, Erwin, WA (1995-02). Became known for my innovative ideas and ability to find ways to increase productivity and efficiency while overseeing the performance of approximately 40 employees.
- Trained and then supervised employees in the winding and warping stage of the manufacturing process.
- Managed operational areas which included preparing payroll figures and conducting inventory.
- Oversaw the quality control and safety inspection activities.
- Developed and implemented a production tracking program through which employees were motivated and morale improved, resulting in a decrease in absenteeism.

PERSONAL   Excel in molding individuals into teams which can be counted on to achieve high standards of productivity and efficiency. Am a detail-oriented and well-organized professional.

Date

Mr. Ray Smith
Technical Team Leader
Matthews Tire Company
54670 Fifth Street
Parnassus, NY

Dear Mr. Smith:

With the enclosed resume describing my experience and skills, I would like to formally initiate the process of being considered for a position within the Quality Assurance Department.

As you will see from my resume, I offer a track record of distinguished service within the Matthews organization which I have served as a Tire Builder, Area Manager, Labor Trainer, and Builder/Sorter. I am proud that I have helped to achieve some of the highest production records within the organization, and I have played a role in hiring and training personnel who are today some of Matthew's most valuable employees.

Throughout my personal life, I have demonstrated a drive to excel in all I take on. Prior to my employment at Matthews, I served my country briefly as an enlisted soldier and rose to E-5 in under two years, a nearly unheard-of accomplishment. As a youth, I was encouraged to skip the eighth grade because of academic excellence and went on to graduate from Cleveland Vocational High School and O'Fallon Technical School where I specialized in Commercial Sheet Metal Pattern Drafting. With my formal training in pattern drafting, I became accustomed early in life to working within close tolerances.

At Matthews, I have earned the respect of my supervisors and peers, and, I have also earned a reputation as a perfectionist, because I always take the attitude that a job should be done right the first time.

I strongly believe I could make valuable contributions to quality assurance within the Matthews organization. With a reputation as a resourceful and creative individual, I am confident that I would be highly effective in implementing new ideas, solving stubborn problems, and identifying new opportunities for improved safety, quality, and cost control.

Please let me know if you would like me to make myself available for a personal interview to discuss the possibility of my contributing to Matthews in some position related to quality assurance.

Sincerely,

Keith M. Boulder

KEITH M. BOULDER

1110½ Hay Street, Fayetteville, NC 28305   •   preppub@aol.com   •   (910) 483-6611

OBJECTIVE

To continue my track record of contributions to Matthews Company by combining my strong interest in quality assurance and quality control, my understanding of the company's manufacturing policies and needs, as well as my cross-training in multiple functional areas.

EDUCATION

Completed college courses, Parnassus Technical Community College, Parnassus, NY, 1988-present.

While in military service, completed courses related to supervision and leadership, maintenance and quality control, and other areas.

Graduated from Cleveland Vocational High School and O'Fallon Technical School specializing in Commercial Sheet Metal Pattern Drafting, 1975.

EXPERIENCE

Have contributed to the Matthews Tire Company, Parnassus, NY while excelling in the following positions (1982-present):

TIRE BUILDER. (1994-present). Proudly played a key role in achieving numerous plant records for production, control of waste, and safety while building R3 type machinery.

Am versatile and cross-trained with the ability to expertly perform a variety of jobs related to the following:

R-1	R-1 RLT BBR-2 ISR-2	R-2
code changes	production service	sorting/labeling

AREA MANAGER. (1989-94). As a Vacation Replacement Area Manager, managed activities in the Tire Room for 1st stage and 2nd stage while section managers were out; worked on various shifts on constantly changing schedules.
- Motivated the builders who worked for me to set new historic production records.
- Achieved section builds that were the highest ever attained at that time.

LABOR TRAINER. (1988-89). During this period, hired and trained people who have turned into some of Kelly's most outstanding tire builders; made recommendations about hiring or not hiring personnel and then trained new employees.
- Gained valuable insights into the qualities and skills needed by efficient tire builders.

BUILDER/SORTER. (1982-88). Learned to build R-1 type tires; was cross-trained to sort tires; and also learned to build ISR-2s.

Other experience:

MAINTENANCE MECHANIC. Worfield, MA (1981-82). As one of eight mechanics on the third shift, worked with new machinery and helped to field the then-new "WEEFAC" printer.

ASSISTANT MANAGER. Jansen Stores, Worfield, MA (1981-82). Supervised up to 20 employees while controlling inventory, planning and implementing sales promotions, and handling timekeeping for employee wages. Responsible for implementing the bar code system.

GENERAL MANAGER. U.S. Army, locations worldwide (1977-81). Promoted to E-5 in under two years – an unusual accomplishment; took pride in serving my country.

PERSONAL

Proficient in operating a wide range of equipment including micrometers, dial gauges, depth gauges, calipers, gas and electric trucks, forklifts, band saws, drill presses, sanders, routers, planers, jointers, lathes, and band/table/radial arm saws.

Date

Mr. Ray Smith
Technical Team Leader
Matthews Tire Company
54670 Fifth Street
Parnassus, NY

TOOL & DIE MAKER   Dear Mr. Smith:

With the enclosed resume describing my experience and skills, I would like to make you aware of my interest in seeking employment as a Tool & Die Maker.

As you will see from my resume, I have worked for only two organizations in my life as a Tool & Die Maker. For a major home furnishings manufacturer, I utilized my knowledge resourcefully as I invented several new items which the company patented. Subsequently in a milling environment, I have applied my expertise in helping the company resolve a wide variety of production and manufacturing problems.

I have recently relocated to your area and am seeking an organization that can benefit from my expert skills related to tool and die making. Please let me know if you would like me to make myself available for a personal interview to discuss the possibility of my contributing to your organization.

Sincerely,

Woodrow Forrest

WOODROW FORREST

1110½ Hay Street, Fayetteville, NC 28305 • preppub@aol.com • (910) 483-6611

OBJECTIVE

To offer my technical and natural mechanical skills to an organization that can use a self-motivated professional who possesses a reputation for reliability, attention to detail, and the ability to relate to and get along well with others.

EDUCATION & TRAINING

Graduated from Wyoming Technical Community College: studied subjects including:

mathematics, including trigonometry	physics
machine shop theory and application	tool and die making
blueprint reading	electricity

Completed two years of study at Crossington State University in pursuit of B.S. in Mathematics.
Graduated from Magnolia High School, Tucson, AZ.

CERTIFICATION

Am certified as a Journeyman Tool and Die Maker, 1976-present.

EXPERIENCE

TOOL AND DIE MAKER. King Co., Tucson, AZ (1994-present). As a Tool and Die Maker, created custom dies according to engineering specifications.

- Operated a wide variety of standard and specialized manufacturing equipment including:

Wire EDM	Drilll Presses
Lathes	Dial Calipers
Pipe Threaders	Comparator
Shaper Machines	Depth Micrometers
Grinders: Blanchard, OD, ID, and Centerless	I.D. Micrometers
Band Saws	Press Breaks
Height Gauges	Torque Tools
Rockwell Hardness Tester	Honing and Boring Equipment
Punch Press	Milling Machines
Measuring Machine	

- Through training and experience, became familiar with welding and metal fabrication; hardening and quenching of tool steels; tempering, carbonizing, and annealing.

- Became skilled in the design, construction, and repair of jigs, fixtures, and dies.

- Have been recognized on numerous occasions for my natural mechanical abilities.

TOOL AND DIE MAKER. Mountain Home Manufacturing Co., Lawson, AZ (1976-1994). Worked as a Tool & Die Maker for a major manufacturer of home furnishings and fixtures; created several new products which the company patented and which vastly improved productivity.

Highlights of other experience: In addition to my years of experience as a Tool and Die Maker, served in the U.S. Army for three years.

AFFILIATION

Am a Life Member of VFW Post 230.

PERSONAL

Have a strong interest in science and technology. Am a team player who gets along well with others. Highly creative problem-solver who has frequently developed new tools which are tailored to specific industrial issues. Excellent references on request.

Date

Mr. Ray Smith
Technical Team Leader
Matthews Tire Company
54670 Fifth Street
Parnassus, NY

Dear Mr. Smith:

With the enclosed resume, I would like to make you aware of my interest in exploring employment opportunities with your organization.

As you will see from my resume, I most recently have worked in manufacturing environments. In my current job the company depends on me as its Traffic Specialist, which makes me responsible for organizing shipments of manufactured telecommunications products to customers all over the east coast. In my previous position, I worked for a company which manufactured bottles used by major soft drink companies, and I was in charge of assuring that major customers received on-time delivery of their orders.

In both the positions above I made significant contributions to profitability and efficiency through my ability to solve problems resourcefully. I am well known for my intense dedication to the highest standards of safety, quality, and cost control.

Prior to entering the manufacturing industry, I excelled as General Manager of a country club, where I was responsible for supervising up to 40 employees. I offer highly refined supervisory and communication skills.

If you can use a dedicated professional with a sincere desire to make enduring contributions to the bottom line, I hope you will contact me to suggest a time when we might discuss your current and future needs and how I might serve them.

Sincerely,

Liana Rasco

LIANA RASCO

1110½ Hay Street, Fayetteville, NC 28305 • preppub@aol.com • (910) 483-6611

OBJECTIVE	To benefit an organization that can use a motivated professional with experience in the management of human and physical resources, interviewing and hiring, training and staff development who also offers exceptional data entry skills.
EXPERIENCE	**TRAFFIC SPECIALIST & MANUFACTURING LIAISON.** Westfall Manufacturing Center, Atlanta, GA (2000-present). Started with Westfall working part-time in Data Entry and then quickly advanced, first to a full-time position, and then to the Traffic Department, where I am currently excelling in handling all aspects of load scheduling for this busy regional manufacturer of telecommunications devices.

- Schedule all loads to be dropped and assist the gate by locating and providing load numbers when the driver doesn't have a load number.
- Sign all freight bills, and update receivers by keying additional information from the freight bills into the computer.
- Enter all Void To Return (VTR) items into the system, removing merchandise that has been slotted in the wrong physical location so that it can be reentered into the computer and slotted correctly.
- Generate and reconcile the 4631 & 4632 reports; check the physical warehouse to verify whether or not stock has been slotted, then ensure that receivers for merchandise that is already slotted are keyed as complete.

PACKAGING COORDINATOR. Morgan Bottling Company, Morgan, GA (1995-2000). For a company which manufactured bottles used by major soft drink makers, coordinated all aspects of the packaging, loading, shipping, and delivery of products to customers all over the east coast.

- Accepted customer orders for delivery on the next business day from bulk accounts drivers, then keyed these orders into the system to generate loading cards.
- Sorted printed loading cards, organizing them according to the order in which the deliveries were to be made. Contacted customers in order to schedule delivery times; provided exceptional customer service to all vendors.

DATA CONVERSION OPERATOR. United States Postal Service, Atlanta, GA (1990-1995). Provided data entry services at this large regional distribution center, encoding mail for Atlanta, Macon, and Savannah plants through the use of computer-generated images.

- Maintained a 98% accuracy rate while keying more than 1,000 pieces of mail per hour; facility goal is 750 pieces per hour.

GENERAL MANAGER. Payne Country Club, Payne, GA (1988-1990). Oversaw all operational aspects, including human resources, purchasing, events coordination, and bookkeeping for this local country club.

- Supervised 40 employees, including the kitchen staff, bartenders, and wait staff.
- Performed all bookkeeping functions, including accounts payable, accounts receivable, payroll, W-2s, income tax reports, and ABC reports.
- Conducted periodic employee appraisals and wrote weekly employee schedules.
- Interviewed, hired, and trained all new employees.
- Booked parties and scheduled special events; was responsible for purchasing.

EDUCATION	**Associate's** degree in **Accounting**, Los Angeles City College, Los Angeles, CA, 1988.
PERSONAL	Excellent personal and professional references are available upon request.

Date

Exact Name of Person
Exact Title
Exact Name of Company
Address
City, State, Zip

USDA FOOD INSPECTOR, FOOD MANUFACTURING FACILITY

Dear Exact Name of Person (or Dear Sir or Madam if answering a blind ad):

With the enclosed resume, I would like to introduce you to my background as a highly trained professional whose exceptional planning, organizational, and analytical skills have been proven in challenging food inspection positions in processing plant environments.

As you will see from my resume, I have recently been excelling as Food Inspector for the Food Safety Inspection Service of the USDA at the world's largest pork processing facility. I have become very familiar with food processing operational policies and procedures, and have worked with facility management and other USDA officials in developing HACCP and SSOP policies.

I have completed a number of USDA training courses related to food inspection. These included training in the Hazard Analysis Critical Control Point (HACCP) Program and Workplace Lockout/Tagout Awareness, Basic Livestock Slaughter Inspection, and Introduction to Civil Rights.

In a previous position with the U.S. Department of Agriculture (U.S.D.A.), I worked as a commissary Food Inspector at Fort Rucker, AL. Throughout my career in Food Inspection, I have demonstrated exceptional attention to detail and have been cited for my keen observation as well as for error-free accuracy of documentation.

If you can use a highly skilled professional with exceptional analytical skills and the ability to quickly master and apply complex rules and regulations, I hope you will welcome my call soon when I try to arrange a brief meeting to discuss your goals and how my background might serve your needs. I can provide outstanding references at the appropriate time.

Sincerely,

Gerald A. Knight

GERALD A. KNIGHT

1110½ Hay Street, Fayetteville, NC 28305 • preppub@aol.com • (910) 483-6611

OBJECTIVE

To benefit an organization that can use an experienced young professional with exceptional organizational and analytical skills who offers a background in the inspection, documentation, and troubleshooting of products and programs in food processing environments.

EDUCATION

Completed one year toward Associate of Science in Biology, Gulf Coast Community College. Earned a two-year vocational certificate in Precision Machining, Haney Vocational College, Panama City, FL, 1992.

Completed a number of military and USDA training courses related to food inspection, including: Hazard Analysis Critical Control Point (HACCP) Program, 24 hours, 1997; Advanced Food Inspection Preparatory Course, 24 hours, 1996; and Basic Food Inspection, U.S. Academy of Health Sciences, 8 weeks, 1995.

CERTIFICATIONS

Hazard Analysis Critical Control Point (HACCP) certification, 1997.

Certified in Community CPR (Adult, Child, and Infant), scheduled to renew certification 2002.

EXPERIENCE

USDA FOOD INSPECTOR. Troy Packing, Troy, NC (2000-present). Conduct regular inspections of plant facilities and equipment, raw materials, and product in various stages of processing, to ensure compliance with USDA and federal, state, and local rules, regulations.

- Assist with the development and implementation of the facility's Hazard Analysis and Critical Control Points (HACCP) program. Perform preoperative inspections and monitor operational sanitation in all departments, verifying adherence to the facility's Sanitation Standard Operating Procedures (SSOP).
- Oversee quality control procedures for the facility, evaluating plant logs and verification tests to ensure that the operation strictly adheres to USDA standards.
- Perform net weight checks, formulations, pumping checks, and other tests to ensure compliance with policies, procedures, and regulations of processed meat inspection.
- Observe packaging and labeling of variety meats, chits and casings, etc., ensuring accuracy of labeling data and compliance with regulations and applicable standards.

FOOD & SANITATION INSPECTOR. U.S.D.A., Fort Rucker, AL (1995-2000). Provided a wide range of food safety and inspection services to the Fort Rucker Commissary.

- Inspected incoming shipments of produce, meats, poultry, and dairy products, checking for proper temperature and monitoring compliance with quality assurance standards.
- Conducted sanitation inspections of the warehouse and dining facilities on a daily basis, to ensure that storage areas comply with federal, military, and USDA regulations.
- Operated food inspection equipment, including various types of laboratory equipment.

Highlights of earlier experience:

APPRENTICE OPTICIAN, LAB TECHNICIAN, and **SALES ASSOCIATE.** Various locations, Panama City, FL. Assisted customers with the selection, purchase, and fitting of new eyewear, as well as grinding lenses and installing them in frames.

SALES ASSOCIATE. Barton Shoes, Panama City, FL. Performed a wide range of sales, customer service, and administrative tasks for a branch of the national shoe retailer.

AFFILIATIONS

Nominated to receive a 2001 **Distinguished Service to Special Olympics Award** for Outstanding Adult Volunteers – Special Olympics' highest honor.

PERSONAL

Excellent personal and professional references are available upon request.

Exact Name of Person
Exact Title
Exact Name of Company
Address
City, State, Zip

**VICE PRESIDENT OF
MANUFACTURING**

Dear Exact Name of Person (or Dear Sir or Madam if answering a blind ad):

Can you use a highly skilled executive with the proven ability to solve problems, develop new business opportunities, and manage complex manufacturing operations for maximum profitability and customer satisfaction?

In my current position as Vice President of Manufacturing, I am providing management services to a company which manufactures abrasive products. I played a key role in boosting profitability so that the company became an attractive acquisition target. Although I have been offered a key management position on the team of the acquiring company, I have decided to seek employment elsewhere.

In my previous position, I rose to the position of President of a company which manufactured grinding wheels and ceramic filters. I oversaw every aspect of internal operations and external relationships while guiding the company in producing $5 million in sales with 75 employees. During my tenure as President, I turned around a negative cash flow situation through an aggressive strategy which reduced costs while extending terms with vendors. I offer a proven ability to restore profitability to ailing operations while designing efficient new processes, tools, and physical facilities.

If you can use an astute strategist who has the ability to see "the big picture" while meticulously managing the details, I would enjoy an opportunity to meet with you to discuss your needs. I can provide outstanding references at the appropriate time.

Sincerely,

Paul H. Wordsworth

PAUL H. WORDSWORTH

1110½ Hay Street, Fayetteville, NC 28305   •   preppub@aol.com   •   (910) 483-6611

OBJECTIVE

To contribute to an organization that can use a highly resourceful manager who offers a proven "track record" of restoring profitability to ailing operations and troubleshooting stubborn productivity and manufacturing problems, as well as designing new processes, tools, and physical facilities that improve efficiency and output.

EXPERIENCE

VICE PRESIDENT OF MANUFACTURING. Eastern Abrasives Products Company, Aberdeen, NJ (2000-present). After the company was sold, my services were retained on a contract basis; manage all plant operations including maintenance and upkeep of the equipment, buildings, and grounds for this busy manufacturing company

- Develop operations/production schedules, determining staffing needs, machine and equipment requirements, tooling needs and development methods, and time standards.
- Plan and implement programs and procedures to ensure compliance with OSHA and EPA regulations and guidelines regarding plant safety and materials handling.
- Direct research and development projects for new products and equipment.
- Manage and coordinate the purchasing of raw materials, equipment, supplies, and services, including procurement of capital equipment and negotiation of contracts.

PRESIDENT. Quality Manufacturing Company, Trenton, NJ (1984-1999). Reported to a board of directors while managing operations of a company which manufactured grinding wheels and ceramic filters; became president in 1987 after excelling in jobs as plant engineer and plant manager.

- After taking over as president of a company which had a negative cash flow in 1985, aggressively reduced costs while extending terms with vendors, a strategy which produced a positive cash flow in less than two years.
- Developed or refined written procedures in these various operational areas in order to assure that all company procedures "on the ground floor" were consistent with strategic goals for short-term profitability and long-term growth:

  sales techniques   engineering purchasing process   quality control
  inventory control   compliance with safety, OSHA, EPA   preventive maintenance

- Oversaw every aspect of internal operations and external relationships for a company with $5 million in sales and up to 75 employees.
- As plant **manager** from 1985-87, improved overall output by 15% and, through new equipment which I designed and built, increased one product line by 1000%.
- As plant **engineer** from 1984-85, developed engineering and maintenance controls, developed and built new equipment, and reorganized manufacturing processes with the net result that operating efficiencies improved by 30%.

PRODUCTION MANAGER & PLANT ENGINEERING MAINTENANCE MANAGER. Glover & Son, Athens, PA (1979-84). Began with this auto-building company as a Production Foreman and Maintenance Foreman overseeing 45 employees and responsible for a $1.5 million profit center; promoted to oversee a $6 million profit center with up to 150 employees working in a union shop.

EDUCATION

Completed extensive college-level and executive development course work sponsored by numerous industry groups and associations as well as my employers.

PERSONAL

Believe that the kind of creativity and vision I possess give me the ability as a CEO to formulate strategy and anticipate problems before they occur. Am known for my integrity, compassion, and desire to work toward perfection..

Date

Rita Smith
Personnel Manager
Buy-Mart Distribution Center
5557 Dune Drive
Lamont, MS

**WAREHOUSE
ACCOUNTABILITY
SPECIALIST**

Dear Ms. Smith:

I would appreciate an opportunity to talk with you soon about how I could contribute to your organization through my experience and knowledge as well as through my strong interest in the field of warehouse operations and manufacturing support.

As you will see from my enclosed resume, I am presently working as a Warehouse Accountability Specialist for a wood products company. In this job I provide assistance and support for both the shipping and receiving departments while checking pallets of finished products for the proper amounts, bin numbers, and serial numbers. My eye for detail allows me to contribute to the process which ultimately ensures that the customer receives the items he needs for his particular project.

In earlier jobs as a Warehouse Clerk/Retail Sales Clerk for a nonprofit organization and as a Telecommunications Operations Technician in the U.S. Army, I was also known as a reliable and detail-oriented individual. My years of military service taught me to take responsibility for my own actions and also to work together with others to achieve success as a team. I was entrusted with a Secret security clearance and worked on radios, telephones, and switchboard systems handling sensitive information.

If you can use an experienced professional who offers a strong desire to succeed and willingness to work hard to achieve individual and corporate success, please contact me to suggest a time when we might meet to discuss your needs. I can assure you in advance that I could rapidly become an asset to your organization.

Sincerely,

Carol Ann Guest

CAROL ANN GUEST

1110½ Hay Street, Fayetteville, NC 28305 • preppub@aol.com • (910) 483-6611

OBJECTIVE
To contribute through a combination of skills and experience in warehouse operations and communications operations as well as my reputation as a detail-oriented professional known for versatility and dedication to providing support services.

EDUCATION
Completed nearly three years of college course work in General Studies, Lamont Technical Community College and Austin Peay Community College, Lamont, MS and Ft. Campbell, KY. Finished one year of course work towards a Dental Laboratory Technician certification at McCarries School of Health & Science Technology, Philadelphia, PA, 1996.

TRAINING
Completed a 10-week training program for communications specialists.

SPECIAL SKILLS
Offer knowledge related to teletype and COMSEC (communications security) equipment operation, installation, and troubleshooting.
Was entrusted with a **Secret** security clearance.

EXPERIENCE
WAREHOUSE ACCOUNTABILITY SPECIALIST. Everly Brothers, Lamont, MS (2000-present). Ensure wood products have been cut to proper lengths and that the correct number of items are bundled together as they arrive in the shipping department and then assist in the preparation and packaging of items to be shipped.
- Check each pallet of wood as it arrives and determine if amounts are correct and if the items are marked with the proper bin and serial numbers.
- Assist in both the shipping and receiving departments while applying my eye for detail and ensuring proper procedures are being followed at all stages.

WAREHOUSE CLERK & RETAIL SALES CLERK. Salvation Army, Lamont, MS (1997-99). Handled multiple duties which included sorting incoming donations and placing them in bins for shipment to different stores, loading and unloading trucks, and stocking items in the store.
- Chosen for my willingness to accept responsibility and for displaying organizational skills, was entrusted with opening and closing the store.
- Completed paperwork including receipts for customers to use to claim tax deductions.

TELECOMMUNICATIONS OPERATIONS TECHNICIAN. U.S. Army, Ft. Campbell, KY (1992-97). Became known as an adaptable young professional while contributing my skills related to the installation and operation of radios, switchboards, and telephones.
- As a unit-level communications maintainer, completed troubleshooting on radio systems, repaired telephones, and installed WD-1 wire for the telephone systems.
- Ran telephone lines which were then connected to the switchboard in addition to operating a 24-line switchboard.
- Prepared work orders for all types of equipment under my control.
- Installed field antennas in support of the radio systems.
- Operated the PRC-77 field phone switchboard system which provided secure communications links as well as single-channel LOS (line-of-sight) radios.
- Became skilled in the operation, installation, troubleshooting, and maintenance of equipment and systems including PRC-127, VIC-3, KY-57, KYK-13, and SINGARS.

PERSONAL
Am knowledgeable of warehouse operations and of providing data processing support. Received the National Defense Service Medal and a Good Conduct Medal for my professionalism.

CAREER CHANGE

Date

Director of Personnel
City of Chesterfield
Grayson Hall, Suite 123
Chesterfield, VT 98231

WAREHOUSE MANAGER

This warehouse manager seeks a career change into the firefighting field.

Dear Sir or Madam:

With the enclosed resume, I would like to formally initiate the process of becoming considered for a job as a Fireman within your organization.

As you will see when you read my resume, I have excelled in every job I have ever taken on. Currently I am a member of the management team for one of the area's largest and oldest furniture stores, and I have become skilled at problem solving and decision making. I began with the company in a part-time job, was hired full-time after one week, and have been promoted to increasing responsibilities because of my proven ability to make sound decisions under pressure.

While serving my country in the U.S. Army, I was promoted ahead of my peers to a job as Telecommunications Center Operator and earned numerous commendations for my management ability and technical skills. I was praised on numerous occasions for my ability to "think on my feet" and to remain calm and make prudent decisions under stressful circumstances. I was entrusted with a Secret NAC security clearance.

Throughout my life, I have been known as a highly motivated self starter with a strong drive to excel in all I do. Even in high school, I was on the All-Star baseball team and was elected Captain of the football team in my senior year.

I am sending you my resume because it is my strong desire to make a career in the firefighting field, and I am willing to start in an entry-level position and prove myself. I am always seeking new ways in which to improve my skills and increase my knowledge; for example, I am learning Spanish in my spare time because I feel Spanish language skills will be an asset in any field with our growing Hispanic population. I can assure you that I would bring that same level of self motivation to firefighting as a career field, and I hope you will give me an opportunity to show you in person that I am a dependable young individual who could become a valuable part of your organization.

I hope you will contact me to suggest a time when we might meet to discuss your needs and how I might serve them. I can provide outstanding personal and professional references. Thank you in advance for whatever consideration and time you can give me in my goal of becoming a professional firefighter.

Sincerely,

Jorge Perez

JORGE PEREZ

1110½ Hay Street, Fayetteville, NC 28305 • preppub@aol.com • (910) 483-6611

OBJECTIVE	To contribute to an organization that can use a hard-working young professional in excellent physical condition who offers a proven ability to make prudent decisions under stressful conditions and within tight deadlines.
LANGUAGES	Working knowledge of Spanish and German; am highly motivated to better myself and master new skills, and am learning Spanish in my spare time.
EDUCATION	**College:** Completed two years of college course work concentrated in History and Liberal Arts, University of Maryland. **Military:** Excelled in more than a year of college-level training sponsored by the U.S. Army related to electronics and telecommunications, safety and quality control, and management. **High School:** Graduated from Jamestown High School, Jamestown, RI, 1989. • Was an **All-Star** Baseball player, **Captain** of the Football team in my senior year and a starter on the football team all three years of high school. **First Aid:** Obtained First Aid and CPR Certification through ROTC training.
EXPERIENCE	**WAREHOUSE MANAGER.** Fancy Furniture, Chesterfield, VT (1995-present). Began in a part-time position and was offered full-time employment after one week; worked in the warehouse and learned the "nuts and bolts" of warehouse operations while working my way up from warehouse worker to driver's helper; was selected as Assistant Warehouse Manager after eight months. • Supervise, train, and evaluate seven warehouse employees while also filling in for absent employees as needed; operate 24-foot truck and forklift. • Oversee security of a furniture inventory worth half a million dollars. • Have become skilled in problem solving and decision making while handling public relations and solving customer complaints; am now entrusted with the authority to make numerous management decisions independently. • Have refined my planning and organizational skills while earning a reputation as a prudent decision maker who thinks well on my feet and who excels in maximizing efficiency and productivity. **INDEPENDENT CONTRACT REPAIRMAN.** Bath and Kitchen Fixtures, Chesterfield, VT (1994-95). Increased new business accounts by 30% through my outstanding sales and customer service skills. • Traveled from store to store that sold bath and kitchen fixtures and provided personal demonstrations and testimonials of my repair work; accounts skyrocketed through my personal selling skills. **TELECOMMUNICATIONS CENTER OPERATOR.** U.S. Army, Ft. Bliss, TX (1989-93). Learned valuable work habits and acquired a disciplined approach to work while becoming promoted ahead of my peers to Telecommunications Center Operator; earned numerous commendations for my excellent coordinating and management skills. • Held a Secret NAC security clearance.
PERSONAL	Outstanding personal and professional references. Strong work ethic.

Date

TO: Diamond Corporation

With the enclosed resume, I would like to request that I be considered for the position of Distribution Assistant Supervisor. I am a flexible and adaptable individual and am to work any shift including second shift. I have worked with oil, filter, and rubber products of Diamond Corporation.

As you will see from my resume, I am extremely proficient with the CIM system. I began working for Diamond Manufacturing Company as a temporary worker through Hudson Personnel, and I am now employed as a permanent employee. I have become known for my strong attention to detail and I am regarded as an internal expert on the CIM system.

A licensed forklift operator, I also offer proven supervisory skills and an extensive management background. I previously worked as the Lead Person in the shipping department of another manufacturing company.

I am certain that I could make a valuable contribution to the distribution operations of the Diamond Corporation, and I hope you will permit me to formally interview for the position.

Yours sincerely,

Ray C. Abrams

RAY C. ABRAMS

1110½ Hay Street, Fayetteville, NC 28305   •   preppub@aol.com   •   (910) 483-6611

OBJECTIVE

I want to contribute to a company through my knowledge of warehouse operations and dispatching functions, as well as shipping and receiving.

SKILLS

Forklift: Skilled Forklift Operator
Computers: Knowledgeable of computers and skilled in warehouse applications.
- Responsible for calibrating scales and counters as well as operating the UPS computer.

EDUCATION

Waywright Technical Community College (WTCC), graduated from the program in commercial art and design, 1997.
- Named to President's List for academic excellence.
- Represented Waywright at the National Student Advertising Conference.
- 1995 Rising Star, two awards
- 1994-95 member of the Waywright American Advertising Federal Club.
- Waywright Alumni Association Member.

Extensive technical training and professional development courses sponsored by the U.S. Army related to supply management, inventory control, and distribution operations.

EXPERIENCE

MANUFACTURING ASSOCIATE. Diamond Manufacturing Company, Waywright, AR (2000-present). Responsible for shipping, receiving, picking, packing, stock keeping, and inventory to include delivery and bin-stocking material for a major manufacturer.
- Was commended for my ability to work in a fast-paced environment which utilizes computerized manufacturing, shipping, receiving, and picking processes.
- In preparation for an internal audit followed by an ISO Inspection, I rearranged and produced tags for all material in the warehouse while also writing procedures on shipping and packaging for several major manufacturers.
- Received six separate awards for perfect attendance, quality assurance results, high production levels, and lowest observed defects.
- Have learned to safely operate a variety of manufacturing machines used to manufacture oil filters and other automotive products.

PRODUCTION ATTENDANT. Area Services Corporation, Waywright, AR (1996-99). Responsible for ordering and shipping components to be assembled by Keene Production Company; served as **Lead Person, Shipping Department.**

TECHNICIAN. Arcade Amusement Center, Waywright, AR (1995). Diagnosed and repaired various video arcade games.

TACTICAL COMMUNICATIONS CHIEF. U.S. Army, Ft. Bragg, NC (1974-95). Was promoted ahead of my peers in a track record of advancement to jobs in which I excelled in handling complex technical responsibilities as well as challenging managerial duties.
- Planned, supervised, coordinated, and provided technical assistance in the installation, operation, management, and unit-level maintenance of radio, field wire, and switchboard communications systems.

PERSONAL

Can provide outstanding personal and professional references on request.

WELDER MECHANIC   Dear Sir or Madam:

Please accept this letter along with my resume as a formal indication of my interest in the maintenance position.

As you will see from my resume and application, I have extensive experience using the latest diagnostic test equipment and welding technology used for many mechanical needs. In addition, I offer a proven track record as a Welder Mechanic, a primary trouble-shooter, and a liaison with outside dealerships and vendors necessary for repairs on city equipment.

I hope you will contact me to suggest a time when we could meet to discuss your needs and goals and how I might help you. I can provide outstanding personal and professional references. Thank you in advance for your time.

Sincerely yours,

Thomas D. Moon

THOMAS D. MOON

1110½ Hay Street, Fayetteville, NC 28305 • preppub@aol.com • (910) 483-6611

OBJECTIVE   To contribute to Smith-Dale Tire Company as an experienced Welder Mechanic through my experience, strong interest, and mechanical abilities.

EXPERIENCE   **WELDER MECHANIC.** The City of Hayward, SC (1998-present). As a Welder Mechanic, I have extensive experience with various types of equipment.

- Because of my exceptional mechanical abilities and expertise, was *Promoted to Welder Mechanic, 1996.*
- Maintain and operate a wide range of equipment including tractors, industrial mowers, fire trucks, and heavy equipment; repair supply parts including cylinders, lines, valves, and pumps.
- Apply my problem-solving, decision-making, and analytical abilities when troubleshooting problems and rebuilding equipment within the hydraulic system.
- Offer expertise as a Welder and Fabricator; familiar with ARC, Mig and Tig welders.

FLEET MAINTENANCE AUTOMOTIVE TECHNICIAN II. The City of Hayward, SC (1996-1998). Within 30 days of beginning as an Automotive Technician II, was promoted and placed in the position of Lead Technician, and now work at the Master Technician level on both light and heavy vehicles.

- Assisted technicians with problem repairs; functioned as the Master Technician in his absence.
- Served as one of two primary troubleshooters on complex computer-controlled automobiles, heavy trucks, and other equipment; functioned as a primary liaison with outside dealerships and vendors to facilitate repairs on all types of equipment.

AUTOMOBILE MECHANIC. Mitchell's Auto, Inc., Dolan, SC (1995-96). Performed all aspects of automobile repairs, both major and minor, including the following:

- Electrical diagnostic repairs on computer-controlled engines and brake systems; minor welding repairs; engine and transmission overhauls.

AUTOMOTIVE MECHANIC. Jerry's Auto Sales, Dolan, SC (1994-95). Coordinated repairs needed to prepare cars for resale, including minor body work and engine repair or replacement.

- Gained additional experience in selling cars and in completing the necessary paperwork including titles during the absence of the owner.

EDUCATION   Attended Dolan Technical Community College, Dolan, SC, 1993-94.
Studied arc welding as well as oxygen and acetylene welding.
Graduated from Deer Valley Senior High School, Dolan, SC, 1993.
Completed three years of study in architectural drafting and two years in auto mechanics.

CERTIFICATIONS   Hold the following certifications:

North Carolina Inspectors License   Forklift Operations License
R12 Recovery Recycling Certification   CDL Class A Driver's License
ASE Certified in brakes, air conditioning, suspension, and electrical

SEMINARS   Attended seminars on Fuel Injection Systems and ABS Brake Troubleshooting.

PERSONAL   Became interested in automobile maintenance at a young age. Began working on cars at 13.

Date

Exact Name
Exact Title of Person
Exact Name of Company
Exact Address of Company
City, State Zip

WIRING TECHNICIAN   Dear Exact Name:

With the enclosed resume, I would like to make you aware of my desire to seek employment with your organization.

As you will see from my resume, I have most recently gained valuable knowledge related to the operation of compressors and machinery while building motor control units for a major manufacturer. I have been credited with making contributions which allowed the company to reach its goal of "zero defects" in on-time shipping.

Known for my strong personal initiative and resourcefulness, I have volunteered to serve on numerous corporate committees which have been established to analyze and make recommendations about vital corporate issues. I played a key role on a committee which facilitated the company's ability to qualify for ISO 9002 certification.

If you can use an experienced professional with an extensive background related to manufacturing operations, I hope you will contact me to suggest a time when we might meet to discuss your needs. I can provide outstanding references at the appropriate time.

Sincerely,

Wynona T. Limans

WYNONA T. LIMANS

1110½ Hay Street, Fayetteville, NC 28305   •   preppub@aol.com   •   (910) 483-6611

OBJECTIVE

To offer excellent technical electronics skills to an organization that can use a self-motivated team player who possesses a high degree of initiative, attention to detail, and planning skills along with a strong bottom-line orientation and desire to increase productivity.

EDUCATION & TRAINING

Excelled in more than 780 hours of U.S. Air Force technical training which included a 696-hour Electronics Technician Program emphasizing communications and navigation systems as well as courses in hazardous material handling/disposal and data entry operations.

TECHNICAL KNOWLEDGE

Avionics: Ability to troubleshoot and repair to the component level, computer systems, and electromechanical devices with analog and digital circuitry.
Program, install, maintain, troubleshoot, and repair F-16 avionics systems including communication, navigation, penetration aids, fire control radar, and flight controls.
Hold COMSEC (communication security) certification on all F-16 systems.
Computers: Am skilled in word processing and computer applications using the AS400, the Windows operating system, and Microsoft and Delrina FormFlow software.
Other: Use office equipment including typewriters, computers, and multiline phones.

EXPERIENCE

WIRING TECHNICIAN. Norse Industries, Waterloo, IA (2000-present). Gained valuable knowledge related to the operation of compressors and machinery while building motor control units for this manufacturer.
- Read wire diagrams, schematics, and engineering order specifications in order to ensure units were completed according to requirements and proper standards.
- Applied my computer skills while accessing inventory information and obtaining data about the availability of needed parts.
- Was credited with making contributions which allowed the company to reach its goal of "zero defects" in on-time shipping.
- Was a member of a department which was successful in qualifying for ISO 9002 certification.
- Played an active role during new-employee orientation.

JOURNEYMAN AVIONICS TECHNICIAN. U.S. Air Force, Shaw AFB, SC (1994-99). Became skilled in performing services including the analysis of malfunctions, inspection, installation, and maintenance of avionics systems on multimillion-dollar F-16 aircraft.
- Earned recognition for my bottom-line orientation and technical skills displayed by developing a suggestion for a modification to the IFF (Identification Friend or Foe) system which was accepted and resulted in millions of dollars in savings.
- Received the Air Force Outstanding Unit Award and the Southwest Asia Service Medal.

FULL-TIME STUDENT. Drake College and Des Moines Area Community College, Des Moines, IA (1990-93). Studied Music at Drake College on a full academic/music scholarship and completed one year in DMACC's Paralegal program before military service.

ADMINISTRATIVE ASSISTANT, CASHIER, and **INVENTORY CONTROL CLERK.** Sam's Grocery, Des Moines, IA (1988-91). Received training and gained knowledge of book-keeping, accounting, and record keeping while assisting in several functional areas in this supermarket; controlled health and beauty aid product ordering and stocking.

PERSONAL

Was entrusted with a Secret security clearance. Work well independently or as a member of a team to meet corporate goals for safety, productivity, and quality. Operate forklifts.

ABOUT THE EDITOR

Anne McKinney holds an MBA from the Harvard Business School and a BA in English from the University of North Carolina at Chapel Hill. A noted public speaker, writer, and teacher, she is the senior editor for PREP's business and career imprint, which bears her name. Early titles in the Anne McKinney Career Series (now called the Real-Resumes Series) published by PREP include: *Resumes and Cover Letters That Have Worked, Resumes and Cover Letters That Have Worked for Military Professionals, Government Job Applications and Federal Resumes, Cover Letters That Blow Doors Open,* and *Letters for Special Situations.* Her career titles and how-to resume-and-cover-letter books are based on the expertise she has acquired in 20 years of working with job hunters. Her valuable career insights have appeared in publications of the "Wall Street Journal" and other prominent newspapers and magazines.

PREP Publishing Order Form

You may purchase any of our titles from your favorite bookseller! Or send a check or money order or your credit card number for the total amount*, plus $4.00 postage and handling, to PREP, Box 66, Fayetteville, NC 28302. You may also order our titles on our website at www.prep-pub.com and feel free to e-mail us at preppub@aol.com or call 910-483-6611 with your questions or concerns.

Name: _____

Phone #:_____

Address: _____

E-mail address:

Payment Type: ☐ Check/Money Order   ☐ Visa   ☐ MasterCard

Credit Card Number: _____ Expiration Date: _____

Check items you are ordering:

☐ $16.95—REAL-RESUMES FOR MANUFACTURING JOBS. Anne McKinney, Editor
☐ $16.95—REAL-RESUMES FOR AVIATION & TRAVEL JOBS. Anne McKinney, Editor
☐ $16.95—REAL-RESUMES FOR POLICE, LAW ENFORCEMENT & SECURITY JOBS. Anne McKinney, Editor
☐ $16.95—REAL-RESUMES FOR SOCIAL WORK & COUNSELING JOBS. Anne McKinney, Editor
☐ $16.95—REAL-RESUMES FOR CONSTRUCTION JOBS. Anne McKinney, Editor
☐ $16.95—REAL-RESUMES FOR FINANCIAL JOBS. Anne McKinney, Editor
☐ $16.95—REAL-RESUMES FOR COMPUTER JOBS. Anne McKinney, Editor
☐ $16.95—REAL-RESUMES FOR MEDICAL JOBS. Anne McKinney, Editor
☐ $16.95—REAL-RESUMES FOR TEACHERS. Anne McKinney, Editor
☐ $16.95—REAL-RESUMES FOR CAREER CHANGERS. Anne McKinney, Editor
☐ $16.95—REAL-RESUMES FOR STUDENTS. Anne McKinney, Editor
☐ $16.95—REAL-RESUMES FOR SALES. Anne McKinney, Editor
☐ $16.95—REAL ESSAYS FOR COLLEGE AND GRAD SCHOOL. Anne McKinney, Editor
☐ $25.00—RESUMES AND COVER LETTERS THAT HAVE WORKED.
☐ $25.00—RESUMES AND COVER LETTERS THAT HAVE WORKED FOR MILITARY PROFESSIONALS.
☐ $25.00—RESUMES AND COVER LETTERS FOR MANAGERS.
☐ $25.00—GOVERNMENT JOB APPLICATIONS AND FEDERAL RESUMES: Federal Resumes, KSAs, Forms 171 and 612, and Postal Applications.
☐ $25.00—COVER LETTERS THAT BLOW DOORS OPEN.
☐ $25.00—LETTERS FOR SPECIAL SITUATIONS.
☐ $16.00—BACK IN TIME. Patty Sleem
☐ $17.00—(trade paperback) SECOND TIME AROUND. Patty Sleem
☐ $25.00—(hardcover) SECOND TIME AROUND. Patty Sleem
☐ $18.00—A GENTLE BREEZE FROM GOSSAMER WINGS. Gordon Beld
☐ $18.00—BIBLE STORIES FROM THE OLD TESTAMENT. Katherine Whaley
☐ $14.95—WHAT THE BIBLE SAYS ABOUT... *Words that can lead to success and happiness* (large print edition) Patty Sleem
☐ $10.95—KIJABE An African Historical Saga. Pally Dhillon

_____ **TOTAL ORDERED (add $4.00 for postage and handling)**

PREP offers volume discounts on large orders. Call us at (910) 483-6611 for more information.

THE MISSION OF PREP PUBLISHING IS TO PUBLISH
BOOKS AND OTHER PRODUCTS WHICH ENRICH
PEOPLE'S LIVES AND HELP THEM OPTIMIZE THE
HUMAN EXPERIENCE. OUR STRONGEST LINES ARE
OUR JUDEO-CHRISTIAN ETHICS SERIES AND OUR
BUSINESS & CAREER SERIES.

Would you like to explore the possibility of having PREP's writing
team create a resume for you similar to the ones in this book?

For a brief free consultation, call 910-483-6611
or send $4.00 to receive our Job Change Packet to
PREP, Department SPR2002, Fayetteville, NC 28302.

QUESTIONS OR COMMENTS? E-MAIL US AT PREPPUB@AOL.COM